EVERYDAY
CHAMPIONS

UNLEASH THE GIFTS GOD GAVE YOU, STEP INTO YOUR PURPOSE, AND FULFILL YOUR DESTINY

JOE HORN

DEFENDER

CRANE, MO

Everyday Champions: Unleash the Gifts God Gave You, Step into Your Purpose, and Fulfill Your Destiny

Defender Publishing
Crane, MO 65633
©2019 by Joe Horn
All rights reserved. Published 2019.
Printed in the United States of America.

ISBN: 978-1-948014-17-5

A CIP catalog record of this book is available from the Library of Congress.

Cover photo by Justen Faull Cover Photography.
Cover design by Jeffrey Mardis.

All Scripture quotations from the King James Version unless otherwise noted.

Special thanks to the following pictorial contributors:
Sue Abelein
Holly Harris
Darlene Osban Hundtoft
Wanda Duncan
Debbie Short
Alicia McDermott-Yanik
Whitney McDermott
Barbara Phillips
Linda Hoard

DEDICATION

This book is dedicated to Jesus Christ, who has given me life abundantly and purpose. To my beautiful wife, Katherine, who has stood by me through so much; my amazing children for bringing me unspeakable joy; my parents for loving me throughout some very difficult chapters; and the countless real-life heroes and mentors who stood in the gap of this once-unruly youth.

CONTENTS

CHAPTER ONE

The Day That Changed Everything

There are many ways to obtain an education in this world, the initial concepts of which typically associate to some kind of institutionalized learning in a building or online where students report for class. Students who apply themselves to meeting the requirements of the teacher or professor's format will achieve an exceptional grade, whether or not they retain that knowledge for years beyond the date the class reaches completion. However, another form of learning is at least equal, if not superior, to institutionalized education on many fronts, as it bestows both knowledge *and* wisdom, and it almost always guarantees that students will retain the skills obtained for the remainder of their life here on earth. It's called, for lack of a better term, the "school of hard knocks."

Textbooks and reading materials can train students for countless futures and careers, but no manual is thorough enough to prepare students for life from all conceivable angles in the daily scenarios this world will throw at them. Personal experience is the most valuable hindsight manual for the future when the skill needed is wisdom and common sense. Fortunately for me, I have kept my own "hard knocks" manual updated and have chosen to revisit the lesson outlines of my past each time I've been confronted with something new. Over time, in *some* areas, this made me stronger and smarter going forward than I would have been had I flown straight back into danger's path and allowed myself to repeatedly be fooled or taken advantage of. *Unfortunately* for me, however, my attitude has often been such that each hard knock took me well past a lesson learned and straight into a cynical outlook on the world and the people around me. I became almost entirely focused on placing walls between myself and anything that smelled like a counterfeit, and I'm afraid to say my perspective on much became imbalanced.

"Fool me once, shame on you…"

You know the drill.

Over time, and in *most* areas related to being used by the Lord for His Kingdom purposes, this made me weaker and more pessimistic, and for at least a couple of decades, my ability to minister was stunted by the towering walls of self-preservation that I had forged.

It wasn't always that way. I began my life as trusting and earnest as any child, loving the Lord and His people as sincerely as any boy raised in a perfectly healthy Christian home. But as a minister's child, with all the pressures that implies, I inherited a front-row seat to the "show" that a few churches were putting on around me during some of my early, formative years of spiritual development—and the effect that had on my concepts of Christianity and ministry was profound.

To make matters more dramatic, I was raised Pentecostal.

Pentecostalism…there always seem to be cons amidst the pros on any list describing that denomination. Yet the authentic demonstrations of God's intervention remain in existence for us to observe in every generation…

Throughout my journey, I observed two realities as they played out in front of me: 1) human men and women engaging in the hype of a false movement of God (often this escalated to the peak of blatant heresy during church service); and 2) the undeniable evidence of the Holy

Spirit's influence upon people who would never stretch the truth of His intervention in their lives. The former reality was extremely frequent, only peppered here and there with legitimate supernatural manifestations. I spent most of my childhood, teen years, and early adulthood trying to iron out what I was even looking at during church half the time. The things these people said were "from God" or the events that occurred "in the Spirit" were at times so unbiblical—and occasionally outright blasphemous—that they stirred a heavy doubt within me, one that bubbled up into my spirit's sensory gullet like an acidic bile I couldn't swallow back down. My distaste for the hype of "religious experience" grew intense.

Yet, each time I began to think that these events around me were *all* sensational reactions to mankind's hunger for a connection with God, I would see the effects of a true and lasting touch of God on the life of someone I knew, and the result was undeniable.

At one point early on, the person "touched" was me—though I had not been seeking it—and the effect would last a lifetime.

The book you hold in your hands is *only in part* my journey through these extremes. It is crucial to understand that I am not sharing these memories to entertain (although it has already been brought to my attention by those who have read this book that my story is quite entertaining and frequently humorous). I share these memories because, through everything I've faced, God has given me a message ripe not just for my own generation, *but for every generation of believers alive on this planet today.* My life's circumstances have placed me in a unique position. Because my father was a state leader in one of the largest evangelical organizations in the US, and because he was (and is) also an extremely successful author in the Christian world with ties to countless big names in the media, since I was very young, I've seen the exposed *and* hidden sides of some of the celebrity-status Church megastars. I've observed both ends of the spectrum—from simulated "acts of God" to authentic, Holy-Spirit-guided intervention—and the Lord has equipped me through the "school of hard knocks" with a mission to awaken dormant Christians to the good fight of the faith as it pertains to the gifts of the Spirit in such a time as this. To drive my message home with cohesion and strength, I must share with my readers what I have observed in my short time on earth. A college lecture might teach students the cold facts and figures about an academic subject, but only by sharing my life experience can I fully communicate the depth of the revelation God has given me to impart upon today's Church Body.

To bring balance to a story that is otherwise fraught with internal struggle, I will begin with "the day that changed everything"…

The church I was attending was brand-spanking new because of a merger. Carpets were light grey, unlike the 1970s burnt orange I had been used to in so many churches prior. Pews weren't "pews"; they were interlocking chairs the contemporary color of milk chocolate. The worship song display was state of the art: We had *printed* lyrics instead of those archaic, hand-written pages for the overhead projector. At the highest point on the walls towering around the enormous auditorium, sound-reflecting foam had been installed to ensure only the greatest acoustics during service. Ministers had traded in corded microphones for wireless ones.

This church was cutting edge.

On this particular Sunday, the congregation was several hundred strong, with attendees gathered to hear the anointed sermon from the lips of a man who had been revered throughout the country…a man who, to avoid petty slander, I will simply call "Reverend Peter." He had been with us as keynote speaker for an entire revival conference that had begun on Friday evening and featured services throughout Saturday and Sunday. This was his final sermon.

Reverend Peter had a great reputation as a man who could enter the doorway of a church and irrevocably storm the gates of hell, setting loose the congregants who had spent years of their tormented lives in the captivity of devils and principalities of darkness. His pulpit-pounding oratory style held the nation spellbound. The pews weren't even cold before the strongest recommendations were made from one pastor to another from one border of the US to the other, exhorting ministry colleagues to do anything they had to do to get Peter into their own places of worship.

Throughout the entire Satanic Panic era of the 1980s and early '90s, Reverend Peter was considered the deliverer of souls. The soldier of heaven. The enemy's biggest threat. The illustrious captain of the progressive Pentecostal stronghold in this ongoing and invisible war between the forces of good and evil.

His personal story was likewise inspiring, and those who normally fought the temptation to nod off on a typical Sunday were riveted. With crowds numbering nearly a thousand in many of the establishments he visited, Reverend Peter limped around the stage and regaled his audience with a tale so fascinating and so motivating that even Rip Van Winkle would have been alert on the edge of his seat.

"I'm sure you're all wondering about my wooden leg," he would begin. "I'll get straight to the *meat* of it."

This joke, when it was delivered in my own church, didn't catch on right away, but he paused for effect. Once a few people began to chuckle, however, everyone else slowly arrived at the punchline and there was a corporate "Ohhh" followed by the icebreaker laugh.

Wooden leg. Getting to the "meat" of it.

Get it?

Nothing like a corny joke to get things rolling before the bodies hit the floor...

His leg, Reverend Peter said, had been injured "back in the day," when he had been a professional Major League MVP (most valuable player) in baseball. He was the only wooden-legged player to go on to be deemed MVP by the league in a World Series playoff game. I don't recall what team he claimed to play for or how, specifically, he claimed to have injured his leg, but the damage was such that amputation and prosthetics were the only answer. After the installation of his wooden leg and several months of healing, Peter was miraculously reinstated to his position on the team, where he continued to hit numerous home runs, causing full-stadium ovations and uproarious cheers.

When he grew tired of all the fame, attention, and lunch outings with his alleged best buddy, Babe Ruth, Peter was "radically called into the ministry." After surrendering his life to the Lord, he began serving as a chaplain to the Los Angeles Lakers, or so he plied. It was during this stint that he "performed many a number with the Oak Ridge Boys," the old-gospel quartet well known for famous song titles such as "I'll Be True to You," "Ya'll Come Back Saloon," "Bobbie Sue," and "Elvira." Another detail of Peter's story included how he had worked directly under the infamously celebrated evangelist Kathryn Kuhlman, who had trail-blazed one of the greatest healing crusade ministries in history from the '40s to the '70s. (This was before people could fact-check a person's story online from their handheld cell phones. Had that technology existed at the time, these claims and many others would have been refuted before Peter ever stepped off the stage.)

One tale Peter told involved a man who had been "slain in the Spirit" (when a believer falls to the floor as a result of a touch from the Holy Spirit) at one of his services: On his way down, the man had cracked his skull on a pew. Blood was everywhere, yet the man remained oblivious in a state of prayer. Peter held his hand over the man as he lay there unconscious and, according to his testimony, shouted, "There will be no injury!" When the man eventually rose, the leadership of that assembly washed the blood out of his hair and there was no sign of the wound.

In another tale, a terrible storm was headed for the church in the middle of a revival. Peter's wife didn't want to get her nails wet (a detail that inspired a humorous response), so she sent Peter outside to pray. With the authority of heaven, Peter said, he stomped right out into the thick of the storm, pointed at the sky, and commanded the squall to stop. The skies cleared within seconds.

In testimony after testimony, Reverend Peter shared how he had observed miracles at his many meetings.

Anyone with the anointing upon his or her life—anyone who is willing to daily consecrate himself or herself to the Lord and rebuke the devil—can and will be called to similar greatness, success, and prosperity, Peter said. This was the core of his message, and it was met with unanimous enthusiasm. At the end of every sermon, he would hype up the congregation with "Are you ready to take this revival to the next level?"—and then he followed that with various ways the congregants could "earn" God's blessing by supporting Peter's ministerial plans. By giving to *him*, he said, the people were "giving as unto the Lord."

The audience bought the lies and our church continued to take in enormous offerings for all of Peter's plans, convinced that he had been sent by God to do earthly wonders even more astounding than being the only MVP baseball player with a prosthetic leg.

During the altar call on that final Sunday session, so many congregants responded that they packed the aisles all the way down to and around the back row of chairs. Reverend Peter limped from one responder to the next, praying deliverance and blessing over people of all ages.

Almost every time he touched someone, he or she fell to the floor. So many fell that day that the people in the back of the line had to step over splayed limbs to get to the front. Our home pastor's wife was scurrying about the building placing burgundy altar cloths over the knees of the women who had fallen in skirts and dresses (to protect their modesty), and several of our strongest men gathered to catch the falling responders and lower them to the floor between the others lying motionless on the new carpeting.

As a typical nine-year-old kid, I couldn't even begin to understand the spiritual implications of what was happening around me. I had been in Pentecostal churches since I was in diapers. The concept of people falling at the altar was not new to me, and although I innately knew that something powerful was going on, by this time I had been indoctrinated with the "sit still and be quiet during service" creed for so long that I couldn't value being deeply alert like I would in my later years. To me, this was just another Sunday evening—an electrifying one for sure, but when you're nine, you can only comprehend so much, and by the tenth falling person, I figured I had pretty much seen it all and my mind once again wandered to more important things like Saturday-morning cartoons and tacos.

I wasn't a disrespectful child, but stick any boy in a setting like this for nine years straight, and eventually you'll see him go through the same weekly process I did, which goes a little something like this: *Sit still. Remain quiet. As soon as the minister begins talking, find something entertaining to think about while looking at the walls of the room. When the minister pounds the pulpit and shouts about the tongues of fire on the Day of Pentecost in Acts, the adults will be captivated: That's the green flag to begin doodling on the tithing envelopes, but it must be done discreetly to prevent disapproving stares from the elders. When the minister gives the altar call, implied consent has been granted for the children in the building to visit quietly until we leave for home—but don't get caught laughing, or Mom and Dad will separate us…*

So here's how much of a cheeky dork I was that day with Reverend Peter…

Josh, the boy sitting next to me, had the same denominational background, and I could see that he was equally unphased and oblivious to the effects of Reverend Peter's altar calls. For a few minutes, we whispered about your average boy interests—action figures, wrestling, insects, and machine guns—and then I got a fun idea.

"Hey Josh," I whispered. "Wanna play cowboys?"

"Right here?"

"Yeah! Check it out."

I sat for a moment as Reverend Peter railed against the wiles of the enemy over a middle-aged man in a suit. When I saw Peter's hand reach out to touch the gentleman's forehead, I knew my moment had arrived. I pulled out my invisible lasso, whirled it in circles above my head, and let it fly. When the man fell, I mimicked by jerking my arms back. Josh squealed a quiet "yeehaw" in delight and immediately equipped himself with his own rope.

What morons we were…

As a quick aside to the reader, I originally decided against sharing this portion of my memories of that day because I don't want to paint the picture that I was play-acting anything dark. Much to the contrary, with men and women falling down in the Spirit all over the building, and with Josh and me as standard little boys who were trying to entertain ourselves quietly, this was nothing more than a timing game. You "win" if you time it right, and you "lose" if the person remained standing. We honestly meant no disrespect as we made the most of yet another Sunday that involved supernatural events so far above our heads that we felt forced to come up with something new so the adults could pray. In those days, boys played "Cowboys and Indians" and "army guys" regularly without the culturally branded fear from parents that exists today. We were never psychoanalyzed seven ways from Saturday in my youth for playing boyish games, and role-playing such silly things as a lasso during a Pentecostal service wouldn't have been seen as anything more than kids being kids. In the end, I decided to share this after all, because the picture it *does* paint is of a little boy who went obediently to the altar without even the slightest interest in or expectation of receiving a touch from the Lord.

After minutes had gone by and our latest "cowboys" game got old, we sat quietly, swinging our feet below the chairs while our thoughts scavenged from our brains' deepest crevices any inspiration whatsoever for something to do or talk about. It was then that Reverend Peter called all those remaining in their seats to the front of the church. God wanted to bless *everyone*, Peter said—even the youth and children. I turned to look at my father (the associate pastor of this church at the time) for guidance, who was by now standing at the very back, in front of the partition that split the sanctuary from the gym in this enormous, multipurpose room. He didn't return my gaze, and I could tell he was deep in thought.

I would find out later what he had really been thinking…

Obediently, I went to the aisle and stepped over the bodies to make my way to our guest minister. As soon as I found an opening where I could remain still on the far side from where he was praying, my thoughts began to wander again in my impatience. I looked down at my shoes for a moment, contemplating my awesome clothes. (This was during my "Fonz clothes" phase: I was far too young to grasp the humor of the *Happy Days* show, but I was old enough to see Fonzie's James-Dean style and recognize its flair as the perfect balance between modesty and bad-to-the-bone edge. While I was on this kick, I would wear anything black, because black was "cool." We weren't allowed by any stretch of the imagination to conform to the ways of the world around us, so wearing black clothes was my innocent way of being a rebel on the inside.) My avant-garde appearance only held my attention for a minute or two, when my sleeveless shirt reminded me of a recent advertisement that Hulk Hogan of the World Wrestling Federation (WWF) had been in. He was always wearing that bright-yellow, sleeveless tank top that he gloriously ripped in half every time he took to the ring—and as usual, in the ad, he started his sentences with, "Let me tell you something, brother!"

Of course, *that* thought only led to another, which was the most exciting thing I had ever experienced: Dad had bought tickets for the whole family to see a live WWF event. One of the key matches was between Hulk Hogan and King Kong Bundy, but there were also many other legendary entertainment wrestlers in the ring that day, including Big John Stud and the Junkyard Dog. Michael Buffer, the notorious ring announcer—who was not usually a WWF ring announcer but who just happened to be at the Portland Memorial Coliseum that night—sounded just like he did over the television before each match as he delivered his immortal catchphrase, "Lllllet's get ready to rumbllllle!" But the match that kept coming to mind as I stood there was when Tito Santana went up against Adrian Adonis. Tito continued to repeatedly chop Adrian in the chest, which was such a humorous thing to see between two musclemen.

So there I was, standing at the altar amidst a crowd of people who were at least several decades older than me, waiting my turn to be touched or prayed over by the minister of power. My body might have been still, but my thoughts were firing all over the place. I was physically present in a building with highly supernatural occurrences all around me, but I was anything *but* mentally present or engaged when Reverend Peter approached me. I was there out of a blend between obedience and curiosity, but I was far more interested in fantasizing about meeting famous wrestlers than I was in participating in the service. I didn't expect a touch from God any more than Adrian expected Tito to stop chopping him in the chest and bow out in defeat—which is what my thoughts were focused on at the moment.

I closed my eyes in reverence while Peter prayed over me, but I can't honestly say I was listening to his words. Either I wasn't listening or I don't remember what he said, but as far as any potential blessing or declaration he pronounced for me, I'll never know. I vaguely remember that he was going down a line with a corporate blessing, and I was just one of the people standing there, so it's likely that he didn't say anything about me specifically. Eventually, I felt his hand touch my forehead softly, directly above my right eyebrow. It wasn't a shove, as some Pentecostal preachers have been known to do, and there wasn't anything forceful or leading in that moment. It was gentle enough that it could have been a butterfly and I wouldn't have known the difference.

For the life of me, I can't explain how or why this happened, but the second Peter's hand made contact with me, I entered an experience

I can only describe as weightlessness. I felt like I was floating peacefully in total serenity. An electric tingling shot through me like a strike of lightning from my eyebrow to my toes. It was as if the world moved into slow motion and my body drifted downward. (If what I felt during this encounter was even a glimpse of what heaven feels like…words fail to describe how euphoric it will be.) The sensation lasted less than a split second, and before I hit the floor, I was coming out of it. It was over before I even landed. Although I immediately recognized my surroundings, I felt like I was awakening from anesthesia: I knew where I was, but my brain felt like it had been disconnected from my consciousness, and it took me several seconds to return to reality.

I remained on the floor for several moments, flabbergasted. *What in the otherworld had just knocked me over?* A couple of people nearby were looking at me, and I felt the underlying pressure of expectation.

Okay, I'm on the floor. Now what?

My immature coping mechanism returned to the advice a young mind often returns to: "Do what others are doing." Peeking over at a friend who was about my age, I saw that he had covered his face with his hands. *Looks like a good idea.* I proceeded to mimic the gesture. I didn't know what else to do, and now that I was once again myself, I was once again thinking the thoughts of a nine-year-old, the manifestation of which translated to covering my face for no apparent reason other than the lack of a better idea.

Everything up to the moment my body fell had all been clownery. I had been a typical kid buffooning my way through another service, from Tito Santana to staring at the ceiling. I hadn't been seeking to instigate what happened to me in any way, and I had never thought about going to the altar for a spiritual touch. Even while I waited in that line, I had been counting down to the moment I would once again be free to return to my "lasso game" nonsense. When I fell, I had collapsed like a deadweight. I hadn't experienced any nervous muscle-clench that would normally coincide with a trust fall, and I don't know if there was anyone behind me to catch me. I had surrendered to the weightlessness and descended like a brick, though I felt no pain anywhere. Then, when I eventually stood, our family left as though it had never happened.

On paper, this comes across as the most anti-climactic, abrupt, and confusing ending to that episode fathomable, and I admit I felt that, too, at the time. This defining moment held none of the poetic revelation that so many talk about when they've experienced the supernatural. For weeks following, I continued to wonder: *Why would I receive a touch from God that simply took me to the carpet so I could lie there and cover my face? What did that accomplish, and what message was God trying to send me?* The questions in my young mind were numerous, and my bewilderment over the whole ordeal was intensified when I mentioned Reverend Peter to my dad later on.

"The guy's a fraud," Dad said firmly.

"What do you mean?"

"He's a fraud. Plain and simple. Mark my words. He didn't do any of that stuff he claimed to do."

"He is? He didn't?"

"No way, man." Dad shook his head. "I know the whole country is excited about this guy, but he's lying out the mouth, and it's a matter of time before his balderdash catches up with him. Major-league baseball on a wooden leg? Nah. He's making it up."

Dad went on to explain that Reverend Peter had hyped up the crowd with astonishing tales, and then asked them to give generously to the offering plate to fund his ministry. People are more willing to pull out their wallets for a man with lofty connections. *That's* a man who's "going places," people think. There wasn't an ounce of truth to Peter's claims, Dad said. Additionally, Peter had promised to stick around for another week to preach—an announcement I missed in my easily distracted attention span—and that bolstered the congregation's willingness to give a larger offering on that final night, since they believed he would see him again and could hear about how he planned to use the money.

Peter was so blessed by their generosity, he said, that he couldn't think of leaving until he had given them the specifics of what their money would accomplish for God's kingdom. The offering plates came in full, and he was beaming…but he disappeared before morning.

"I tried to warn them," Dad said.

"You mean you knew this would happen?" I asked, eyes wide.

"Not down to every detail, no," he answered. "But I had an uneasy feeling about him from the beginning. His story never added up, and well before he came here, I advised the board to reconsider bringing him."

"Aren't you the pastor? Don't you decide these things?" I had no idea how church governance and administration worked. I only knew that my dad had been "in charge" for years prior to this.

Dad went on to explain that he was currently in the process of resigning from his position at the church. When the churches merged, he planned to stay long enough to help smooth out all the transitional wrinkles, but he had long since handed the reins over to the new board and newly incoming senior pastor. His position as the associate pastor was temporary. He had shared his reservations about Peter with the new leaders, but it hadn't been his place to call the shots while he was on his way out. The board members heard Dad's warning, but when the decision had been put to a vote, Reverend Peter was the man of the hour, and there was nothing Dad could have done about it. When Peter arrived on the scene despite Dad's misgivings, Dad's only option was to stand aside and pray for discernment.

As the next few years would prove, Dad's gut check was absolutely right. Reverend Peter *was* a fraud. He continued to travel from place to place, asking people to help him in his various ministerial endeavors, and he finally got into real hot water when he started promising parishioners that he would return their investments thirty- and fifty-fold. Hundreds of thousands of dollars were handed to him freely with the understanding that it would all come back in spades. But, following this, nobody would hear from him again. As a sad addition to his investment scam, several allegations surfaced indicating that he had used his flash-in-the-pan popularity to seduce several young women in many churches.

Now that we have the Internet, any Johnny-come-lately can look into every Kathryn Kuhlman and major-league baseball record in history to find that Reverend Peter's name doesn't show up in all the places where he said he established fame. I looked him up recently out of curiosity (remember, "Reverend Peter" is not his real name, in case you were planning your own search), and the last scam on record that he pulled was in 2006. That fiasco landed him in court, where he was forced to agree to reimburse his latest round of victims. Whether he ever followed through is anyone's guess. But it's no wonder to me now that Dad stood at the back of the church quietly ruminating that day.

Nevertheless, I know beyond the shadow of the darkest doubts that I did *not* fake that altar experience. If I had, I would have done something "spiritual looking" when I fell. I might have wept or started imitating "speaking in tongues" (another Pentecostal term that describes a manifestation of the infilling of the Holy Spirit wherein an unknown language is spoken; more on this later). That is something I certainly could have done if that had been my intention, because I had heard people speaking in tongues around me in church services many times before. Further, I might have shaken, moaned, or tried to stir up spiritual excitement in those around me. All of these behavioral displays were familiar territory.

The truth remains as ingrained in me now as it did then: A power beyond all humanity came over me that day, and it wasn't one I asked for or even knew how to pray for. The whole experience ended so abruptly that I couldn't find any sense in any of it. How awkward and out of place I felt on that floor, looking around and seeing all those unresponsive people, wondering why God's greatest will for me as it manifested then was for me to be horizontal instead of vertical!

It would be years before I could connect the dots and see for myself what I needed to know about that day.

When I was in my teens, the Pentecostal enthusiasm continued to escalate, and when the Brownsville, Texas, and Pensacola, Florida, revivals hit the country, the Holy-Spirit manifestations were at an all-time high. I know that some of these occurrences were truly of God, because I knew some of the people who had traveled to those places, and I believe they weren't making up the stories they later shared. But for as many tangible experiences that were being talked about, there seemed to be as many fake experiences as well, as later evidence showed. Things were happening in the Church across the nation that were purely heretical—not of God—because people in the company of men like Reverend Peter were too eager to embrace hype in trade for a genuine focus on the Messiah of the Gospel. Observing this, my faith in the whole idea of God's outpourings was waning. But every time I was tempted to dismiss modern-day miracles or the idea of the gifts of the Holy Spirit being present and alive today among believers, my doubt was always challenged by "that day when I was nine."

As I reached adulthood and took a job working for a Christian youth camp, many ministers would come and "storm the gates of hell" just as Reverend Peter had been known to do, and people all around me were running all over the place with stories of what had transpired in the chapel. Later, many of these same "power ministers" would be caught in scandal, show their true colors to my fellow staff behind the scenes, or steal from the camp facilities in the middle of the night. This nonsense went on for five straight years, and every time I was tempted to dismiss the testimonies of those who were touched by these fraudulent ministers, my doubt, once again, was always challenged by "that day when I was nine."

I couldn't let go of the experience I had that day, and as God has taught me, I was never *supposed* to let go of it. When I fell so long ago, I wasn't swept up to heaven and entrusted with an earth-shattering revelation of His will. The ceiling never parted. I didn't see any angels. Nothing glowed. It appeared to me at the time like the most ambiguous thing in the world that the Lord would touch me—through this scam artist, no less—*just* so I would fall down.

But as the years have flown by, I have concluded that my experience that day wasn't ever about potential deliverances or spiritual revelations caused by the Holy Spirit's touch. God's touch, *in and of itself,* was the message: God is real and His power is real. It's not through the power of the surrogate minister that we catch glimpses of God's supreme authority; He will reach out and grab His people's attention in His own divine timing and for His own purposes. God knew what my life was going to throw at me, and He knew that I would need to be left with just one baffling but undeniable show of His all-consuming power.

It was the day that changed everything.

CHAPTER TWO

The Need for Heroes

The purpose of this book is to focus on a deeper understanding of the spiritual gifts given to the members of the Body of Christ through the Holy Spirit. These giftings have often been misunderstood to be limited to what 1 Corinthians addresses: "word of wisdom," "word of knowledge," "faith," "healing," "miracles," "prophecy," "discerning of spirits," "divers kinds of tongues," and "interpretation of tongues" (1 Corinthians 12:8–10). Perhaps with the exception of "faith," this section of the Word appears to modern interpreters to list sensationally super-natural manifestations of God's power in the lives of believers.

Yet, it is crucial that we revise our concepts to include *all* of what the Bible says on the subject of spiritual gifts, not just those that arouse a dramatic reaction amidst the Body. Later in this work, we will visit some commonly discounted "gift verses" and look at the importance those Scriptures have in the supernatural realm, but I believe it's helpful to show how I came to appreciate these truths, because I believe my story is one that *many* Christians or individuals who have been injured by the "ministry" can relate to today.

I didn't come to value or understand the gifts of the Spirit through a Bible study group, a cluster of sermons, or books. I had, of course, spent most of my life hearing about these giftings as a child of the Church, but it was through personal experience *only* that the Holy Spirit led me to whole new level of comprehension. When the Church leaders spoke of these gifts throughout the '80s–'90s, they placed an enormous emphasis upon the gifts that result in immediate and visible proof of God's supernatural intervention within our earthly lives (such as miracles, healings, speaking in tongues and the interpretation thereof, etc.). Whereas those gifts, as well as their results, are irrefutably genuine and important in every age, I believe the Body's focus during my childhood had shifted from experiencing a relationship with the Risen Christ to experiencing the manifestations and demonstrations of the Holy Spirit during church service or at revival meetings. These two can be related as they stem from the almighty power of one Godhead, but as they correspond to an individual motive in seeking God, they are not the same. One is healthy, and one is misleading. (In truth, I'm excited to see evidence that the Church is moving away from this unhealthy pattern. We are starting to see cultural symptoms of a generation that yearns for an authentic relationship with Christ, not just with the sensational events of a lively service gathering—and this is a very good sign.)

Pursuing Christ first and witnessing the subsequent miraculous effects of that relationship with Him produces a lifelong strength that can withstand anything the enemy throws against it. Pursuing the experience of a supernatural event at an altar because everyone is hyped up about signs and wonders produces a weakness that limits one's understanding of God—it depicts Him more as Santa Claus or a magician and reduces Him to a performer who reacts to our wishes or whims. If we don't "get" the number of healings or miracles we expect to see in the time limit we've set, then He is "not the God we thought He was," and/or "the evidence of His provision is lacking."

But God is not a "show" that we can buy tickets to see; He is a Deity we should strive to know—and if we get that wrong, we can get addicted to the "high" of supervising miracle-shows. Likewise, as we float from one revival meeting to another, if God doesn't reveal to some people the Holy Spirit gifting assigned to them by the time such a revelation is expected, then these individuals might be tempted to assume they were never given a gift by the Lord in the first place. They were the "overlooked" minority. If taken to the extreme—which several people in my life have done—some may erroneously conclude that God hasn't gifted some of us because He doesn't plan to *use* some of us.

This tragic misconception has led many away from the Lord. *Every* believer is given gifts to use here on earth, and while in service to the Kingdom of God, but if we focus on gifts that produce immediate and fantastic results, all other gifts may be unheeded or viewed as marginal. A true, divine, and healthy Body of Christ at work on earth requires all giftings to be considered of equal importance, working together in supreme mutuality. Paul was clear about this in later verses of 1 Corinthians 12 (bracketed notes are my own reflections):

If the foot shall say, "Because I am not the hand, I am not of the body"; is it therefore not of the body? And if the ear shall say, "Because I am not the eye, I am not of the body"; is it therefore not of the body? [By this, Paul illustrates that all members are equally part of the ideal functionality in the Body of Christ.]

If the whole body were an eye, where were the hearing? If the whole were hearing, where were the smelling? [It takes all parts, and therefore *all gifts*, to operate perfectly.]

But now hath God set the members every one of them in the body, as it hath pleased him. [God is pleased by this arrangement.] And if they were all one member, where were the body? [The human body cannot function if it's made up of only eyes; the Body of Christ cannot function if it's made up of only one archetypal gifting.] But now are they many members, yet but one body.

And the eye cannot say unto the hand, "I have no need of

thee": nor again the head to the feet, "I have no need of you." Nay, much more those members of the body, which seem to be more feeble, are necessary [no one Body member is more important than another]:... That there should be no schism in the body [there should be no fighting over who has which gifts and which ones are better than others as they contribute to the main goal of the Great Commission]; but that the members should have the same care one for another [supreme mutuality and equality for precise function].

And whether one member suffer, all the members suffer with it; or one member be honoured, all the members rejoice with it. (1 Corinthians 12:15–22; 25–26)

As we go along in this study, we'll spend more time reflecting on the gifts that our modern Church has marginalized, as well as considering the proof I've witnessed that the more sensational gifts are as real today as they were for the Church of the first century. However, before we dig more deeply into those truths, I want to show the reader a few comprehensive examples of how these so-called "lesser gifts" proved by far to be the most important in *my* life. God does use instantaneous and irreversible deliverances to change a person's life forever, but more often, He uses longer, more interminable methods and circumstances to shape our character. Sometimes it's the less emotional but more durable and steady platform upon which lasting changes occur in people's lives. My spiritual worldview was gradually shaped by those who served at these life posts diligently, patiently, and with the utmost devotion, even though they never spoke in tongues, cast out demons, made the lame to walk or the blind to see, or displayed any supernatural signs and wonders.

These people were, as the chapter title relates, my "heroes." Without them, I may never have been able to establish a healthy link between the "day that changed everything" with Reverend Peter and the man I became through the subsequent years I perceived to be a spiritual drought.

I was one of "those kids"—one who had everything handed to him in all the right and healthy places, and still managed to be internally troubled. Let me explain…

My family was amazing. Mom and Dad were kind to me always and at every turn, and at all times they recognized and bolstered my talents. Year after year, we celebrated my birthday with love and as many gifts as my parents could afford. My parents never fought around or in front of me, and overall, nobody in my family ever squabbled with each other over any substantial issues. With my sisters as close friends, despite stints of normal sibling rivalry, Donna and Allie were the first people I ran to when life's conflicts required me to lean on someone for support. Minus the white picket fence, our family was the epitome of the all-American dream. Had we been followed around by a camera crew as I was growing up, our *Horn House* TV show might have competed with *The Andy Griffith Show* or *Mayberry R.F.D.* Every day was filled with innocence, laughter, love, and happiness.

Nevertheless, I was almost irreconcilably distressed in my youth. For no evident reason, and in spite of my idyllic childhood, I fought daily against an internal anxiety that harassed me to the point of acting out against the world. Mind you, I don't mean to infer that I was under any kind of spiritual attack. Something was going on in my body's chemistry that the medical world wasn't equipped to deal with at the time.

Today, we see many young kids unnecessarily medicated for Attention-Deficit Hyperactivity Disorder (ADHD). Numerous scholars have pointed out that the disorder has become a go-to diagnosis for many doctors at the first signs of a child being troubled, but other contributing factors that may cause the symptoms of ADHD aren't being investigated and treated at the root. For example, an unstable home life may create a distracting environment that carries into school or daycare, and the real "medicine" in that case would be peace at home, but the child is instead placed on meds for ADHD to help him or her focus. There may be another underlying reason a child is distracted or anxious—such as a dairy allergy that triggers fatigue and lack of concentration, another processing disorder, or a number of other influence issues—but because awareness of ADHD was raised in the 1990s and early 2000s, many parents and doctors have grown to suspect ADHD as the answer at the onset, and misdiagnoses of this disorder have reached a higher level. After looking at the symptoms that I had, however, and knowing that my issue was not caused by trouble in my home life, allergies, or anything else, there is no doubt in my mind and in the opinions of medical professionals I've spoken with recently that I was one boy who truly suffered from severe ADHD…and my will was *strong*.

I *was* the little boy who inspired such parenting help materials as Dr. James Dobson's *The Strong-Willed Child*. Even though Mom and Dad were incredible parents, it was as if I had been formed in my mother's womb with the innate will to challenge everyone and everything around me at all times because I could not focus for longer than a second on anything I wasn't inherently passionate about. At school and church, I was like Jim Carrey's *Ace Ventura: Pet Detective* or *The Grinch* movie characters on the inside, flailing like a clown in a hundred directions at once, completely bored with everything around me and clinically incapable of harnessing my pent-up energy.

God knew from the very beginning what brand of people I would need to have around me to temper these characteristics.

One of my first heroes was a woman at church whose name I can't remember. She led worship on the piano prior to my dad's sermon each week, and would allow me to sit up on the stage with her. I was four years old and fancied myself a guitar player, but I had no clue that playing one required anything of the left hand other than to hold the instrument's neck. I had no idea what a "chord" was. I had been two years old when I had laid down my first single—a little ditty I called "I See, I Saw," (nearly the only words in my vocabulary and therefore the song's only lyrics)—and since that time I had always weaved my melodies around whatever harmonized with the open strings while my left hand served no other purpose than to hold the guitar steady. Every "song" I wrote blended immaculately with open tuning, and I developed the idea that the guitar would magically flow together with any melody. So, by the time I was four, my idea of joining the worship band was to strum the open strings repeatedly throughout the song, forever stuck in A11/E—a chord that appears infrequently in any music other than jazz.

As I sat onstage with this woman, my tiny ears could tell that I wasn't in sync with what the others were playing. Instead of concluding that I needed to do something different on my end, I assumed the guitar was perpetually out of tune. Between each song, week after week, I would approach the woman and whisper, "It happened again. My guitar is out of tune." She would always smile, lean over, twist one of my tuning keys, and then wink at me to let me know it was "fixed" and ready to play the next number. I would continue to strum the open strings, hear that my instrument wasn't harmonizing with the others, and, at the close of the song, I would return to her side: "It happened again…" The woman treated me like a member of the worship band with equal importance to anyone else on stage, and I'll never forget what it felt like to "lead" the corporate Body of Christ in "worship" at age four. She always took the time to make this experience fun for me, and I believe my later confidence as a musician traces its roots to her repetitious "retuning" and treating me like a legitimate member of the team.

I may not remember her name, but I'll never forget her service to me and the church.

But my younger years don't always paint such an endearing picture of people surrounding me in love and building me up. Much to the contrary, being the "pastor's son" was often an enormous challenge, and in every congregation, there were those who found more reason to be disappointed in me than to be proud of me. One man, whom we will call Luke, glared down at me no matter what I did. That man simply *could not* be pleased.

If I giggled or whispered during a forty-five-minute sermon, it was guaranteed that Luke's eyes would land on me from anywhere in the room. He was so quick to cast his scornful gaze upon me that I could almost hear the reverberation of a spaghetti-western whip-crack as his head snapped in my direction. If I defied him by meeting his gaze without the instant and shame-faced deflation back into my seat next to Mom, the edges of his eyebrows would raise into a sharp arch, like a nomadic hunter drawing the bow on an unsuspecting deer. Then, his bearded chin lowered and his eyes narrowed to slits just before releasing the all-too-familiar arrows of condemnation. If the disciplinary arrow found its mark, coercing me to put my head down and return to silence in defeat, he would adopt the next condescendingly victorious "that's better" expression before returning his attention to Dad's sermon. If the arrow missed and I didn't react, I earned the slow, methodical head-shaking of a man observing a certified future-delinquent-in-the-making. On the days I did my very best—with hands folded on my lap and my mouth silent through the whole, painstakingly long sermon, determined to show Luke that I could amount to something in life—the best response I earned came after the service, when he would raise only one eyebrow and frown at me with an "I'm watching you" glare.

Luke was always getting on to me and my sisters. Because we were the "pastor's kids," we had to show the better example. On the playground, the designated place for running and playing: "Slow down. This is a playground, not an insane asylum. You're the pastor's son." In the classroom, where *every* child took turns drawing on the blackboard at some point: "Put that chalk back. It's not a toy. You're the pastor's son." In the parking lot, where families loaded up hyper kids: "Stay away from those cars, hear? You're the pastor's son." In the kitchen, where every kid got into the cupboards after each service: "You know better than to use those paper cups. Save those for potlucks. Use a real one and wash it when you're done. You're the pastor's son."

The "pastor's son" had to set the example by sitting rigid and silent next to Mama at all times. Anything less, and it wasn't just my soul in danger; I was leading *others* into eternal judgment as well, should the Lord catch *those kids* acting like children in the house of God as a result of my villainous influence.

On many occasions, when the service was over and every kid in the neighborhood was running rampant in the sanctuary during those few precious free moments before the parents would round us up to leave, Luke's heavy gaze would shoot past thirty-five other children and pierce my soul with reprimand. Every other child in the building could be laughing, playing tag, jumping over the pews, and engaging in loud, rhythmic, hand-clap games, but if I wasn't standing perfectly still next to my mother, he was staring me down with scorn. Running was a sin. Giggling was out. Even smiling earned the warning arrow.

After a while, these constant, high-bar expectations became what my family and I came to call the "Pee-Wee on a train" effect. In 1985, Warner Brothers paired with Tim Burton and Danny Elfman to produce the film *Pee-Wee's Big Adventure*. One scene involves Paul Reubens' central character and then-beloved American hero, Pee-Wee Herman, carrying a classic, red and white hobo stick, catching a ride on a moving train. A rough-looking homeless man keeps Pee-Wee company on the way to his next destination—and when they first meet, they're caught in the throes of what appears to be the beginning of an everlasting friendship as they burst into "She'll Be Coming 'Round the Mountain." Their attention each to the other is precise as they alternate call-and-response singing parts and swing their legs off the edge of the moving train car. Pee-Wee is ecstatic about this newfound relationship. The journey he expected to make alone and afraid is turning into an exhilarating voyage with excitement and new friends around every corner. A few miles down the road, however, Pee-Wee is a little less enthusiastic during "Oh Susanna" while the homeless man is still singing at the top of his lungs. Farther on, Pee-Wee is no longer responding to his shouting companion (who is hugging Pee-Wee around the shoulders) as he enjoys a vociferous blast of "Skip, Skip, Skip to My Lou." Miles later, by the time Pee-Wee's new friend is delivering an unnecessarily loud and emphatic rendition of "Jimmy Crack Corn," Pee-Wee screams and throws himself off the train just as the homeless man yells the lyrics "and IIII. Dooon't. Caaare!"

Moral of the story: Too much of anything unsustainably jazzed or "high octane" brings an "I don't care" result. At the onset of Luke's disapproval, I was Pee-Wee-on-the-spot with my call-and-response reaction: He shot me a warning stare, and I would deflate in my seat to please him. If I thought for a moment that I was successful, I was encouraged to try again. Miles later, as his silent yet simultaneously voluble arrows continued to fly at me through service, I became less enthusiastic about trying to make him happy. Even farther down the tracks, when I realized that there was no stopping him from keeping his expectations of me at a 10, I was Pee-Wee jumping off my own train car, resigned to being myself and letting him continue the ride in his solitary disappointment. Too much of the same suspense from the same relationship all the time—always hoping that it will improve yet never seeing improvement—eventually leads a person (and especially a child with little patience) to give up. It's the law of diminished returns. It's why every jump-scare movie has to insert—between scenes of monsters emerging, car accidents, bombs, etc.—certain "reset" scenes that give your emotions and your nerves a chance to calm down so the next monster behind the victim has the capability of ramping your emotions and nerves back up to a 10. (This is also true with emotional highs, which we will get into later.)

Luke wasn't alone in being impossible to please; it's just that he was the most memorable because others came and went during Dad's days as a pastor. Luke was faithful to attend every service as the self-appointed deputy monitoring the pastor's unruly offspring.

One woman happened to be standing nearby when my sister, Donna, and I were laughing about something—again in the midst of almost fifty other kids engaging in the high-volume laughter and chatter of a recess setting. The woman's reaction is one I've reviewed in my memory many times since. Without any explanation as to why we had offended her, she shook her head disdainfully and exclaimed, "My lands! Kids these days. My heavens!" Donna looked at me and asked what we were doing wrong, and I defaulted to the same "no idea" response that had become the norm during my own Pee-Wee adventure.

At that moment, Donna's face grew dark as she glanced back at the woman —who was now out of earshot—and whispered, "Oh no…"

"What's wrong?" I asked. I was surprised that Donna was concerned. We weren't unfamiliar with the random chastisement of near strangers who had discovered we were the pastor's kids.

"Joe… Her *lands*! Her *heavens*!" Donna smirked sarcastically. "We've offended them both! What ever will we do to correct the damage we've done to that woman's lands and heavens?"

Catching on, I adopted the sarcasm. "I know!" My eyes widened in mock surprise. "I suppose you don't know first aid for lands or heavens, do you?"

"Sadly, no."

We had a good chuckle and moved back to our playtime.

I shared that to say this: When there was no satisfying the adults around us and our only options were to laugh or cry, we learned to laugh and enjoy our lives despite how much worse that rendered our "transgression."

The thing is, we were almost never told *why* we were a disappointment, nor were we encouraged or shown how to do better; we were just made to feel that we always fell short. Learning not to try anymore was easier than trying to decipher the unattainable secret codes behind fixing the problem. *Outside* the walls of our church, people would frequently comment that we were "so well-behaved" and "such good, respectful children," which made Mom proud, but all that praise from others fizzled when we were once again in the presence of the Christian deputies…

Mom and Dad were amazing at keeping us balanced, however, and both were proud of us no matter what anyone at church said. There were occasions when they encouraged us even in front of those who unnecessarily corrected us, but usually, to keep the peace and respect, they waited until we were in the privacy of our own home to deal with the never-ending injustice.

"You guys were just playing," Mom would say. "I know you didn't do anything wrong. Luke can be a little rough around the edges, and he means well. He just wants to make sure the church is an organized place. Just bear with him and let it go."

"But Mom, he was glaring at me again! He's always glaring at me!"

"I know, I know. And it's not fair. But it is what it is. Just do your best to be good and let Luke worry about Luke."

This was the basis of most conversations we had on the subject, whether it was Luke or someone else (and the list of "deputies" was long). Mom and Dad were quick to let us know if *they* thought we were in the wrong, while still upholding the value of good behavior, but it usually came back to Dad's summation: "I'll let you know if it's something you need to worry about."

Over time, my sisters and I concluded that people in the church were likely to be judgmental—but I *did* have a few heroes who kept me grounded in right thinking. And it's a good thing I did, because as it turned out, I was going to need that support when I entered school.

I can't begin to stress how much I hated school, almost from the very beginning. Preschool was fine, because "coloring in the lines" and earning "gold stars" for completing the letter charts was toddler stuff. I breezed by without a wrinkle in those days. First grade was similar, and held few challenges. But by the time I entered second grade, I cast aside any endeavors for gold stars and began to wonder why "prison" was a legal educational requirement in my country for children so young. My mind went in every direction *except* where it was supposed to go, and the anger I had begun to feel against the faculty of "the education system" was heavily increasing because they were the cogwheels in the machine that forced me to "sit down," "be quiet," etc.

During one eye-opening afternoon, my teacher commanded me to sit down and be quiet, but I was so outraged by her order that I picked up my chair and threw it across the room as hard as I could. It went over the other students' heads and hit the wall, causing a twenty-five-pound clock to shake loose and fall to the floor. After it shattered into a million pieces, my shocked teacher immediately informed me of her plans to tell the principal and my parents. In that moment, however, I truly didn't care, and I shouted this fact to her face. I wasn't even afraid of the trouble I would be in; I was just so angry that I couldn't control myself, so I flew into hysterics. The clock may have been the only school property that I damaged in those days, but this incident was not even remotely my only trip to the principal's office. In fact, in the second grade alone, I brought home pink slips, referrals, and notes from the staff describing their exasperated attempts to work with me.

School was a nightmare, and my educational evaluations reflected that.

Prior to this year, the grading system had consisted of only three letters: E, N, and P, which stood for "Excellent," "Needs Work," and "Poor Performance." In addition, the subjects we were graded in were no-brainers, like "visual/motor development" and "social/emotional development." All I had to do to get straight-E progress reports was show that I could toss a ball and agree not to have meltdowns in the middle of "carpet time." Now that I was in the second grade, I learned that a C on the new paper called a "report card" did *not* stand for "Commendable"; D didn't mean "Distinguished"; and F most certainly did not mean "Fantastic." School success wasn't about coloring inside the lines anymore, and my parents were somehow already privy to the letter-grade method of measuring my success on report cards. How they came to know what these new marks meant was beyond me, but when I came home with my first F, Mom wasn't buying the idea that we should celebrate how "Fantastic" I had been at completing my work.

But how could I possibly excel at what they were making me do? Everyone kept telling me I was going to love school, and they had *lied*!

The adults in my life hyped it up: Mom and Dad bought me clothes specifically for attending classes in this building of knowledge each August, and whenever the subject came up, they made the purpose of school clear: "It's where you learn to read and write." By the time I reached the third grade, I already knew how to read, and my writing was as legible as any other kid's, so I believed I had already arrived at the end goal of the system as it had been advertised every summer. But now there were these new subjects I had to submit my mind to, and the injustice was more than I could bear.

Math seemed pointless. I realized that everyone needs to know how to count, so I cooperated in the first few years of school because I understood the value of being able to add up those handfuls of beans the teachers put on my desk. But beyond that, what was I ever going to need to know about the relationships between numbers? Calculators are dirt cheap, and every household owns at least five of them, so what clandestine motive did our government have for enforcing each child to *be* one?

Likewise, what was with all that "history" my teacher was talking about? Why did the past matter if those events couldn't be changed anyway? Christopher Columbus sailed on boats, pioneers lit fires, and we all had turkey dinner. Hit the fast-forward button and we all live in America. My teacher explained that it was necessary to learn about history or else it would repeat itself, but why was that a bad thing anyway? Based on that logic, and on the happy-Pilgrims-hugging-the-natives imagery portrayed in the curriculum, we might just find a new island and have another feast with the natives if history repeated itself. New land, new friends, more turkey.

Then there was science, with so many complicated words like "database," "nucleus," and "cells"…plus something called a "solar system" doing things with planets, and the water cycle bringing rain. We were even supposed to learn the names of different clouds and where they were located in "the atmosphere"—a highly complex term that could have just as easily been called "the sky" in my opinion.

And then there was health class… all the details about the digestive system and how it works; knowing how and why exercise is important to the body; understanding the difference between veins and arteries and how the heart keeps the body alive, and so on. These facts were unnecessary when compared to the much simpler and comprehensive lesson: We eat, and then later on, we use the toilet. If we gain weight for eating the wrong thing, then we should stop eating the wrong thing. We shouldn't forget to run around (as if *any* child needs that kind of advice). I could have taught that class in five minutes, and we all could've gone back home.

I just couldn't wrap my brain around why all these subjects were considered a mandate for my own edification. Why must we, as fragile children in our earliest developmental years, be shackled like captives to our desks for seven hours per day, five days per week, learning things we would never use? When I raised that question, I received all kinds of explanations about the "progression of our world toward a brighter future through a generation of younger minds" and other similar answers, but none of the explanations had anything to do with *me*. Why was I personally being punished and imprisoned by this legal establishment just because other kids might want to grow up and be scientists? If the others wanted that for themselves, then *they* could go to school, but it wasn't my fault that the future relied on people my age to learn. Furthermore, if school just had to happen, why didn't people my age get to choose the kind of school we might be interested in? Why couldn't I go to guitar school or wrestling school? Why did this American institution of knowledge only teach boring stuff?

Day after day, I rapidly became more loathe to return. I couldn't fathom why my sisters were always swinging their backpacks with a happy song at the bus stop. Weren't they as aware as I was that they were about to be picked up by the scholastic police and delivered to their cages? Didn't they also see that this place called "school" was only a collection of proudly displayed "Knowledge is power" billboard propaganda?

The signs the teachers hung… They were *so* misleading. They made promises without a shred of evidence that they could deliver. I might have read "Today's student is tomorrow's president" every time I entered the foyer, but nobody was pulling the veil over my eyes on that one. We had hundreds of students and only one president at a time, so I knew *that* was a lie. The hallway might have held a banner that said, "Mistakes are proof that you're trying," but if you didn't try in the first place, you wouldn't make mistakes: *another* lie. If the phrase, "You are free to choose, but you are not free from the consequence of your choice" had even an ounce of truth, I would have been free to choose to go home and play video games—the consequences of which I was more than prepared to deal with later. I had a big beef with "I won't promise it's always going to be easy; I will promise it's always going to be worth it." According to whom? I could guarantee that the advantages of school were *never* going to outweigh its torment.

Worst of all, however—and it was hung in *every school I attended* (which was many in my youth, since we moved around a lot)—was the poster that proclaimed: "Learning is fun!" The grandiose level of this lie made all the others pale in comparison. The illustration accompanying this phrase varied from place to place: Sometimes it portrayed a boy and a girl flying into space in a pencil-rocket; other times, it was an open book with all sorts of intriguing images floating off the pages. There was even one with a drawing that depicted twenty smiling kids in a classroom, with each student's hand raised in anticipation of being called to answer the teacher's question. But whatever the imagery, the "learning is fun" ruse was eternally deceptive. Was I the only one who saw past the flimsy "education" mask to the covert, governmental operation of executing all childhood happiness—all youthful imagination and creativity—in trade for another generation of dull grown-ups?

So, you can see I was deeply troubled, and from the earliest age I had developed more than a healthy level of cynicism. My *word*, my attitude was awful.

Looking back, I feel terrible for my mother. She withstood more whining and groaning from me about school than should ever be forced upon anyone. How she never blew up and abandoned me in a forest after the sixth, seventh, eighth, and ninth months of my agonizing droning is a mystery. Dad didn't have to hear it as often because I knew he wouldn't put up with it, but Mom always would, and I milked her patience to the bitter end. Every time I arrived home with another note or another bad mark on my record, Mom had to hear all the excuses for why it wasn't my fault—it was the system, or the teacher, or the distracting classroom, or a miscommunication about what was expected of me. My teachers saw through the smokescreen and knew I was just being lazy, but when that report reached my mother, I swore oaths with the tenacity of a bulldog that I was truly applying myself. If Mom doubted my side of the story, I would take my theatrics to a whole new level, lamenting to her through mock heartbreak that I had been a failure at birth and even my greatest efforts only brought shame to myself and the family.

Eventually, this big sob-job backfired, although I didn't see it that way at the time. Mom and Dad agreed to pull me out of the public system. It wasn't just the clowning and the tomfoolery that led them to make that decision, nor was it merely my acting up. We simply moved around so often that by the time I was failing in only the second grade, it made sense to them to pull all three of us out of school so we could at least have a stable education as we moved between houses. I remember when our parents first sat down and explained to us what homeschooling meant, but despite all their warnings about the downsides—which landed on me like the same "wa wa wa, wa wa wa" warnings given by adults in the Charlie Brown cartoons—I responded with enthusiastic promises that this new plan was going to solve everything. School at *home*! What an advantageous concept! With Mom as my teacher, I could play stupid and she would be swayed to give me hints. I would only have to pretend to work half the time, and if I was really good and got through all my work in only a few hours, I would be free to play from lunchtime onward.

Mom was so sweet. During the time between the day our plan was set in stone and our first day of learning at home, she visited several office supply stores and bought all sorts of maps and charts. Some of her choice wall hangings held similar lies as the "learning is fun" posters, but I so believed in my scheme of floating through responsibility that I was no longer offended at the clichéd themes. In a way, they held fresh meaning to me, because skating through life might prove to be a fun alternative to actually applying myself.

On the first morning, after breakfast, Mom called us to report to class. I rushed to my dresser, put on my best clothes, and ran to the secondhand desk she had found for me at a garage sale. I sat up straight with a wide, excited smile and folded my hands attentively. Mom greeted us as if she'd been a schoolteacher for years, gave us a few announcements regarding the layout of the curriculum, and then proceeded to hand out our first worksheets. I don't remember what my first day required of me, but to my own shock and dismay, Mom wasn't responding to my manipulations. Every time I was given a task, I played stupid. Mom would explain the process of the work again and stay beside me until I could show that I understood how to solve the problem. Then she would walk away and leave me to it. When she returned to ask why I hadn't made any progress, I couldn't claim that I didn't know *how* to complete the work because I had already illustrated otherwise, so I was cornered into the lamest admission I could come up with: "It's too hard!" That didn't work, either, as Mom knew me better than my teachers at school had, so before the first day was over, I had already earned a couple of gentle lectures about "applying myself." The only way out was to complete the assignment.

It was just like "real school" all over again—with projects, duties, and tasks—except this time I had a teacher who knew me and my capabilities well enough to know when I was playing it up.

How could I have walked right into this trap?!

The next morning, when Mom called us to the classroom, I wore my pajamas and a scowl (and that's how it would be for the next nine months). Only weeks into this homeschooling arrangement, I realized the expectations of me were even higher than they had been at public school, because at home I was one of only three students. That meant Mom was checking on me more often, and I had to produce results at the end of each study subject. If not, she didn't just send me to sit in the hall like I had been in "real" school; she grounded me from video games and wrestling action figures if she caught me skirting my work. It was a horrible dilemma and I didn't see any escape routes—except by doing my work, which was an unacceptable hitch in my plan.

At one point, when Mom was busy with something else for a few days and we kids had to self-govern our class time, I thought I had figured out a way to outsmart the routine. I took the worksheets and, without even reading the questions, filled each blank with the first thing that came to mind. The curriculum was Christian-based, and one worksheet asked questions about the Bible. I skimmed the first one long enough to know it was asking me something about Abraham, so I wrote in, "the stars." Another one asked something about the first six days of creation, and my answer was simply, "He created it." On my math worksheet, I scribbled in random numbers without even looking at the problems. In science, I wrote in nonsensical words that sounded intelligent, like "stratosphere," "thermal energy," and "phases of the moon." This was my method for all subjects.

I knew if I told Mom at that point that I was finished, she would suspect me of cheating and check over my shoulder to discover my shortcuts, so I waited until she left the room to tend to her consuming project, wandered away from my desk, and played with my wrestlers for several hours before reporting to her that I was finished to make it look like I had been working diligently the whole morning. For several days, she told me she was impressed with how quickly I was getting my work done, and it saddens me a little to remember one comment she made: "It looks like this homeschooling might just be working out well for you!" (Poor Mom! I'm so sorry!) But when she completed her project at the end of the week and was able to check my answers, I had to face the music. I heard my name called from the other room and knew my charade was over.

"What in the world is all this?" she asked angrily. I don't remember my response, but I can recall that in the following weeks I paid for my actions in spades. My stunt had only served to increase the attention Mom gave to my work, and her suspicions about my lack of "applying myself" (oh, how I hated those words!) at my previous public school skyrocketed.

The jig was up. I had exposed myself as the scam artist I was training myself to be. Now, even if it took all day and into the evening hours, I wasn't getting off the hook until I produced legitimate schoolwork. I thought at the time that these were the most miserable days of my life, but I quickly discovered that homeschooling got even more demoralizing. Not only did I have to read, write, calculate, and show that I had learned facts about history, science, literature, and social studies, but I had to do it all alone, *without* anyone to whisper with or pass notes to. Toward the end of the third grade, Mom started noticing that I was socially immature and the solitude of my home classroom was having a negative effect on me. Long term, even if I was struggling in public school, at least I would be engaging in a healthy level of interaction with fellow classmates, so my parents decided I should go back to fourth grade in a "real" school in a new district so I could "socialize with peers." After all, we had moved—*again*—and perhaps this could be my "fresh start."

Well, socialize I did, but not how Mom and Dad pictured it.

I was miserable, and the fact that I had become the school punching bag made it far worse. Kids were brutal to me. In the hallways, they would pull my books away from me, throw them down the stairs, and shove me against the wall. In P.E. class, I was relentlessly bullied when the teacher wasn't looking. I was ruthlessly shoved into my locker, smacked in the back of my head and ears, tripped in the hallways, and thrown to the ground at recess. I was never invited to play with anyone, but keeping myself company a quiet distance from the others didn't curb their interest in making my life torture. If I managed to get my hands on a basketball for a few seconds, the other kids would steal it from me just before they pushed me to the asphalt and ran away in laughter sharing high-fives. If I was running anywhere near most of the other kids, they would hold their feet out to trip me and then explode into a fit of giggles when I stood to reveal a skinned knee. On the rare occasion when I was given a turn at jump rope, it was only so they could observe my subsequently entertaining face-plant when they intentionally increased the spinning rope to an impossible speed.

I was hammered daily, and the faculty of the school was useless in preventing the abuse. Even during class, these students were allowed to verbally slam me without rebuke. If I raised my hand to answer a question, they would sneer and mumble little critical comments: "Oh look here guys, stupid *Horn* thinks he has something valuable to say." The teacher's biggest response was a calm and ineffective, "Quiet down now, kids. Go ahead, Joe." Of course, that never did a thing to stop them. When the teacher passed out worksheets to all the students, the negativity escalated when she arrived at my desk: "Stupid *Horn* thinks he's gonna participate in class, guys!" "Doesn't the teacher know there's no point?" "Yeah, you have to have a brain to fill these out." These moments, too, were met with another calm and ineffective, "Okay now, boys. That's enough." I was called every profanity in the book, including words I wouldn't understand for years, and there was nothing I could do but continue swallowing this treatment down while the teachers sipped coffee and laughed in the breakrooms. With every out-of-class shove, trip, or smack I endured, the in-class disregard for respecting my teachers intensified. From my perspective, the school staff proved daily that they didn't care about *me*; they were only interested in seeing me do my work and hit the government standards of education so it wouldn't be *their* necks on the chopping block if a student was failing in class. (Thinking back, I believe my teacher simply didn't know what I was going through physically or emotionally.)

I detested having to face the beat-down from my peers every day, and the fact that the staff was allowing it to go on stripped away any likelihood that I would ever respect them as authority.

I think God knew I would need a boost midway through the following year, because, after another rough start in the public system, my heroes really began to emerge.

CHAPTER THREE

Heartbeat of the Body

M rs. Phillips was an unbelievable teacher. At first I didn't think much of her, because she, like the teachers before her, knew I was capable of accomplishing more than I was, and she wasn't about to let me play dumb. Once again, I found myself having to do my work or face the consequences, and this time Mom knew the game, so at first Mrs. Phillips was just another fifth-grade teacher to me: another "sent by the establishment to rob me of my childhood" accomplice.

The commonly used desk design at the time was called the "lift lid desk," which was fully closed like a box, with the writing surface opening as a lid to the inside. This year, however, I had the alternate "open front" kind, which is fixed shut on the top and hollowed out near the student's abdomen, allowing access to the materials by sliding them in and out. I discovered early on that if I held my pencil just inside the opening and flicked it around, it made a different sound when struck against the bottom, the side, and the top edges. The bottom, where my schoolbooks lay, produced a thin "tic, tic, tic"; the top, which was wooden, sounded with a "knock, knock, knock"; and the side gave a metallic, hollow "thoom, thoom, thoom." When the three sounds were interchanged rhythmically, it sounded like a drum set to me.

At the start of each day, before the kids had settled down quietly, I would sit to myself and drum a beat. Only days into this activity, I started beatboxing with my mouth as well (way before beatboxing was popular), and then I gradually added a base-rift melody at the back of my throat. Soon, I had become a one-man band at the desk any time we weren't engaged in a lesson. However, eventually this became such a habit that even when the class *was* in session, I inadvertently drifted into another round of music.

Mrs. Phillips started the year patiently: "Joe, your drumming sounds awesome, but this isn't the time or place. Would you mind waiting until you get home to make your cool music sounds? Thanks." Five minutes later, I would be at it again, and her gentle reminder would repeat.

At eight o'clock in the morning, I was Vanilla Ice drumming the immortal number "Ice, Ice, Baby": "knock-knock-knock, knock-tic-knock, thoom." By nine, I was Batman: "tic-tic, knock-knock, tic-tic, knock-knock, thoom-thoooom." Ten rolled around, and I was M. C. Hammer, performing the illustrious "Can't Touch This": "thoom-thoom-thoom-thoom, knock-tic, knock-tic." I couldn't help myself. To me, any environment where I was forced to learn about subjects I believed I would never use was nothing less than a hostile environment, and like a self-appointed victim, I escaped into a happy safe-haven of the mind.

After several months of the same disruptive rap beats materializing from the center of the room during a math test or reading assignment, Mrs. Phillips' warnings grew more tiresome. "Mr. Joe Horn, we're testing. If you do it again, you're out in the hall. This is your first and last warning of the day." I can't say I blame her, and even at the time, I knew that what I was doing was obnoxious, but I wasn't cognitively setting out to get on anyone's nerves. I honestly wasn't. Sometimes I didn't even know I was at it again until I heard my teacher's protests. I told her as much, and at the time I didn't think she believed me, but when the first-quarter parent-teacher conferences were held, I realized she knew what was going on even more than I did…

When the scheduled meeting began, I watched as Mom and Mrs. Phillips shook hands in greeting. I took a seat at my desk, grabbed my pencil, and started doodling on a paper. Try as I might to resist the urge, I found myself drumming again. I was trying to be on my best behavior, but a part of me had already resigned to accepting the inevitable. Mom sat down, exchanged superficial details of the day and a few courtesy laughs with the teacher, and then it came…the moment another of my teachers would fill Mom's ears with a million reasons why I wasn't "applying myself" and had to "shape up or else," and so on. By only the fifth grade, I had memorized the drill. I knew I was in for it.

"Mrs. Horn," my teacher began, "Joe has a hard time paying attention in class. That much is true. And I acknowledge that his grades reflect that. However…"

The word "however" grabbed my attention from across the room like a hovering promise. I stopped drumming and turned my attention to the women. What on earth had I done in Mrs. Phillips' class to earn the elusive and illustrious "however"? The very word insinuated that maybe, just maybe, I wasn't going to be fed to the proverbial wolves by another teacher like I had anticipated.

"That boy…" Mrs. Phillips pointed at me, "…that boy is going to be a musician. He's going to be an *excellent* one." She leaned forward in her chair to increase the intensity of her eye contact with Mom. Her expression was serious. Firm. I was on the edge of my seat as she spoke with the authority of a prophet: "There's no stopping this. It absolutely *is* going to happen. It runs in his blood. He can't *not* drum on his desk and make music, because it bubbles up from inside him. There is no off switch, and there is no cure. It runs deep. It's in his DNA. Do you get what I'm saying here?"

Mom nodded, but it was clear by how her eyes danced about the tabletop between them that she wasn't grasping the relevance of Mrs. Phillips' observations.

"I need to be very careful how I say this, Mrs. Horn." Mrs. Phillips leaned back again. She held her hands out in the air casually, as if searching for a way to drive her point home. "I am certainly concerned for Joe's grades in math, English, history, social studies, and these subjects that, as his educator, it is my responsibility to ensure he's learning."

"Right, right," Mom responded with a nod.

"But, um… Your son is *gifted*. Joe's the real deal." Mrs. Phillips' gaze rose to the ceiling and slowly back down as she contemplated how her following statement should be worded. Then, with the same authority as before, she blurted: "He may not be excelling in the areas the state or government considers to be standardized learning, but *this* school is not equipped to even reach Joe in the areas he was born to excel in. He's special, and I don't say that lightly. We might have choir for these kids, but that's not enough for Joe, you know? The failure here is not your son, the failure is in the limitations of the system. He was born for something higher than all this." Her arms gestured about the room. "There's no outlet in school that accommodates his interests or passions, and he's not the average child."

Mom was beginning to understand. She glanced over at me with a proud smile. I blinked in disbelief. Could it really be that Mrs. Phillips was able to see another side to my insufferable and constant disruptions than just the characteristics of another belligerent, "go-nowhere" delinquent? Was a teacher—*a teacher, for crying out loud*—really on my side for a change? Was she, as it sounded like she was, *truly* sharing that she believed in me and saw potential in me beyond my grade performance? And was she *right*? *Was* there something special about me? I had never thought about this before, and I certainly had not *heard* this before from anyone other than my parents.

"Mrs. Horn, we need to do all we can to ensure that Joe applies himself." I swallowed back the bile those words inspired, determined to hear where she was going with this. "But we also need to do all we can to understand who he's hardwired to be. He's a composer, and he's simply waiting for life to open the door and provide the outlets for him to channel his talents into the proper place. Until that happens, his ability to follow the outlines of class will be challenged; but it's for good reason, not only out of rebellion."

Validation.

Finally!

At this, Mrs. Phillips glanced over at me with a knowing look. I beamed. The implications of that one exchange was enough to give me new respect for her as a mentor, because it drew me up from the "lost cause" boy to someone worthy of an elder's attention. I might not have been her equal in the classroom, but I now knew that she considered me equal as a person with internal value. She *believed* in me, and she had showed that by choosing not to write me off as an inconvenience or as a lesser human just because I hadn't "applied myself" yet to her teaching. In order to apply myself, Mrs. Phillips was wise enough to recognize, I would have to be given a motive first. She not only knew that I needed to be reached with a different approach; she praised me for *why* I needed that different approach, and now we were on the same team—no longer rivals. I wasn't "above" the system, but I didn't fit into the cookie cutter the system had been formed into, either, and now I was able to identify a *partner*—as opposed to another dictator—who believed in me enough to rise up and do the unthinkable: apply myself in class.

(Years later, I would recognize many ministers-in-training in a similar situation: young men and women of God who do not fit the mold and must understand the motive *behind* the cause before they can apply themselves *to* the cause. I'm grateful for the lesson.)

When we left, Mom was as happy about the outcome of the meeting as I was, and the grades on my report card were a non-issue. Mom could already tell by the bounce in my step that we had reached a breakthrough.

For the rest of that year, I followed Mrs. Phillips' directions as well as I could. My grades went up and the distraction went down. I caught and stopped myself from drumming sometimes even before she had to remind me, and whenever I was asked to stop messing around and pay attention, I did so agreeably. That is not to say I was perfect from then on, but I had found a reason to try to be my best. Someone saw potential in me. I liked that feeling, and now, I was far more devoted to not letting her down.

Because of Mrs. Phillips, a musical seed planted in me at birth was sufficiently watered. That patient woman at church who always tuned my guitar and treated me like a bona fide member of the worship team brought the sunshine needed to sprout my roots and draw my budding sapling of musical talent to the surface. Sometimes, as adults, we don't know *why* we do the things we do or why we have the interests and passions we have; we just follow them without thinking about what influence others may have had along the way in tempering our talents into full fruition. Music was "in my DNA," Mrs. Phillips had said. I "couldn't stop it," she had said. So I guess, in some deeply rooted way, I never tried to stop it or remove that tendency from my essential makeup, and now music has become the longest and greatest passion of my life (apart from family and fatherhood). I have never been forced to practice or study playing my guitar. I have never had to be cornered by an adult with a lecture about applying myself. I had the same access as anyone in my generation to video games, toys, and other entertaining distractions, but those outlets for the mind didn't hold my heart in a grip like composing did. I don't know how much of all that can be attributed to these women, but I did become a zealous musician, and it's an art I've used for the Lord from the beginning.

Then there was Bob, the principal of the school I attended in the seventh and eighth grades, and another of my heroes.

Throughout the seventh grade, my experience was agony as usual. More bullying. I had gotten pretty good at making sure I was never alone in the locker room—or anywhere else, for that matter—to avoid being ambushed by the thugs in my grade. By this time, I had become adequate at self-defense, as I had taken karate lessons for a couple of years, so I wasn't always the one to walk away with an ice pack on my face, but I was still the one who found a way to disrupt the class. My teacher—whom I will simply refer to as Miss O'Brian—was worse than any I'd ever had. (Donna had her a few years after I did, and she still remembers how miserable that woman was all the time. At least in this case, I know I wasn't completely responsible for all my teacher's woes. As an adult, after many years to reflect, I can honestly say she simply wasn't cut out to be a teacher. She may have been intelligent, but kids made her uncomfortable, and it showed each time she scolded someone for the most menial offenses.)

Miss O'Brian had a snarky, catty way about her, and every word out of her mouth was as sharp and as cutting as a chef's favorite serrated blade. She never talked, she snapped. Every time. I wasn't the only one who grated on her nerves (again, Donna got along with every teacher *except* her), but I was without a doubt the worst in my homeroom. Because infuriating her was the only way to get back at her for her constant barking at me in front of the student body—and because I had already concluded that I was never going to make her happy—I went out of my way to make her mad. I started by deflecting my internal anxiety through humor: When I learned I might get lucky and earn a chuckle or two from my peers, I quickly developed into a model class clown. Before long, I became astute at turning every moment of the day into a big joke. It didn't make me any less a target of bullies outside of the classroom, but it at least afforded me a temporary comedian crown I could wear during the draining hours of "learning," and life was that much more livable.

Eventually, I pushed Miss O'Brian to her limit. As God is my witness, after I smarted off to her for the four-hundredth time, she slapped me in the face in front of all the other students. She really did. That's no exaggeration, and it happened in front of more than twenty onlookers who gasped in response. (Remember, this was not the 1800s. This was the 1990s. Teachers were *far* removed from the use of physical discipline by this point.) I deserved a slap, that much is true; but there is no circumstance on the planet that justifies a teacher in the United States educational system striking a student's face out of frustration.

There was much talk following this incident between my outraged parents and the school board, and some of the discussion involved legal repercussions, but at the end of the day—for reasons far too complicated, lengthy, and irrelevant to this book to explain herein—we all decided to let it go and move on. I share this, however, to show how obvious it had become that I was quickly developing into the school's most problematic student, and something had to be done. During that year, I spent more time in the principal's office than a hermit crab spends in his conch. Principal Bob was so tired of seeing me by the end of the second semester of seventh grade that, over the summer, he developed a plan for my next year…

I had only been in the eighth grade for two or three days when I heard my name over the intercom: "Joe Horn to the principal's office, please. Joe Horn to the principal's office. Thank you."

What have I done this time?

It was possible that I *had* done something wrong, because by then I had made getting into trouble such an art that I didn't always remember what I was guilty of. But on this occasion, I had only been in school for a couple of days, and now that I was in the eighth grade, I didn't have just one teacher; the days were divided into "periods" of classes that were taught by different lecturers. I had no doubt that in the coming weeks I would be back to visit Principal Bob after I had executed some other knuckleheaded and disrespectful demonstration of absurdity, but I hadn't even been in my classes long enough yet to determine which of my teachers were worthy of my grandest displays of buffoonery. And since we were only just learning the layout of the building and hadn't had any papers due, I hadn't had a chance to get an F on anything, so that explanation for being called over the intercom was ruled out as well.

As I walked down the hallway to my familiar doom-room, I couldn't think of a thing I had done wrong. Then again, the previous year had been *so* rough with Miss O'Brian, it wasn't entirely impossible that I was going to be given a stern, preventative talk about why this year needed to be better than the last.

Yeah, that's probably what it is, I thought, approaching the office. How disappointed Mom and Dad would be to find out that I couldn't make it a week without visiting the principal!

But, to my shock, when I walked in to his office, Principal Bob stood to greet me like I was a fellow business executive: firm handshake, professional smile, and a gesture toward a black leather office chair.

"Have a seat, Joe. I'd like to talk to you about the plans I've made for our current school year."

"Okay…" I slowly sat down, appreciating the comfort of the high-backed, swivel-seat armchair, as I had anticipated being forced to sit at another mercilessly rigid detention desk for the rest of the day. I had no idea why I was being welcomed so formally, nor did I have a clue what he meant by including me in his "plans," but Principal Bob didn't appear the slightest bit agitated as he walked around his big oak desk and sat across from me. He folded his hands and got straight to it.

"I've been thinkin'… You're a funny guy, right?"

"Umm…"

"Come on, you like to make people laugh, right? People think you're funny?"

"I mean…I guess so. Sometimes."

"How do you feel about being the school mascot this year?"

"The *mascot*?!"

My first thought was of those goofy, oversized costumes that acrobats wear on the ballfield during sports events. For a moment, I froze in fear. Was I going to be asked to attend *extracurricular* school events?! I mean, the costume was fine and all, but the idea of being required to report back to the prison grounds during the precious hours of freedom I had been awarded every day after three o'clock? Inconceivable…

Please, God, I prayed silently. *Please no. I can't fathom it. Tell me this*

49

is a dream. Has he already appointed me to this position? Is there any undoing it? I can't be forced into this, can I? How can any person ask this of me? They're gonna make me go to school even when school is out? MORE school? Is he pulling my leg?

My gaze fell on the principal's steel pen as the world spinning around me slowed to a crawl. Conversations in the background muted to the same echoing, low-pitched, molasses drone from the horror movies. My mouth went dry. Sweat toyed with the edges of my brow as my heartbeat thundered in my ears.

I'll have to learn the significance of the school colors and the purpose of those coats with letters stitched on the front. I'm gonna have to use devious, allegorical terms like "school spirit" and "school pride." I'll be cornered into knowing about programs I have zero interest in, like the color guard. They'll make me memorize phrases I don't believe in, like "There is no 'i' in 'team.'" They'll make me paint signs and posters about how "learning is fun" and strong-arm me into "saying a few inspirational words" during sports-uniform fundraisers on the weekends!

Then another thought hit me…

Oh dear God, no… They'll make me a part of "the system" that robs young people of their imagination and innocence… Say it isn't so! It goes against everything I believe in! How can the principal ask me to become a traitor to my fellow man?!

Throughout my childhood, when I had been coerced into attending extracurricular school activities my sisters were involved in, I faced the events like Stephen King's John Coffey character walking the Green Mile to his execution. My sisters and their classmates may have been singing fifty choir songs in three languages, but from where I sat, throughout the whole event in my ADHD-wiggle-bottom mode, Chopin's "Funeral March" floated up around me, suffocating the happiness and life out of me until the final note of my sisters' performance resonated off the walls of the auditorium like a glorious release. That was the moment of victory.

I was so callously bored to tears in these events that I clung to the program printouts as if my life depended on the grip I had on the paper. The first thing I did after our family got settled on the bleachers was to count how many performances there would be, and then, after each number crawled to its conclusion, I lowered my finger to the next song on the list. Each presentation that came to a close was a gift, because it meant we were one act closer to leaving—my little reward from the universe for holding steadfast during the trial of monotony. As such, I had started referring to these proceedings as the "countdown-to-victory" events. Mom would tell me that Allie's choir had a concert, and I would beg her not to make me go to her "countdown-to-victory." Donna would have a part in an elementary school program about the pioneers, and I would grumble all the way there about being made to attend another "countdown-to-victory." (This phrase is still in use in my family anytime we refer to a function we're obligated to attend when we'd rather stay home.)

Anyone who knew me knew how quickly I ran in the other direction to avoid extracurricular school gatherings, and now I was being asked to become a *mascot*... I was going to have to be present at *all* of them!

This was more than I could stand. I was Pee-Wee on that train, and the homeless man was shouting "Jimmy Crack Corn." I was seconds from screaming and jumping into the unknown—

"Joe? Your thoughts?" Principal Bob said, interrupting my anxiety.

My attention snapped back to the office. "Uh, well...a mascot? What exactly would I be required to do?" I asked timidly. "Do I have to go to games and do 'school spirit' stuff?"

"No, no, no," Principal Bob said, leaning back in his chair. "There are lots of different kinds of mascots. You wouldn't be required to be involved in anything outside school hours or off-campus."

Relief surged through my body like rainfall in the desert. I felt my heartbeat start to slow down as Principal Bob had a good laugh. After taking a deep breath and slinking into the black leather of the luxury chair, I opened my mind to what he had to say.

"There are thematic mascots as well, and I have an idea that I think might work out very well for you. This *could be* really slick."

His excitement was visible, and looking back, I realize he must have been planning this conversation since well before the start of the school year.

"I wanna know if you'd agree to be the school's stand-up comedian. At each semester's pep rally, we'll have you start us off with a comedy routine, and occasionally you'll report to my office first thing in the morning to greet the whole building over the intercom with something funny. I'll even allow you to work on new material during the fourth-period study hour. What do you think?"

After I picked my jaw up from the floor, I excitedly agreed to this new plan. It was unfathomable that someone in "the system" had discovered a way not only to *allow* my foolhardiness, but to *feature* it! I couldn't believe the ingenuity of Principal Bob's strategy in that moment.

Ten minutes before entering Bob's office, I had been a troubled kid wondering what I was in for *this* time. But now, I was reborn into a brand-new, glittering layer of celebrity skin. And it changed *everything* for me that year...

Within weeks, word spread all over the school that "Horn" was the new mascot, and it didn't take long for everyone to catch on to my sense of humor—which was intentionally the most outrageous collection of the worst comedy ever. Sarcasm had always been my native language, and now that I had an official outlet for it, I channeled it as flamboyantly as I could. I picked through joke books and chose only those that had potential of being disgracefully bad. The material I used was always clean, but never once funny—and that was the point. There may have been students or staff who didn't know me and therefore didn't "get" why people were laughing in the beginning, but after a while of seeing the reactions of those who did know precisely what I was up to, everyone caught on.

I was "trolling" before "trolling" was a thing...

I can't claim that I understood the psychology of purposefully telling bad jokes at the time, but I recently looked it up in a behavioral science book out of curiosity, and the information perfectly described my social position in the eighth grade. People who write their own comedy material do so at their own risk: If their humor is not accepted, their art expression is rejected—and by extension, they feel rejected—so there is a great layer of vulnerability in producing something new. A person who steals preexisting material that *is* funny is nothing more than a thief who swipes someone else's art. However, if a person uses well-known, overdone comedy that stinks before it's uttered, and if every listener knows the punchline before the lines are delivered, then the following happens: Because the joke is not expected to be funny in the first place, there's no personal or social risk to the comedian if the material is rejected, because the comedy is *in* the rejection of the material—i.e., both the audience and the comedian join in a laugh about how bad it was to begin with. From this approach, the challenge lies in trying to make the *next* joke even worse than the former one; the worse the jokes get, the funnier they are, because the audience is waiting with bated breath to see if the comedian can outdo himself with a bit that grates on the nerves more than the last one. In professional comedy clubs, this kind of humor is a career killer, because the audience expects hilarious, original material. But in a nonprofessional social setting like school, this kind of humor has the power to unite a student body in anticipation of laughing over how bad the worst jokes in history really are.

I didn't analyze this at the time, and I'm not sure everyone thought it was amusing, but I instinctively approached it as the best move. I wasn't well-liked in school, so if I had *tried* to come up with funny material on my own, I would have filled my "haters'" arsenals of insults to pummel me with later: "Hey everyone, here comes 'Horn the comedian.' What a loser. Even as a *clown* he can't make people laugh." Everyone knew I was sarcastic, and what I got the biggest kick out of at the time was making fun of things that I thought were drab or boring. As such, my new schtick as the school comedian was, in a respectful and tasteful way, to sardonically present drab and boring jokes and include the rest of the students in my "how bad can it get" challenge. Nobody could really make fun of my efforts, because I wasn't "trying" or "applying myself" in this position, and if a student commented about how terrible my material was, another one would come to my defense: "That's precisely the point, dude. Joe's *trying* to stink this place up, and I personally think it's hilarious." I disarmed the weapons my haters were pointing at me, and anyone who couldn't appreciate my humor was becoming a socially vulnerable minority.

I remember one of the first times I was handed a microphone at an assembly.

"Why did the chicken cross the road?" I asked.

For a moment, I stood quietly, as if I was going to give the student body a chance to respond. As a couple of bolder kids started shouting out popular answers about "getting to the other side" and so on, I abrasively shouted the punchline straight into the sound system, startling everyone in the room. "He *didn't* cross the road! He was stupid, so he got hit by a car… Because, you know, he was a stupid chicken."

This response caught everyone off guard; after the expectations of my giving a new-generation answer to the age-old conundrum of the chicken and the road were dropped, the class body started chuckling amidst themselves, and their laughter grew more intense as I allowed the ridiculous punchline to linger. Several kids called out for another joke, and I met the demand with a few additional doozies I'd been baking, each more absurd than the last.

This approach was risky, for sure. I was lucky that it worked out, because my awful jokes could have given bullies a reason to mock me that much harder. But in the end, I was (by the grace of God, I'm sure) more accepted for my invisible accomplishments than for tangible gags: I had united a corporate crowd in becoming better than the now-intellectually-inferior classic joke. This was a new era. This was the 1990s!

We weren't *children* anymore, right? We were smarter than that now. Too *cool* for that old chicken. United, we could kill the chicken for good and demand better, more stimulating material fit for our level of turning-of-age maturity.

Who was laughing *now*? Heh…

That's not to say that I instantly became the most popular kid in school, but at least I started receiving respect from my peers. When I spoke over the intercom the words "Knock, knock," I could hear voices from classrooms up and down the hallways shouting, "Who's there?" When I stood in front of an assembly and asked about chickens and roads, I could see the smiles appearing. When clusters of students in the cafeteria saw me coming and started laughing, they weren't laughing *at* me anymore; they were joining me in my appreciation for terrible humor. In class, even the teachers recognized me for what I brought to the table: I was still the class clown, but now that wasn't a derogatory or annoying function; it was a jovial one that brought lighthearted camaraderie to an educational atmosphere, and it was proving to increase efficiency in some students (myself especially). I was literally, legitimately, and oh-so-ironically bringing "school spirit" about by poking fun at "school spirit."

For example: Art was one of the only classes I did well in, because I basically got to color and never had to study anything except fun stuff, like shading and blending. My art teacher approached me one day and said, "Mascot, your art is actually very good. I would like for *you* to choose what our next theme is going to be."

I didn't have to think about my answer. "The theme is, 'School's fun!'"

My teacher knew I was being cynical, and that I openly despised school (or at least I had before my mascot days; I had something to ease the suffering of it now), but he didn't take it disrespectfully, because it was "the mascot's" sense of humor. Nor did the teacher deny my idea, because whether or not the students got the joke, the message of the next art theme would be positive. As promised, he announced the theme the next day, and for the following several weeks, the entire art division of my school produced hand-painted posters that said "School is Fun!" or some equivalent, and then posted them all over the walls. Donna remembers walking down one hallway and seeing an especially colorful poster that read, "Learning helps me grow!" Over the words, the student had sarcastically painted the depiction of a baby growing into an adult, as if the phrase was meant to apply in a physical way. Donna didn't understand the painting, which is reasonable, since learning only helps a person grow internally, and a friend of hers told her it was a joke…one that her brother "Horn" had gotten started all over the school.

This also gave other students who found school challenging an outlet to laugh about their frustrations as well, and the teachers began to appreciate that these frustrations were being channeled into a harmless, upbeat direction instead of through negativity. It was a well-rounded, win-win situation, and it came not through *my* ingenuity, but through Principal Bob's.

Bob saw a floundering child of the system—a child who had shown only signs of failing in an environment that was stifling his creativity and imagination—and he adjusted the system to match the child. With only one small tweak in the school's organizational strategy, my social life, as well as my grades, were redeemed. Although I was still the clown and would never be the most popular kid, when I walked down that aisle at the end of the year to accept my eighth-grade diploma, the mascot earned some of the loudest applause of the evening.

It was one "countdown-to-victory" event that I was sad to see the end of.

Bob was a true hero—one of the greatest in my life, because he, like Mrs. Phillips, saw my failure as a sign that I was born to excel in ways the system wasn't built to accommodate. But he also trusted me with something at his own risk. I could have used my horrible attitude to get on the intercom and tell an X-rated joke just to get a big reaction before my mascot title was stripped from me. I could have stood before the pep rally assembly and told "stupid principal" jokes. Principal Bob was a smart enough guy that he knew a troubled kid like me might do many destructive things with the small pellet of power he gave me that day in his office, but instead, he *trusted* me to use my new post intelligently and maturely. That was not the brand of confidence I had been used to getting from authorities at school *or* at church. Because *he* believed in me, despite the risks that would have placed on him had I abused the mascot role, I believed in myself. Having an adult shake my hand like a business partner and offer me a mutually beneficial deal like he did twenty-five years ago made me want to live up to his expectations. I couldn't possibly let him down, because he believed I was worth more than a string of Fs and Ds on a report card.

The tiny moments of making children believe they're worth more than the world or the system tells them have the power to redirect them toward success and happiness for the rest of their lives. The true heroes know how to keep Pee-Wee on the train until the next destination.

Music and humor became the core of my being, and they're second on my list of ministry priorities. My first is being the jovial, slapstick "big brother" to those who need encouragement. Thanks to Bob, through humor, I've found a way of reaching through the seemingly impenetrable walls of others' sadness and pulling them into believing they, too, are worth more than the world or their own grading systems say they are.

But I would not fully grasp or develop this gift of mine without one lengthy, eight-year season of observing one of the greatest of all heroes outside my family...

His name is Dave Hoard.

After the church merger I spoke of earlier, when Dad retired as a pastor, our family continued to attend that church for several years. The kids' programs on Wednesday nights were fashioned after the Girl Scouts and Boy Scouts, but they had different names: The girls went to "Missionettes" and the boys went to "Royal Rangers." Our district in Oregon had many outposts that made up our section of the Royal Rangers, and our church was home to Outpost 64. We wore uniforms similar to those of the secular scouting clubs, but the mission of our programs were Christ-centered. Royal Rangers' vests featured designated spots for badges we could earn through hard work, Scripture memorization, community service, and learning various survival skills (like building a fire, tying sailors' knots, etc.). Additionally, we memorized mottoes, pledges, and codes of righteous living. If a boy completed the entire program (which took several years), a flag ceremony would be held in his honor, wherein he would stand in front of the church congregation and display what he had learned. The elders would pray over him and, should he wish to remain in the program, he would then become a Royal Ranger Commander so he could teach the younger generations. I was a Royal Ranger under Commander Dave from the age of seven to around eleven, but went on to observe him until I was fifteen when I left that church.

Commander Dave had an instinctive way of reaching the boys that nobody else could mimic. It was something instilled within him that can't be trained. No matter who he was teaching from Wednesday to Wednesday, he extended his welcoming presence to all equally. When he spoke to children, his speech was methodical and gentle in its steady rhythm: never sluggish, but not as hyped as a typical children's ministry leader, and *never* too fast for a kid to follow and understand. His volume was the same as any other speaker, but his voice was permanently perched on the edge of a partial whisper: thoughtful, deliberate, intense, and reflective, as if every word he said in response to his young listeners had been meticulously planned for days. Each time Dave responded to a child's ideas or comments, he delivered his words with sincere astonishment, as if his young companion had just dispensed a level of insight that history's grandest oracles had yet to discover.

As an example, a boy named Billy from the neighborhood once visited our Royal Rangers outpost. Billy's hair was matted to his head as if he had played in the mud a week prior and hadn't bathed since. His clothing was filthy and torn, and his shoes had giant holes in the toes, showing all the way through to his bare feet within. As he walked past me into the room, I noticed he had a powerful odor to him. He found a chair and sat down, scratching his flaking scalp. It's highly probable, under normal circumstances (outside of our class), that fellow peers of Billy (at public school, etc.) would have responded to his odor and disheveled presence with heckling. But when Dave was around, nobody was higher or lower than anyone else. As soon as Billy had taken his seat, Dave's radar picked up the signal of a little boy who likely didn't have anyone back home to look up to or pattern his life after.

"Well hello!" Dave said, walking from his place at the commander's table to our new visitor. In full uniform, he pulled up an empty kid-sized chair and sat next to Billy, bringing his large, towering body down to his height. "My name is Dave. What's yours?" he asked in his nonthreatening and half-whispery tone.

"Billy."

"Billy, oh… Wow…" Dave acted as if even the boy's name was a great revelation. "I love that name. That's a name of a true soldier."

The boy chuckled.

"And how old are you?"

"Nine."

"Oh, I would have guessed thirteen," Dave said, looking at the rest of us as if he was dumbfounded. "You look mature enough to be thirteen at least. I bet you're smarter than thirteen though, aren't you?"

"Um…" Billy looked around at the other faces in the room for a moment. "I don't know."

"Well I do. I can tell." Dave took his time in the conversation, ensuring that Billy would be given a greeting worthy of a king before the class continued. "I'm looking at a future scientist or inventor, I bet. Perhaps an NFL player. Yes, you've got the markings of a professional sportsman *for sure.*"

Dave reached out and gripped Billy's hand in a tight handshake, completely unphased by the child's dirty appearance. He could care less if Billy had germs or smelled bad. Dave was only ever interested in the soul beneath the outward person, and his interest in making them a part of everything was always genuine and never condescending. "I'll tell you what, it's a good thing you came tonight." Dave gestured to the rest of the outpost. "We all knew we were gonna have a great time, but now that *you're* here, it's gonna be incredible! Let's welcome Billy to Outpost 64, boys!"

As was customary in these moments, the rest of us smiled, waved, clapped, and shouted "hellos" from throughout the clubroom. Billy smiled and waved back. Most of the other boys went back to what they were doing, but I allowed my gaze to linger on Billy for a moment. In the five seconds it took for Dave to get back to his table and continue talking with the visitor, Billy kept smiling, though his eyes were locked on his knees. A happiness radiated from behind his simple expression, and I began to suspect it was a happiness he wasn't used to. In less than one minute, Dave had done it again: A boy whom I suspected might not fit in anywhere—a boy the world likely rejected—was experiencing that rare feeling of belonging.

"Guess what we're gonna do tonight, Billy?" Dave asked. Billy looked up and shrugged awkwardly. "We're gonna learn about David and Goliath. Do you know about them?"

"I think so," he responded tentatively. "Wasn't Goliath a giant?"

"You got it!" Dave said, running across the room again for a high five. Billy held his hand up to receive Dave's token of congratulation, and after the sound of the clap was over, I looked at Billy's face again. The smile had returned. No answer in Dave's class was ever wrong, but the right answers—even those that came after the easiest questions— were a cause for celebration, and it always left the children in his class feeling like victors over a great challenge. In this moment, Billy was the giant.

"Now, David was a warrior," Dave said, passing out the Ranger worksheet that featured a picture of the young David with his sling, standing near his sheep. A lion lay dead just behind him. Under that were several fill-in-the-blank questions that would help steer our learning that evening. "Joe," Dave handed me a pencil. "I'm not sure I know the answer to this first one, but I bet you do. Can you help me out?"

I read the question aloud. "David killed a *blank* to protect his sheep, first Samuel 17:34–36." I looked back at Dave. "The answer is 'lion.'"

"Yes!" Dave shot his hands in the air like a football coach whose team had just scored the winning touchdown. "See? I *knew* I could count on Joe to have the answer. Joe is a champion."

Randy, another boy in our club who frequently had an attitude problem, piped up. "Whatever. You don't even have to know the answer. There's a picture of a dead lion right there on the worksheet."

Dave intervened in his gentle way, without scolding Randy. "I know, but Joe is a Bible scholar. He didn't need the picture. He knows *so much* about what the Bible says."

The class went on for a while as Dave hit the highlights of the story, but when it came time to answer the key question of the night, he referred to Billy. "Now Billy, this is the most *important* question of the whole night, and I think I know just the Ranger for the job. Can you help us out with question seven?"

"I guess so." Billy read aloud. "David slew *blank* with a single stone, first Samuel 17:49. The answer is 'Goliath.'"

"Well, well, well. We have another scholar in the Outpost, boys," Dave said slowly, shaking his head in amazement. "I told you, Billy, you're smarter than nine or thirteen. You're smart enough to be *fifteen*!"

I knew he had saved this question for Billy all night because it was one the boy had proved to know at the beginning of the lesson. Dave wouldn't dare place visitors in the position of having to say they didn't know an answer, because making anyone feel stupid was unthinkable. He planned every moment of every meeting to lift each boy into a position of greatness, and even though I was old enough to see that Dave knew exactly what he was doing in saving that question for Billy, it wouldn't be until years later that I would fully appreciate his confidence-building strategies.

When our church ran pinewood derby races, Dave was the announcer. He would stand at the foot of the track and commentate over each race. We had several kids from the neighborhood just like Billy, whose fathers were no doubt unavailable to help them shape and build a derby car. As a result, their cars were slower, bulkier, and wobblier than the cars the rest made with the help of fathers who invested the time it took to make a real racer. But to Dave, every race was a close call.

"And they're off! Number twenty-three is zooming down the track! But look out! Number ten is catching up! Here they go over the hump…"

By this point, the race was over (a fast car could complete the short track in seconds), number twenty-three had won, and the Ranger who owned the winning car was walking over to retrieve it…but Dave was still in suspense mode. "Number ten might just steal the win, boys! Here it comes! Here it comes! Such a fast car!" Number twenty-three was already removed from the track and being turned back in at the tournament line. When number ten finally hit the bumper, Dave called the win. "Ohhh! Number twenty-three by a nose! What a close race!"

It didn't matter that everyone in the room knew that racers like number ten didn't stand a chance. By the end of the night, thanks to Dave, the boys who brought the slowest derby cars were still made to feel like they gave everyone else a real run for the trophies. Nobody went home a loser.

And you simply couldn't pull anything else out of Dave. Even when confronted with outbursts from troubled kids, Dave was a *rock*. One day, when our club was headed to a regional event, Randy (the boy with the attitude) was in the backseat next to me while Dave was at the wheel.

"I hate this stupid day!" Randy said, kicking the back of Dave's seat. "I told my dad I didn't wanna go to this stupid thing!"

"Now Randy," Dave replied in his typical, calm manner. "I know you're gonna have a great time when we get there. You might be feeling a bit challenged right now, but when we get there, you'll have a lot of fun. You'll see what I mean."

"I'm not gonna have fun. This is so stupid! I hate this day, I hate the Royal Rangers, and I hate my dad for making me go to this!"

"I know you don't mean that, Randy. You don't really hate your dad, and if you'll give this a chance—"

"No!" Randy shouted, whipping his head violently into the headrest of the back seat. "I don't have to give this a chance to know that it's the lamest thing ever! I'm just gonna jump outta the car at the next stop light and run home. I swear, I'm gonna do it. I don't even care!"

Dave took a deep breath. "Now Randy, you don't wanna do that, because old Dave can't match your speed, and everybody that loves you is gonna be out lookin' for ya."

"I don't care about that! I don't care about anything! I hate this stupid club!"

"I can see the warrior's spirit in you," Dave said. "You are a true warrior, Randy. But part of being a true warrior is knowing when to fight and when to be peaceful."

I shook my head in astonishment. Even a tantrum earned a child the title of "warrior" when Dave was present. Eventually, Randy went along with us, but it wasn't without a price. He pouted the whole time and had another meltdown on the way home. That evening, it became apparent that Dave *wasn't even capable* of losing his patience. You couldn't *dare* the man to react with anything less than the genuine love of Christ in every situation, and it was an influence I carried with me at school.

Kids were cruel to me within those walls. I know most everyone has some "I was picked on" stories, but mine often ended in fisticuffs. I was no stranger to dealing or receiving a serious punch in the face. As I've said, my family moved a lot, so I went to several different schools, and I was always the "new kid." The most popular clothing style at the time among kids my age was anything that looked like what Vanilla Ice or M. C. Hammer would wear—tough-guy parka jackets, beanie hats, "hammer pants" (named after the pants worn by Hammer in his "Can't Touch This" video), Nike "Airs" (only the high-tops at the time were cool), gold "rapper" chains around the neck, and sunglasses worn even indoors. Anyone who was anyone knew that if you wanted to be popular, you had to look like one of these two icons. (The "leather and zippers" style brought about by Michael Jackson was waning by this time, since his name had been drawn into controversy.) Even kids who didn't follow sports knew they were obligated to choose between the Chicago Bulls and Portland Trailblazers and wear at least one clothing item every day that showed their devotion to their choice team. We didn't have much money, and I often wore hand-me-downs, which meant that I sometimes had no choice but to wear high-water, decades-old corduroy bell bottoms, Ninja Turtles T-shirts that I had outgrown, and clothing my grandmother had made. My grandma was an *amazing* seamstress, and there was nothing she couldn't make, but the fabrics she chose were leftovers from her quilting materials. Bless her heart… It wasn't uncommon that I would get a box from Grandma in the mail: "hammer pants" made of prints with neon teddy bears or Mickey Mouse. *It meant the world to me* that Grandma spent so much time adjusting her patterns to what kids thought was in style so I could attend school and not be made fun of, but because of the fabrics, the other boys at school thought I was even more pathetic.

This book is not about the fights I got into at school, so I won't go into those details, but the point I want to nail down is that I struggled like you can't believe. Each day was an enormous trial. Not only did I barely scrape by with my grades, but I was constantly bullied, at times to the point that blood was drawn. But in the back of my mind at all times, I heard Dave's voice calling me a "champion" or a "warrior." When I got another F on a test, Dave's words repeated in my head: *"You're a scholar…"*

I amounted to something because a hero of mine had told me I would.

Years later, when I became a supervisor of almost fifty staff members at a youth camp in the mountains for five straight years, my own radar clicked into operative mode. Some of the high-school-age kids who came to work for us carried themselves in a way that I recognized as being like myself as a youth: fronting a counterfeit confidence—talking the talk, walking the walk, and at times even wearing the clothes—but deep down, it was clear that they grappled with believing they were worth anything. Before they unpacked their bags each summer, I had already zeroed in on several of them, determined to help them feel like they had value.

Without considering my interactions with them as similar to Dave's exchanges with me and the other Royal Ranger boys, I found myself calling these kids "Champ." If I saw any opportunity throughout the day to build them up, even in the smallest ways, I did. I wasn't just their "boss," I was their "big brother." This truth didn't hit home until one very eye-opening conversation I had with a sixteen-year-old named Jessie.

"Why do you call everyone 'Champ' all the time?" he asked me.

I didn't have to think about my answer—which was strange, because I had never contemplated it before. "Well, there was this guy in church when I was a kid who always called us boys 'Champion' or 'Warrior' or 'Soldier' or whatever, ya know. It meant the world to me at the time because at school I was always just 'loser' or 'Horn,' as if I wasn't worthy of being called 'Joe.' This guy's name was Dave, and he always made me feel like I could conquer the world even though I was just a scrubby kid getting in trouble all the time."

The answer came out of my mouth as smoothly as if it had been rehearsed, but I hadn't thought about Dave's role in who I had become until I heard myself saying it aloud. Afterward, something within me clicked. I realized right then what I had never put together before: Dave was a true hero—and his influence on me had been so powerful that I was unconsciously following in his footsteps nearly twenty years later. His "radar" for seeking out and ministering to those with nobody to look up to was imprinted on my psyche to the point that, even unknowingly, I was adapting to the same practice.

Once we reach adulthood, we don't always know *how* we become who we are or *why* we think the way we do or take the steps we take; we often just walk in a direction that feels familiar on some innate level. As we develop, we take little nuggets from this person or that person, and eventually these moments in our memories accumulate, making a paramount mark upon our shape. But the heroes know that even that one little thing they said to a "Billy" on one long-ago Wednesday night might change the course of a child's life forever.

The gifts of the Holy Spirit certainly *do* include miraculous and sensational applications, and we've seen that manifested repeatedly throughout revival history. However, between those demonstrations are giftings that provide a stable, perpetual stage upon which the performance called "Life" is able to carry on without a hitch.

It's like Paul said: "If the whole body were an eye, where were the hearing? If the whole were hearing, where were the smelling?" (1 Corinthians 12:17). I might rephrase this: "If the whole Body of Christ were prophets who shouted in tongues and cast out demons, where were the Daves, the Mrs. Phillips, and the unnamed women who tune the pastor's son's guitar?" These heroes in my life had the Holy-Spirit-granted *gift of encouragement* (Romans 12:8), and though I never saw them stomp up to the platform and wage war against the principalities of darkness, their influence on me lasted longer and dug in deeper than that of anyone else in my life besides members of my immediate family.

Paul also said, "And those members of the body, which we think to be less honourable, upon these we bestow more abundant honour; and our uncomely parts have more abundant comeliness" (1 Corinthians 12:23). Dave, Mrs. Phillips, and the woman on the worship team in my childhood have a gift that is honorable and beautiful! To people who seek the visible signs of miraculous workings, theirs may never appear to be spectacular from the outside, but their service is *not* inferior than any others. A woman who faithfully bakes peanut butter pies for the church fundraisers and bake sales year after year is as beautiful and honorable in the eyes of God as any Billy Graham the world has ever seen. So, too, is the man who volunteers to drive the church bus week after week to take all the kids in the neighborhood to hear about Christ. The elderly couple who joins hands in prayer for their friends every morning is as vital to the ministry as James Dobson—and, whether they know it on this side of eternity or not, they may cause as many miracles to happen in the lives of those they love.

Think back: Who have been the greatest heroes in your life? Some may be sensational, but I imagine at least a few on your list were simply steady, stable, honorable, and beautiful souls who helped pave the road to your own internal health. *They* are the heartbeat of the Body.

Unfortunately, in the years between Dave and the youth camp, I wouldn't be able to appreciate that. My superficial understanding of the ministry was, at least for a time, shaped by the "Reverend Peters" of the day.

CHAPTER FOUR

We're Off to See the Wizard

Earlier in this book, I talked about the school of hard knocks. Some of the most important lessons I obtained in that training occurred during my teen years. I had received an undeniable touch from the Lord when I was nine, and I had been imprinted with concepts of self-worth by my heroes throughout that season. As I matured from a little boy into a young man, my hunger to know God and to be used for His purposes was insatiable, but the fallible, human side of me misappropriated that hunger, leading me not to the true table of God's presence, but to a phony table lined with an all-you-can-eat buffet of spiritual junk food.

Many in today's societies worldwide live in a constant state of over-indulgence, and the American culture emphasizes a "feast-level" upgrade to nearly everything. We live in an entitlement era wherein we not only *expect* a perpetual Thanksgiving Day feast-level answer for all our needs, we also feel it's what we *deserve*. All we have to do to see this reality is log on to social media or turn on the TV, and all advertisements spanning each product or service—from toaster ovens to family counseling—offer bigger, better, more satisfying results than competitors…or even than what their own services could have provided the day before.

Touching voiceovers in television commercials tell us to indulge, to increase, to achieve, to treat ourselves—and nothing is valid in advertising unless it strongly implies that the product or service will render greater value to our lives than that it can realistically produce. Despite the fact that these depictions can be quite ridiculous, they don't stop American campaigning trends from making extravagant promises. For instance: Yogurt isn't just a food anymore; it's an ecstatic, almost *spiritual* experience, according to the brunette who just slowly and savoringly lifted the first bite of guilt-free strawberry Yoplait into her mouth, tilting her head back and closing her eyes as soon as the silky product lands upon her tongue. The yogurt doesn't just satisfy her belly; it nourishes her soul. Shampoo is not just a hair cleanser; it empowers us to excel in boxing-bag exercises and playing the drums, according to Ellie Goulding's encounter with Pantene Pro-V. It doesn't just clean her hair; it gives her the freedom to more efficiently pursue her life goals. And the Visa and MasterCard commercials promise love, happiness, adventure, and dream fulfillment that never costs a penny up front—but the ads never mention the billions who have fallen for this advertising edge and ended up drowning in suffocating debt as a result. (I don't have an issue with campaigning teams appealing to the human senses in extreme ways to sell what they're pitching. That's their job. It works, also, which proves they're doing well at what they're supposed to do. Unfortunately, however, the result is that we have grander expectations.) These are only three examples of countless ads that come to mind when I think of how our society has gradually adopted the mindset that everything we invest in must give us pleasure and convenience beyond what it is actually designed to give, and when it falls short, we feel emptier than we would have without the hype that sold us on the investment in the first place. We buy Pantene Pro-V and Yoplait and are disappointed that our hair is now waxy and our bellies aren't even close to being full. The "experiences" we buy into fail to deliver.

The same is true for the way the media depicts relationships: If a marriage isn't passionately and sexually charged at all times, it's broken; the pursuit of romance (even to the point of wild parties and sleeping around to find "the one") is a top priority, while the action of the pursuit is fraught with loneliness and the lack of true fulfillment. And concerning diet: We eat more than we need, become overweight, and fall into despair over our health because of the fulfillment we originally sought in food. Then there's spending: We fall into debt before Christmas even arrives, and weddings cost ten grand for the signing of a certificate.

Societal sensory fatigue. Too much. All the time. From everywhere.

We're in a constant state of escalation.

Society has a problem. We have to hype everything across the board to a whole new level every time it's presented in order to keep people's interest. This is a universal truth. Everything is sensationalistic. Everyone has to be crazy in love at all times or the institution of marriage is broken. We must land precisely at the center of our dreams and have every shiny thing we've ever wanted, or we've done something wrong along the way. The world gives false, Thanksgiving-every-day promises, and each time we don't get what we're hoping for, we're left feeling as if we've partaken of the feast and still have intense hunger. Indulgence now, emptiness afterward. Extravagance at all times alongside perpetual futility in the pursuit of superficial gratification. Excess, luxury, pleasure…then aimlessness, hollowness, and meaninglessness.

The thing is, we were never *created* to live in a state of overkill, and God knew what He was doing when He gave us an innate balance. He knows that if we live at all times like a high-octane Pee-Wee on a train, we will jump off before we ever get where we are headed. If we learn the answers to everything now, we'll make a beeline for the end goal and miss the necessary lessons on the journey. God knows that if we get what we want when we want it, we won't appreciate the prize because we haven't earned it. There is a season for the Thanksgiving meal, certainly, but most of the time, we are hardwired to survive on the salads of God's blessings and divine providence. It's those steady trails of God-given, spiritually nutritious breadcrumbs that give the occasional hearty meals meaning. Nobody knew this better than Solomon, the wisest man in the world (1 Kings 4:30)—as well as the richest (2 Chronicles 9:13–28). In his lament in Ecclesiastes, he shared this truth, and it is as timelessly applicable today as it was in Old Testament times (bracketed reflections mine):

> The words of the Preacher, the son of David, king in Jerusalem [a.k.a., King Solomon]. Vanity of vanities, saith the Preacher, vanity of vanities; all is vanity [or, as many modern translations phrase this: "Everything is meaningless"]. What profit hath a man of all his labour which he taketh under the sun? One generation passeth away, and another generation cometh: but the earth abideth for ever. The sun also ariseth, and the sun goeth down, and hasteth to his place where he arose. The wind goeth toward the south, and turneth about unto the north; it whirleth about continually, and the wind returneth again according to his circuits. All the rivers run into the sea; yet the sea is not full; unto the place from whence the rivers come, thither they return again. [All this to say: The world keeps spinning, people work and toil for earthly gain, they die, another generation comes, they repeat the same cycle, but all efforts toward temporal gain is meaningless and vain.] All things are full of labour; man cannot utter it: the eye is not satisfied with seeing, nor the ear filled with hearing. The thing that hath been, it is that which shall be; and that which is done is that which shall be done: and there is no new thing under the sun. Is there any thing whereof it may be said, See, this is new? it hath been already of old time, which was before us. There is no remembrance of former things; neither shall there be any remembrance of things that are to come with

those that shall come after.... I have seen all the works that are done under the sun; and, behold, all is vanity and vexation of spirit. (Ecclesiastes 1:1–14)

This last stretch of verses has been repeatedly misunderstood and misquoted. Solomon isn't referring to the idea that we will never see, hear, or experience anything new in life. (If that were the case, the existence of the Internet [as merely one example] would disprove this.) He's speaking of the cyclical, chemical response humanity engages in from generation to generation when new things are introduced. Mass-produced automobiles might have been new to the world through Ford in the early 1900s, but before that, we had carriages, horse-drawn carts, and so on. The products we employ are different from age to age, but the excitement and sense of adventure reach the same highs—and then the same nonchalant lows—in every generation. What we feel today when we buy our first car is similar to what our ancestors felt when they traded ten sacks of flour for a new horse. However, buying our first car does *not* produce the same euphoric sensation we get when we buy our tenth car later on, so each purchase has to be prettier, glitzier, and more intense than the last in order to produce the same enraptured reaction to the first purchase, and we find ourselves in the perpetual snare of "needing" the increase. There truly is nothing new under the sun as it relates to the human-reaction cycle. Everything this world has to offer holds zero eternal value if the goal is only to feed material hunger. The winds will blow tomorrow, the sun will rise and set, the rivers will keep flowing, new generations will come, and if our epitaph equates to "[insert name] had a lot of stuff," then everything—according to the Word and common sense—is meaningless.

We were never designed to live in a constant state of indulgence. Sadly, however, much of society today is built upon the lie that we aren't happy—and we are not *achieving*—if we don't exist in a constant high.

And when we finally have everything, as Solomon did, that abundance only exposes how lonely we are and how little we actually have in the light of eternity, since we can't bring anything to heaven with us anyway (1 Timothy 6:7; Matthew 6:19–21). We want Thanksgiving-feast upgrades every day…and yet it will never be enough.

The most tragic angle to all of this, however, is how these habits play out in religion…and nobody is guiltier of this than me.

Almost every Christian I have met in my generation can relate to the following process:

1. After sincerely giving our life to the Lord (or, if we grew up in the Lord, after reaching that moment when the relationship with God becomes more mature), a season of passion for a new purpose inspires us to do great works for the Kingdom of God. Simply knowing that we, as Christ-ians, are called to a service great and eternal ignites an enthusiasm to use our God-given gifts and talents as quickly and as powerfully as possible, because we're eager to see others' names added to the Book of Life and to see them experience the presence of the King forever. But then:

2. Although the motive is glorious, this gusto response can mislead us into thinking that our gift(s) must look like someone else's— or appear more grandiose in outward manifestations—in order to be as valuable to the Lord. A minister comes into town and pulls a "Reverend Peter" on the congregation, everyone has a Thanksgiving-feast-level spiritual experience, and the underlying sensation that creeps into the minds of *many* who are present in this kind of demonstration is that we must look like, dress like, speak like, exhort like, and minister like the most explosively visible members of the Body in order to achieve the highest level of personal success in the spiritual realm as it pertains to reaching the lost.

And when we finally get the spiritual-experience feast we're hungry for, our human, cyclical expectations only raise the bar higher. Our *next* spiritual encounter—whether we are the consumers or the servers of the feast—must be grander than the last. However, as discussed in the previous pages, the Body of Christ can't function—in fact, it cannot remain alive at all—if all members carry out the same tasks, and many gifts that appear subtler on the outside are equally efficient in their unique purpose. This is clear by how eloquently Paul compares the Body of Christ to the human body. *Some* members of the Body of Christ, like Dave Hoard, may not ever be viewed by others within the Body as the loudest or grandest of pulpit-pounding ministers, but he made a world of difference to countless young boys—many of whom might have grown up to be the grandest of ministers because of that one little thing he said through the Spirit-given gift of encouragement.

My mom has always said, "Anyone can count the seeds in an apple, but only God can count the apples in a seed." A faithful seed-waterer will likely never get the same attention and fame as a powerful preacher, but, barring a miraculous intervention from God, powerful preachers needs their own heroes to water the seed the Holy Spirit placed in their soil if it is to come to fruition.

In the previous two chapters, I spent some time explaining why these quieter gifts are crucial. Now I would like to extend that thread to include how damaging it can be when we seek more sensational gifts over the ones we are given by God, using my own life as an example.

When I was in my teens, my concepts of ministering to or witnessing to others were skewed by what I had seen in the churches I had attended in my youth. Many a sermon had been delivered that said the equivalent of: "Be bold, and know that the Lord is with you. If you are a coward, your ministry will not be blessed, and you will one day stand before God to answer for those missed opportunities to tell others about Him. When you witness to a nonbeliever, know that every word out of your mouth is being guided by the Holy Spirit. It's not *you* talking to your friend, it's *God* talking to your friend through a human host. But the human host must be willing to open his mouth for God to reach the sinner." These words can be interpreted a number of ways, and if approached with balance and sincerity, messages like these can hold a great deal of truth. However, my youth was immensely affected by revivals occurring in Pentecostal churches across the nation at that time, so the emphasis on spirituality and holiness was such that if we weren't actively telling everyone in our whole town about God—including those who had already asked not to be told—we weren't "being spiritual." If someone *did* reject the message, we were trained to persist to the very end, allowing the Holy Spirit to convict that person toward change…the brand of change that bows the knee to *our own* expectations, not to the Lord's.

The approach to being an active witness of Christ varied a great deal from preacher to preacher in those days (guest speakers were numerous and hot off the press at any Pentecostal church during this era, so even if you attended one church for years, you would hear sermons from hundreds of mouths); but the bottom line, as it was presented to me then, was that I would be hindering the Lord if I wasn't aggressively proselytizing Christianity. If I started to tell people about Christ and they told me they didn't want to hear it, I had to "fight the good fight" like Paul did and keep at them, or else I would be seen as a "coward" who "hindered the Holy Spirit." Likewise, when any well-known minister came to town and delivered a convicting sermon, a concept that manifested in my own thoughts was that there was only *one kind* of minister: a strong, articulate, powerful speaker who drove the masses to the altar in repentance—or drove the one-on-one listener to accept Christ at the first attempt. I had seen a couple of frauds (like Reverend Peter), but I had also seen revered ministers from all over the country inspire immediate change in those around me. (Note that I said "immediate" change… More on this later.) I had been told that we can't effectively share the Gospel without studying and knowing the Word, so that at any moment we might be able to quote Scripture. And again, properly interpreted and correctly *applied*, this is a timeless truth. Improperly interpreted and applied, this means we must learn how to beat our listeners against a wall by dropping verses in their laps that they can't argue with, so they have no excuse for not accepting the Lord.

Folks, this is the absolute *opposite* of showing love to the lost. All it does is trap people. What happens when you corner a canine and provoke him with actions and words he doesn't like to see or hear? He becomes aggressive against the provocation, and he might just bite back. That's all this form of "witnessing" accomplishes, and I was at the center of it for a season of "righteous witnessing" that I wish I could say I hadn't participated in. That is not to say I intentionally set out to hold power over anyone or damage any lost person's concepts of God, but the Church, like school, had its own form of "the system," and I had gotten sucked into it. I don't know how many people I might have discouraged from the Gospel in those days, but I remember one man who got a heavy dose of self-righteous judgment from me…

How I wish I could change that now.

After I completed the eighth grade, my family continued to move from place to place as Dad carried out his "tentmaking." (For those readers who may not have heard this term used in church, "tentmaking" refers to any trade or skill a minister can rely on to make money in support of his or her ministry. The term draws its origin from Paul, who supported his own preaching and church-launching ministry by making and selling tents [see Acts 18:3]. When I was very young, Dad's "tentmaking" was flipping houses, but by the time I graduated from the eighth grade, he was beginning to invest in other support businesses; so rather than explain all the ways Dad made money in order to minister through his writing [because the list is long], I will simply say that he was tentmaking all over the place, anywhere he found an opportunity to make money and channel it back into spreading the Gospel. He may not have been in real estate any longer, but his work took us all over Oregon.) As such, I was placed back in homeschooling, and my anxiety about getting along with teachers was finally over. Mom helped me out a lot through my final years of school, but for the most part, I was able to push myself through it merely because the end was so much closer than it had been when I was in the third grade.

With a completely free schedule, I was available to help my father with his many tentmaking endeavors, and I often worked for him full time while I finished up my high school curriculum on the side.

At one point, our family owned a mobile lunch truck company; we drove to construction sites or manufacturing plants and opened our doors at break time. I had the same route each day, so I grew to know the people who flocked to my truck for a sandwich and a bag of chips when the bell rang. Dad's ministry kept him elsewhere on Sundays and Wednesdays, so we weren't attending the same church; as a result, he wasn't aware of some of the extreme teachings I was being indoctrinated with. I had reached a moment in my developing maturity when God was becoming more real to me, and my role as a soldier in His army was obscure. I knew I was called into His work, as every Christian is, but I hadn't yet wrapped my brain around my gifts. I was so fervent about spreading the Gospel and using whatever gifts and talents God had given me to reach the lost that I tended to be overzealous. My enthusiasm itself wasn't the issue; the real matter was that I misplaced my zeal in an area in which I am not gifted. I was born to be the humorous "big brother" and musician, not the lunch-truck preacher.

One guy, Kevin, always got the same lunch from me every day: A deli sandwich, a Mountain Dew, a bag of chips, and a Rockstar or Starbucks energy drink for later. But on one day, whether he ordered it or not, he also got a sermon.

I had only known this customer for around three weeks, so I hadn't developed any kind of sincere friendship with him. Kevin was always telling me stories about the wild parties that he had over the weekends and about the many women he "hooked up" with. His lifestyle might have been exciting in a temporal way, but nobody ever *truly* finds fulfillment by repeatedly getting drunk and waking up in strangers' beds. I cared about Kevin, and deep down, I really wanted to help him, but the doctrines of witnessing that had been imprinted upon my psyche from church won out over common sense and authenticity, and as a result, I instigated the following unquestionably inappropriate conversation. It was a Friday, and the weekend was coming…

"Hey Kevin, what's up, bro?" I asked as he sauntered around the corner from his rental car office.

"Not much, man. It's Friday, so I'm already makin' plans to paaarrr-taaayy!"

"Oh yeah?"

"Yeah, man. I'm gonna find myself a hot chick and several beers and, well, *you* know, heh heh."

I must pause to share with you how insanely immature my next statement was: I didn't know this man's heart at all; I hadn't spent any time getting to know him, his family, his interests or passions; and I hadn't invested my life into his in any way. Additionally, I didn't wait for a natural segway into a conversation about the Bible or God or anything. The subject had never come up before, and for all Kevin knew, I was just another guy—one who might be interested in hearing about the women and the booze. I'd never given him any reason to believe that his weekend stories were offensive, exciting, or anything else. I gave no explanation or warning whatsoever that would have cautioned Kevin about who I was and what I was about to say. I could have said *anything else* in this moment—from describing what Jesus had done in my life to telling about a funny movie I had watched the night before…*anything*—but I chose the worst possible word-vomit in the universe and slammed him with it.

"You know, Kevin," I began calmly, "In the book of Revelation, we read that if we are lukewarm, we will be spewed out of the mouth of

God. Our actions must be hot or cold, but be they lukewarm, we will face rejection on judgment day."

Since this reprehensible mistake, I've learned much more about the real meaning of this verse, and I no longer believe that I was using it correctly. By no means should a judgment about the Laodicean church—who represented themselves as believers—be equally applied to a nonbeliever, or to someone like Kevin whose conversation openers usually involve beer and women. Comparing him to a tepid Laodicean was no laughing matter. It was intensely shameful. I couldn't have assumed he was hot, cold, or lukewarm about anything to do with his relationship with Christ. That was my first mistake. In addition, by stating that "we" read something insinuated that he had the first clue what the Bible says and a corresponding conviction regarding the God who wrote it. What hubris! What damage!

Kevin wouldn't make eye contact with me after I said that, but he did respond. "Yeah, well, God is good, though. He'll forgive me."

"Actually," my disgracefully relentless mouth went on to say, "God *is* good, and He *does* forgive, but we must turn from our wicked ways and ask Him to forgive us—and it must be sincere. God is nobody's scapegoat." My posture was erect, and my expression was like a mother warning a wayward child. (How condescending…)

At this, Kevin fumbled around at the soda cans for a moment and reached for his wallet. "How much do I owe ya?"

Once the transaction was complete, I never saw him again, except once when I left my lunch truck and wandered into his mechanic shop to find my loyal customer and he fled into a side door to avoid me. (This was my first and only sign that I had come on too strong. Before that, it hadn't dawned on me that I might be someone that needed to be avoided.) After my impromptu mini sermon, I left Kevin with a "Have a good weekend" and drove off feeling like I had won the argument. I had successfully cornered Kevin, and I was proud of it.

My heart *should have been* heavy as I drove away. I should have felt a burden to pray for him—even by sending up the smallest prayer asking God to use my words as a gentle reminder to Kevin throughout his Friday evening that he is loved and cherished by a Savior who wishes to spend eternity with him. But the story gets worse. I wasn't heavy-hearted, and I didn't pray for a potentially lost soul. Instead, I used the time alone in my truck between stops for the rest of the day to plan how I was going to deliver my testimony about Kevin on the following Sunday. It was all about *me*.

When Sunday morning rolled around, I had my speech ready. I stood proudly in front of my youth group to talk about how "God had used me" to minister to the lost. I told the whole story, and even attributed my quick "scapegoat" comeback to the Holy Spirit's leading. My listeners were nodding with encouragement as if I had accomplished a great duty, and when I sat down, my youth pastor gave me props for being bold.

I will say it again: It was no laughing matter. There is simply no excuse for my action that day. Kevin is a *human*. He has a *soul*. My cavalier, battering-ram witness routine might have changed the way he viewed God and His people for the rest of his life.

I have no idea where Kevin is today, and I've prayed many times that the "seed" I planted—one that I thought was Gospel but that in hindsight I understand to be nothing more than self-righteous judgmentalism—will have been replaced by someone else in his path who understands knowing and loving people with the Gospel message rather than cornering them with it.

This is only one example of the kind of "minister" I was becoming in those days. I feel bad for my friends back then who had to listen to me go on and on for hours about why their secular music was putting up a wall between them and God, or why their fathers were "unholy" for watching *M.A.S.H.* on television every night. (Ironically, *M.A.S.H.* later became one of my favorite shows.) I was an unstoppable audio loop of hellfire-and-brimstone nonsense. The God I represented wasn't the same

Christ I would later come to know as I matured. (Nobody was more patient with me during this phase of my life than my best friend from childhood, Jason Pumphrey. He sat through hours and hours and then eventually months and months of my judgmental monologues about whether his standard of living stood up to my parental expectations over his life. Not every friend of mine survived this intolerable chapter, but Jason was, unbelievably, still there when I finally grew out of it.)

To make matters worse, it was around this time when I attended my first youth camp: six straight days of chapel in the beautiful pine hills of Sisters, Oregon, listening to a then-famous speaker known for his "bam, boom" deliveries. And I mean that in a literal sense. When Reverend Lenny (not his real name) presented an altar call, he would stand a couple feet away from someone, and when he thought the moment was right, he would shout "BAM!" or "BOOM!" and the person would fall to the floor. Sometimes Reverend Lenny would blow on the person instead, but the result was the same. I appreciate that, unlike some ministers I'd seen back home, this minister wasn't shoving people's foreheads and forcing them to fall, but for many of the teenagers present that week, the goal *was* "the fall." As another fair credit to the man, he explained his bizarre ministering style so as not to give the impression that it was the *words* causing the effect: "Why do I say 'Bam!'? Because I like the word. Why do I say 'Boom!'? Because I like the word. Why do I blow? Because I like to blow. By themselves, these things are just my own quirks. They do nothing in the spiritual realm. The results you see happening around you are not because I have magic words or magic breath; they happen because the Lord wants to bless you." I'm glad he at least explained *that*, but many other things were going on that he did not explain.

Most of the students in that gathering were immensely immature; by only the third night, there was an underlying sense of competition amongst them to see who could be the "most spiritual" in their visit to the altar. This was as obvious as the nose on Reverend Lenny's face, but he didn't appear to be bothered by it. The teenagers around me may not have said it aloud (nor did he), but the whispers and shared glances (many times from Lenny, himself) were louder than any proclamation: If you didn't go to the altar at all, you were disobeying God. If you went to the altar and didn't have an "experience" (such as speaking in tongues for the first time, getting "slain" and falling, "laughing in the Spirit," etc.), you were either resisting God or something else in your life (likely some hidden sin, or such was the popular explanation) that was keeping you from receiving His divine touch. Something was wrong with you. Clearly Lenny and his crew weren't the problem, because the evidence of their spiritual competence was all over the room, so if God didn't coerce you to the floor with tingling sensations, you were broken and had to be fixed before you could be "blessed" like the others. If you *did* go to the altar and have an experience, yet you didn't follow that up by being the loudest and most hyped camper the rest of the week, your experience wasn't real. Or *worse*, you "relapsed" into your sinful nature immediately, making it plain that the enemy was already taking hold of you again. There were people lying all over the floor for each of the first two nights, and by the third, there was no getting around in that room. So many people had fallen that several had to be "overlapped." I will never know how many of those young people were legitimately reached by the hand of God versus how many were acting this way to draw attention or who were just trying to "jumpstart" the experiences they observed around them, but we all knew one thing to be "true": If you were *really* in love with God, you would become a part of a drastic demonstration at the altar by the end of the week. (For many, the focus was on the manifestations, not on the Lord. Not really…)

By the fourth night, all of this desperate behavior escalated even further. Some of the youth had been so affected by this spiritual-expectation overdose that they started growling and spitting at the altars, portraying themselves as being demon-possessed so they could later be celebrated as having been "delivered." Though I would *never* state that every case was faked, I personally knew some of these teens and what they were up to. A couple were even caught "peeking" to see who around them was watching while they engaged in this dangerous "possession" role playing.

Sure, I was aware that a lot of the youth around me were simply getting caught up in the emotional drama, but there were others I knew (and some that I didn't know, but whose personality and temperament didn't strike me as the kind of people who would fake spiritual manifestations for attention) who went to camp sincerely seeking the Lord and had an authentic experience with Him. This was proven a couple times. For instance, Lenny had a tendency to "know" things he couldn't have known. Donna, who was there with me that week, remembers him approaching a girl from across the room on his first night (before any personal details could have been shared) and shouting, "Purity! Purity! Your body is the temple of the Holy Spirit, not a playground for men!" The girl broke into tears and confessed her promiscuous lifestyle on the spot. (For the record, she was dressed modestly when this transpired.) Another girl was called out: "Stop the secret cigarettes today or they will be secret needles tomorrow!" She immediately went forward and fell at the altar, and later that week gave a testimony that she had, in fact, been stealing her mother's cigarettes and looking at her father's heroin needles with interest. One girl stood stunned when Lenny pointed to her and told her that her use of laxatives was really for weight loss, not for regularity, as she had lied, and that her continual abuse of pills was slowly destroying her organ function. Yet another young man on the second night had his skeletons revealed—although this time, Lenny didn't shout from across the room: "Young man, you've come to the altar to receive from the Lord, but He's waiting for you to put the magazines and videos out of your life first." Later in the week, the boy testified that he had been a three-year pornography addict, a habit he had never told a soul about prior to that moment. (I would like to reiterate that the surrogate minister is not the source of supremacy—the supremacy is in *God*, who meets sincere individuals right where they stand in supernatural and miraculous ways despite the minister. Lenny wasn't "God's chosen psychic," as there is no such thing; God was speaking to these young people because *they* were seeking to be reached by Him.)

If even half of what I saw during that camp was real, there were more miracles in that six-day period than most churches experience in fifty years. As much as I wish I could say my perception of the camping trip was a healthy one, my attention remained on the works of the reverend instead of upon the works of the Lord.

From where I stood in that crumbling chapel building, Reverend Lenny was nothing less than a legend. He had *power* in the fight against the enemy. The way he thrust his hand in the air ten feet away from people and shouted "BAM!" just before they flew to the floor was like a superpower move straight out of a video game or a battle scene from a J. R. R. Tolkien book. When he blew on people from across the room who received the "wind" and flocked to the altar, a secular audience would have thought he was a mystic or a hypnotist mastermind. Between his celebrity status (people traveled the length of the country to see him back then) and his wizard-like stage persona, I felt like I was in the presence of a holy-fire-wielding, spiritually transcendent warrior with authority over the unseen realms. There were "ministers," and then there was *Lenny*—and the two were incomparable.

I'm sure by now you get the picture: I was young. I wanted to win souls for Christ. And there was only one way to go about it. I had to *be* Reverend Lenny.

On the last night of the camp, I went to the altar and asked the reverend to pray for me. I don't recall a specific prayer request, but I was feeling the pressure to have my own epiphany before the week's end. So, regardless of what I told Lenny, I was really up there to receive the keys to my own door of "superhero ministry." When he prayed, I wasn't thinking about who God was or what He wanted for me; every facet of my mind was focused on what my body was feeling. Because of that "day that changed everything," that "day when I was nine," I knew it was possible to have that kind of experience, so I remained in a state of analysis upon the physical. It all happened fast and I don't remember every detail, but I know I tried to jump-start the Holy Spirit by surrendering my muscles. I fell, surely, but it wasn't because God had anything to do with it. Just like everything else in my walk with the Lord in those days, I made it all about *me*. Feeling disappointed and foolish, I remained on the floor long enough to convince those around me that I was as spiritual as they were, then I got up and went to my cabin for sleep. As of yet, I wasn't the "power move" minister. Perhaps they were right. Had God withheld my new super moves because I had hidden sin in my life? (I couldn't think of anything specifically…)

Only time would tell.

I didn't crave power in the traditional sense of the phrase. When that string of words is used in conversation, it typically refers to someone wishing to dominate others for narcissistic reasons, and I was familiar enough with Christ to know that approach would offend Him—something I didn't want anything to do with. Controlling or manipulating others honestly wasn't my motive. However, it would be a lie to say that my desires were entirely humble and selfless. I was as caught up in the "show" of Christianity as many of my peers. These "shows" happened so often in that era that they grew to be the norm: A service with the Lord's true presence would be a dazzling spectacle, or else it wasn't infused with His presence at all (or so was the concept of churchgoers I knew). Bells, whistles, smoke, mirrors, and glitter. Spiritual Thanksgiving every day. It's "what Pentecostal Christianity looked like," you might say.

I, as well as many peers and elders in those days, believed it was a win-win situation to be both the popular, successful celebrity and a soul-winner at the same time: earning bragging rights while checking more souls off the "lost" list. It's simply what the mainstream mentality of the Church Body largely migrated into just off the cusp of the "Prosperity Gospel" heyday of the 1980s. God didn't just want us to spread the Good News, the Church thought, He also wanted us to be superstars, live in mansions, and wear gold rings. Thanks to the "Satanic

Panic" trend of the same time—that period when the message of Christ was temporarily traded in for widespread panic over who was involved in what underground satanic cult—by the early 1990s, it was still "the thing" for traveling ministers to enter town in a blaze of glory with a wild tale regarding the cult they belonged to before they found Christ. Through the doorways of the churches they marched, declaring that their privileged intel of the workings of Satan gave them an edge in fighting him, and they put on quite a display of casting out demons, delivering the masses, and carrying out their own version of the "BAM!" "BOOM!" altar calls. As history does show, many (though not all) of these ministers were busted for fraud a few years later. (Their books were proven to be filled with lies, and many also misappropriated donations as well, just like Reverend Peter.) While they took to the pulpits, however, just like reverends Peter and Lenny, they were the greatest perpetuators of the stereotypical "show pastors"…

And I fell for it.

Hook.

Line.

Sinker.

I can't tell you how bad I wanted it. I *dreamed* of having "power moves" behind a pulpit like they did. I even went as far as to fantasize about what my own "quirk" would be. "Bam," "boom," and "blowing wind" were taken, and I didn't want to be a copycat minister, so maybe my "thing" would be a finger-snap or a clever word. I saw myself standing on a stage with people all over the floor. Once, I even prayed my then-girlfriend would experience the baptism of the Holy Spirit, but the entire time I was praying for her (a half hour!), I was more focused on whether she looked like she was going to fall down or what was emanating from me as a spiritual tool in God's use than I was on whether the Lord was doing something fresh in her life.

For a season, I read my Bible every day and prayed fervently for God to use me. I refrained from listening to secular music, revised my television and film interests, and committed to rebuking every unholy thought that came into my head. All this sounds impressive until you understand why I was adjusting my behavioral patterns. My *actions* were commendable…but my *motives* were not. It wasn't entirely that I wanted to have the Word breathe life into my understanding of God so I could grow closer to Him and appreciate His divine nature—not on the deepest levels, anyway. And if I'm honest, I didn't pray for the sole purpose of developing a relationship with Him. The drive behind my sudden submersion into Scripture and prayer, now that I'm mature enough to admit it, was to find that one verse that would "unlock" the Lenny power within me so I could begin the Reverend Super-Joe ministry I was sure God called me for.

Looking back, I see more clearly what was going on—and, thanks to the showmanship of those ministers, I can liken it to the plot of the classic film, *The Wizard of Oz*. In the beginning, Dorothy is young, vulnerable, and naïve, knowing nothing about life and not asking for more than what the world offers in the natural (much like I was when I was nine). She gets caught up into the whirlwind and lands in a new place filled with vibrant color. Nothing is the same as it had been on the farm; everything is a dazzling spectacle. Supernatural activities are occurring all around—falling houses, glowing bubbles with "good witches" in them, talking trees, dancing scarecrows, living men made of tin, flying monkeys—and, rather than argue the logic behind all the insanity, Dorothy blindly accepts that it is all a perfectly natural extension of the relationships between good and evil in "the merry ol' Land of Oz." (I, too, initially accepted so blindly that all the oddities taking place at the altar were normal workings of the spiritual realm, because I lacked the discernment to see how distorted this approach to spreading the Gospel was. It wasn't about *Christ*, as it should have been; it was about phenomena and competition.) Quickly, Dorothy becomes convinced that the wizard is the only one who can unlock the door to her way home, so she treks the yellow brick road in search of him; she doesn't yet know that she already has the capability of getting back home and that the power she seeks is already there. Every hope she has rests in the wizard's supreme, dream-granting know-how. (I was convinced that the Lennys of the Church had the keys to unlock the power of the grand ministers, so I went to the altar to speak to them instead of speaking to God about what He really wanted for me—which is what I, and any believer, have the capability of doing at all times.) Dorothy's perception of the goal (returning home, in her case) is skewed by the concept that only the wizard can help her get there. (My perception of the goal—ministering to the lost—was skewed by the concept that only the "wizards" [Lenny and other ministers like him] held the key to being *truly* effective in ministry.)

But this is where Dorothy and I differ. Deep down, she just wants to meet the wizard and go home. Deep down, I wanted to *be* Lenny—even replace him, perhaps—and remain in the merry ol' Land of Awe as a celebrity preacher.

Near the end of the story, Dorothy walks the long, glittering hallway to the wizard's room and meets quite a sight. What a marvel the wizard is!

That is, until Toto pulls the curtain back and reveals the trickery…

At this point in my journey with Christ, I was still looking over the hills for the Emerald City, and nobody could convince me that Lenny was just a man behind a curtain. He couldn't have been. I had seen too much "proof" to believe it. The world he was a part of was vibrant, colorful, and filled with wonders I had never seen. He was "the wizard," the great and powerful Oz, the keeper of the keys to every dream. If I could just find the right verse or be prayed over by the right man, I would become the great and powerful Joe…

Around the same time that our youth group was returning home from camp, my church experienced a revival. The passion and excitement were certainly present, but discernment was intensely lacking. In the beginning, I saw occurrences in the congregation that were, without a doubt, radical movements of the Lord. Quickly, however, there began to take root a movement that my gut questioned, but my theology wasn't developed enough to know the ins and outs of what God would manifest during service. It started with a lot of tears, rededications, deliverances, and baptisms of the Holy Spirit, but before a few months passed, it was becoming…concernedly irregular. Everyone had seen the "Yoplait" serving of God and hungered for the "Thanksgiving feast" at the altar. More, more, more. Overindulgence was the only way. Nothing less than spiritual sensory fatigue would satisfy them.

People were "getting drunk in the Spirit," which meant that they would sway, stagger, and laugh out loud at everything they saw during service. A few times, married folks interacted with other people's spouses in a way that could be described as flirtatious, raising an eyebrow or two, but because their actions were the result of "something the Spirit was doing in them," the behavior wasn't questioned. On several occasions, this phenomenon engulfed twenty or more people at once, and the only thing distinguishing the altar atmosphere from a small-town bar atmosphere was the absence of liquor.

I was sure God *could* instigate this kind of behavior if He wanted to, but a small voice inside of me was beginning to ask: *What is the point of this? Whose soul is being reached by these "spiritually intoxicated" activities? What does any of this have to do with Christ's sacrifice on the cross?* Nevertheless, I was so unwilling to let go of my Reverend Super-Joe dream that I—at least in the very beginning—refused to face my concerns. I found it easier to pretend these activities never happened and go on in my personal journey than to stop and deal with whether they were Holy-Spirit-sanctioned. That would require theological study and training, and I didn't have time for that…not with the whole world waiting for me to take center stage.

I went to my dad several times, telling him I felt called into the ministry and wanted to be used in a mighty way—then I would describe some of what I had witnessed in these services. (As I mentioned before, I was going to a different church because I wanted to be with my girlfriend. He and Mom went to a smaller church several cities away, but they supported my decision to attend a different congregation.) Dad was *crucial* at this time in my life for grounding me in reality. He some-how—brilliantly—always knew what I wasn't admitting to myself: I was a leaf caught in the whirlwind of hype. I had gone and landed myself in Oz, and my focus wasn't truly on God, but in becoming a grand wiz-ard for Him. Toto was barking at the curtain for my attention, but my gaze was upon the fire-and-smoke-wizard spectacle. Dad always knew. Always. He never told me as much directly, because he didn't want to influence me toward thinking that Pentecostalism was nothing more than emotional phenomenon. He believed that what transpired in the Book of Acts chapter 2 was real, and he had seen enough supernatural-ism in instances of authentic baptism of the Holy Spirit, speaking in tongues, and falling under the authority of the Holy Spirit's touch that he understood the infinity of God's sovereignty anywhere a sincere heart sought Him. But Dad was also wise enough to know that I only needed one endorsement from him regarding the "show service" and it might warp my theological concepts of God and His Church for many years, if not for life. Dad knew *much* of the Church Body at that time was far too focused on altar manifestations than upon spreading the Good News of Christ to the lost, and he didn't want me in the throes of confusion any more than I already was. So when I approached him for advice, his words maintained the perfect balance between what God can and will do *for* people, and what the Church wanted God to do *in front of* people.

"Here's the thing," Dad said to me one day. "God could make mountains crumble at His mere thought if He wanted to, and there is evidence throughout the Bible that He utilized that authority over nature many times to illustrate His supremacy: Moses and the Red Sea, the plagues, fire from the sky, destruction of the altar to Baal... So it's not a question of whether or not God is *capable* of doing the things you're seeing in church, it's a matter of whether or not those demonstra-tions are real, and whether they are within the realm of His will to begin with. You'll know they're real or not based on what transpires *after* the occurrence, and you'll know they're of His will or not based on what the Scripture says about it."

"What do you mean I will know 'after the occurrence'?" I asked.

"If 'Sister So-and-so' goes to the altar, falls to the floor, gets up weeping and crying and praising the Lord, but then she goes straight back to her vices Monday morning, then her 'deliverance' probably wasn't real. If she has that experience and makes a lasting change in her life—if everyone around her sees something different about how she lives from that day forward—then it was probably truly an intervention of the Holy Spirit. The people you have to look out for are those who are 'delivered from demons' every week, or something to that effect, but who never truly achieve victory over their vices."

I fiddled with my goatee for a moment. "So I have to watch people over time?"

"Well, yes and no." Dad was so balanced. Such wisdom he showed in his words. "First of all, it doesn't have to be any of our business what experiences other people are having—so, no, you're not obligated to be a watchdog. However, you shouldn't be completely blind, either. If you observe false movements of God on a corporate level—and it's my opinion that you are—then you should be careful not to go jumping into any of that nonsense unless you're one hundred percent sure that what you see is really a work of the Lord."

"How can I be sure, though?" I pressed. "Just short of obtaining a seminary degree, there doesn't seem to be a way for me to know what's really happening."

"Well I don't know about *your* church," he said, "so I don't want to make any snap judgments about them, but I can already tell you that I've seen and heard about things going on nationally in the Pentecostal Church that are reminiscent of pagan rituals. I don't think people are always aware of what they're involved in to that degree, but I think they can be deceived or hyped into a movement they don't understand."

"Paganism? You think it's gone that far?"

"Oh sure," Dad said with a chuckle. "I've written at length about this. We're under a major attack right now because the Church is too focused on jumping around to bring the light of the Gospel to the center, and dangerous things happen when Jesus Christ is on the back burner. There's all kinds of weirdness happening right now that couldn't possibly be normal in a God-fearing church. Just the other day, one of my ministry associates approached me and said, 'Now Tom, when you're in the middle of worship service and the demons start crawling down the walls, what do *you* do about it?' I said, 'What did you just say!?' You know, I thought for sure I had heard him wrong."

"Right, right."

"He said it again: 'When you're in the middle of worship service and the demons start crawling up and down the walls, what do we do?' He acted as if it's a typical, Sunday-morning occurrence that demons would be creeping all through the sanctuary right smack-dab in the center of where the Holy Spirit is allegedly conducting His multiple interventions. Criminy… On so many levels, that's just absurd."

I nodded in agreement, and then he continued.

"Some of this will be obvious to you if you read First Corinthians chapter fourteen. Paul talked about the service being in a state of such chaos that if a lost soul wandered in and saw what was going on, they would simply stand back and say, 'Are these people mad? Have they lost their minds?' And what good does that do in the interest of the Gospel? Furthermore, I know you're eager to be used by God, but if your goal is to be the next super-preacher, you really need to ask yourself two questions: First, 'Who am I really doing this for?' and second, 'Will my future ministry *really* help the cause of the Gospel, or will it only serve to dazzle people?'"

Dad didn't know it, but he nailed it. I felt these convictions on my own end, even though I had never read 1 Corinthians 14 with these recent questions in mind. But just as soon as I had added this new truth to my own list of ponderings, my church took things *way* too far.

I'll never forget the "birthing in the bathroom" incident. A guest speaker came to town and spoke about end-time "birthing pains of the Church Body." I can't remember his message, so I have no idea whether his conclusion was theologically sound. I also can't assume that what occurred next was or wasn't via his influence, but I didn't need a seminary degree to immediately recognize it as bizarre heresy.

A grown man was found on the floor of the bathroom "giving birth in the Spirit." He was moaning in agony from "birthing pains," he said. That's what the story was by the time it reached me and my sister, Donna (who was attending church with me at the time). Donna remembers the conversation:

"Did you guys hear what happened to that guy in the bathroom?" our mutual friend Amy baited.

"What 'guy in the bathroom'?" Donna asked.

"Oh my gosh. God totally touched this guy. Okay, so here's what happened: He was just using the restroom like normal, right? Suddenly, he started feeling contractions and he leaned over the counter—"

"Wait," Donna interrupted. She had only ever heard that word in reference to a pregnant woman in labor. "Contractions? I don't know what that means."

"You know," Amy jutted her belly out in mock pregnancy and gestured to the muscles just above the navel. "Like when you're having a baby? It's when the muscles get really tight and start pushing the baby down."

"No, no, no…" Donna shook her head. "I know what *contractions* are, I just don't know what they are when men have them. What does that mean for a guy?"

Amy was a couple years older than Donna, and she took a moment to smirk at me as if we, the older and more mature teenagers, knew what was going on. I assure you, I still didn't. Looking at Donna, Amy leaned forward for emphasis and drove it home.

"That's precisely the point. *Men don't have contractions.*"

Donna and I stood there a moment, expecting just about anything *but* what was said next.

"Anyway," Amy said, bringing back her enthusiastic, juicy-gossip expression. "So he's standing there, the contractions come on hard, right? He leans into the counter, eases himself to the floor, starts *screaming*, and they find him lying on his back in spiritual labor. He was giving birth in the Spirit!"

"Uhh…" I glanced at Donna and back. "What was he giving birth *to*? I mean… What!? Is this for real?" What were we even talking about? It was insanity…

When Amy saw my furrowed brow, she counterattacked. "No, trust me. I'm not making this up. The whole church knows about it. God *totally* touched him. You can ask anyone. This really happened. God really sent that man into labor."

When I didn't say anything, Amy called over some friends who were standing nearby, and they validated the story. One of them, Terra, voiced the only wisdom in the excitable group of girls. Her words were not by any means articulate or polished (she sounded about like your average fifteen-year-old), but she appeared to be the only one slowing down in the midst of all the flurry of what "God" had done long enough to ask some logical questions.

"Hang on though guys. I'm not trying to, like, deny God or His power or anything," Terra paused for a moment to think, "but why would God do *that*? That doesn't make sense. It's not a healing, and it wasn't like a 'speaking in tongues' thing. It didn't accomplish anything. The whole thing is just weird. You know what I mean?"

"God works in mysterious ways, though," Amy disputed.

"I know, I know… But usually when He works in mysterious ways, there's a…there's a… well, there's a *point* to it. There's a reason for it in the end. This guy was just in pain for no reason, and when I asked my mom about it last night, she said there wasn't anything in the Bible about men spiritually giving birth as warnings to God's people or anything. She couldn't figure it out either. I mean, if he had actually *birthed* something, then maybe, but I don't know…" Terra shook her head, suddenly bold. "I just think he wanted attention. I don't even think it was real."

Amy stiffened, rolled her eyes, and crossed her arms. "Be a Doubting Thomas if you want to, Terra. God does what God does, and it's not for us to question Him."

I was as curious as anyone to hear what the pastor would say about the bathroom incident that morning. My head knowledge was too immature to know what the Bible might say, and my emotions wanted it to all be legitimized so I wouldn't have to face the reality of what this "show church" was becoming—but my gut told me that what happened in that bathroom was not only absent of God's involvement, but there was a chance that the episode was very dark…*if* it was real at all. Surely the shepherd of the flock would either denounce the whole matter as heresy that he planned to deal with or he would justify the news with a verse.

When service began, the incident was the first thing the associate pastor addressed (the pastor never said a word that I can recall), but to my surprise, he didn't make a calculated conclusion one way or the other. He gave a quick, nervous comment like Amy's about how God works in mysterious ways, and then moved on to the announcements listed in the bulletin. I don't know if the pastoral team was simply trying to keep the peace or what, but their tolerance made the situation worse. A few weeks later, as I was still marinating on how to react, the same thing happened again—but this time, the second man "giving birth" in the bathroom went as far as to say that he was spiritually becoming Mary in labor, and that the baby "inside" him was the Son of God.

That was it. That had definitely done it, and I was finished with the whole gamut.

What had started as a slow, warning sensation from the heart—one that gained rapid speed with the first birthing tale—suddenly exploded into emergency status. The radar was no longer picking up signals of danger, because the danger had already arrived. I might not have had an ounce of theological training (even though I tried to make people think I did), but I could see the lack of discernment all around me, and I was disgusted that the only person questioning these odd "movements of the Spirit" was a fifteen-year-old who earned the title "Doubting Thomas" the first time she introduced logic to the discussion. The situation was already way out of hand, and just about everyone in the congregation could do anything they wanted, as long as they described what they were doing as "in the Spirit"—and it was not only allowed, it was celebrated! This church easily fit into the category of chaos Paul referred to in 1 Corinthians 14. At once, something within me shattered and my "great-wizard" dream began to look distasteful. What Dad had said was true: If a supernatural sign didn't contribute to people coming to know Jesus Christ—or at least to the discipleship of the Body, which is a part of that goal—then it was a show, and likely a hazardous one, since a corporate group was engaging in activities that could open doors for dark influences.

Besides that, Dad was right about something else... I reflected on all those around me who had shared "God touched me" testimonies, and the same people were still up to no good Monday morning through Saturday night. As only one example: One boy in my youth group gave a testimony three times (the *same* testimony in fact, given on Sunday morning, Sunday night, and Wednesday night, just to be sure the whole church had heard his revelation) about how God had delivered him from listening to profane secular music after he was baptized in the Holy Spirit at the altar. Each time he told the story, he had his own quips he waited to tell about himself: "Before, I was the kid who bought *those* kinds of CDs... You know, the ones with the little stickers on the front? Heh heh..." And everyone would chuckle. We all knew he was referring to the "EXPLICIT LYRICS" warning, and he couldn't wait to get to that part of the story so he could condescend the man he used to be.

Whether he remained delivered from secular music is anyone's guess, because I didn't follow him around, but evidently God had not delivered him from having premarital sex, because he was too loud a braggart for those particular details to remain hidden in the months that followed. Several other teenagers had similar "deliverances" and they would speak openly about their altar meetings with the Lord, but they still engaged in repugnant behaviors and wept bitterly every Sunday or Wednesday about their latest trials.

Everywhere around me, people were claiming to be delivered, but almost everyone remained imprisoned to the same—or worse—behaviors and vices from week to week to week, never appearing to be fully liberated from the chains that bound them to sin and sorrow. What was this accomplishing? People in church took the stage all the time with newfound glory, but a lost person just wandering into a church for the first time would get the idea that the God we serve is weak: He can make people quiver or stagger or fall or jump, but He doesn't have the power to create lasting change in a person's life… In a way, it began to look like the *opposite* of real ministry. Not only was it binding the saved to a demoralizing loop of false deliverance, it was potentially confusing the lost, and nobody knew where he or she *truly* stood with Jesus Christ. There were plenty of superstars and standup comedians, but everything I was seeing was abruptly counterfeit to me.

I didn't want to be the Great and Powerful Wizard of Awe anymore. I'm ashamed to admit it took me that long to conclude that this whole arena of whizz-bang altar experiences was the most superficial goal I could ever have. In hindsight, however, being stationed in the center of all of that for several years was perhaps the greatest step in the direction God would take me, and the message He gave me to share in this book would never have been seasoned to what it is now without those frustrating and confusing days. Everything came to an enlightening peak when I met Debbie that day in Crane, Missouri. My eyes were finally opened, and the word the Lord gave me to share with all of you readers was finally culminating into a cohesive, palatable, and refreshing memo-randum significant for every believer today.

Before I tell you about my unreal encounter with Debbie, I'm sure by now you're wondering whatever came of Reverend Lenny. I assure you, I haven't forgotten that thread. Bumping into him later on was… illuminating, to say the least. People continued to come from all over the country, journeying across their own yellow brick roads to meet the grand wizard, and his reputation as the answer to all their problems was only increasing during that era. But when I saw his true colors, I realized that the marvelous embodiment of spiritual perfection I imagined him to be wasn't reality. He really *was* just a man behind the curtain.

Not "the great and powerful" at all…

CHAPTER FIVE

That Day in Crane

A few years after I left that church where the men were "giving birth" in the bathrooms, I began working as the outdoor recreation director of the same Christian youth camp where Lenny had been a guest speaker. My entire family had been brought there to work in full-time ministry as well, so both sisters and my parents served there alongside me. It was the same hot-spot hive for nationally and internationally revered speakers as it had been when I had been a young camper. Instead of being a part of the services, I was on the serving side with my co-staff, which numbered around fifty in the summer months.

By the time I settled into my job there, I had already become a jaded skeptic of the "bam/boom-style" services, but because I worked and lived on the grounds, I was submerged ever deeper into the continual trails of testimonies during the chapel services that extended throughout the night. A church service seemed to be in session around me at all times, and the judgmental and oppressing expectations of the arriving groups of campers were, at times, overwhelming. There were certainly exceptions to that, but most group leaders arrived in anticipation of being greeted like royalty and having their every whim satisfied, and if we didn't immediately fulfill their demands, some religious-spirited person would corner us on staff, trying to turn material issues into biblical ones.

As one example: The Snack Shack was supposed to close at eleven o'clock at night so the two teenage crew members running it could report to the breakfast grill at six the next morning. One night at closing time, the workers were approached by a group leader who asked if they could keep it open later so the campers just getting out of chapel would have time to buy candy and pop. Chapel was supposed to have ended at ten, but the service was running past that time—in fact, it was expected to continue for another few hours. Our employees explained to the leader that they had strict instructions from their supervisor (me at that time) to close at eleven as scheduled. At this, the leader huffed and puffed and *demanded* to see the supervisor. My staffers didn't know what to do or who to listen to, so they did what anyone in their position would: called me on my camp radio and home phone repeatedly until I got out of bed and agreed to come try to reason with the man. When I got there, his countenance was intense and irrational. He was pointing right in my face and giving me a stern lecture about how the campers were going to come out of the chapel thirsty and hungry, and if our facility was dedicated to ministry as we claimed, then the staff would be Christ-like servants to the needs of the campers (which evidently included making pop and candy available to people around the clock). I tried to explain that there were drinking fountains all over the camp, that the midnight snack the kitchen crew had baked for the group earlier would be available all night long in the dining room, and that my staffers simply needed to get some rest so they could get up and ready to fry eggs in just a few hours. My reasoning still wasn't good enough for the leader.

"Where's your servant's heart?" he asked me in front of a small crowd of nervous leaders who had begun to gather behind him.

They *always* went there…

Any time our camp staff wasn't meeting demands (even when those demands presented a safety hazard, such as the time they asked us to set up rickety ramps at the end of the dock so campers could ride bicycles into the lake, or when they wanted us to leave the pool uncovered all weekend without a lifeguard present), we "weren't being Christ-like servants." God's name, will, and authority were *frequently* used by His people for vain purposes in those days. Anything or anyone that could be manipulated in order for campers to get their way was suddenly placed under the authority of a twisted verse or biblical concept.

People using God's name or authority…for vain or selfish gain…

It brings fresh interpretive light on the Third Commandment, no?

The grievance was exacerbated when the treatment came from the guest speakers—the credentialed, ordained, "chosen" mouthpieces of the Lord who stood in the chapel exhorting God's children one minute and breaking every facility rule in the book the next, as though they viewed themselves as above the law.

Now that I was a supervisor at the same youth camp where I had craved the "Great and Powerful Joe of Awe" title in the past, a certain familiar name popped up on our guest-speaker list. Seven years had come and gone since I had encountered Reverend Lenny, and here he was again: same place, same time, same speaking arrangement. But it was a completely different, eye-opening experience to see him again. My ministerial job description required me to make sure that Lenny had what he needed to make his week of preaching as comfortable as possible. However, it was *also* my responsibility to take care of my staff members all summer. These two duties had a history of conflict during instances when guests were unkind to the crew members, and there was many a moment when I was pulled in to spread the salve.

By the time Lenny arrived, I had seen hundreds and hundreds of reputable Church "celebrities" roam in and out of the campgrounds— many who were class-act people of integrity and many others who were very much *not*—and I realized that you can't truly know people until you watch their "off-stage" treatment of those who strive to serve them. Although Lenny wasn't the most explosive of our "royalty mentality" speakers when he made demands, his air of superiority over the "under-ling" servants was the final straw. I let go of any potential lofty concepts about him that I still might have had in the back of my mind. That's not to say that I have ever—then or now—regarded Lenny with disdain, nor do I doubt the positive effects of his ministry, because I saw them for myself. But, *it says something about a man of God* when he arrives to a week-long commitment to preach about service to the Eternal King, yet he spends that time letting the camp staffers know in not-so-subtle ways that he is above them, and that their sole purpose is to treat him like an earthly king.

Before each meal in the camp dining room, we made an announce-ment about how much food the campers were expected to put on their plates. We were not an all-you-can-eat restaurant, we explained, and we only cooked what we knew would be eaten so we didn't have any waste. Breakfast on Lenny's first morning with us was like any other: We announced that guests should only take one scoop of eggs, one scoop of hash browns, one biscuit, and two pieces of bacon. We particularly stressed the meat limitations, because that was the one selection that guests sometimes pretend they hadn't heard about: "Remember, we only have enough bacon for everyone here at the camp to get two pieces the first time through the buffet line, and then there will be one pan left for those who would like seconds." One of our young, female staff members had been instructed by our food-service director: "If you see anyone tak-ing more than two pieces, speak up and politely remind them they need to wait until everyone has gone through the line at least once."

Lenny was the first to break the rule: He took four pieces of bacon. So, our employee did as she had been asked, alerting him that he was supposed to wait.

Without giving her the time of day or attempting to explain, he grabbed a lanyard from around his neck showing his name on a guest card and held it out in front of her face. She glanced at it, not under-standing what that gesture had to do with anything, and awkwardly turned to her supervisor with a shrug. The head cook walked out from behind the grill and intervened, explaining the bacon rule a second time: "See, we're trying to make sure we have enough bacon for everyone," she said. "We'll have some extras in a few minutes when everyone has had their first plate, but if people take more than…" Her words trailed off as Lenny again held up the lanyard between them, flaunting his name tag as if they were in a heated poker match and he had just drawn a winning ace.

"I'm the *speaker*," he said, lowering the card with a triumphant smile.

The head cook nodded politely and took a breath to continue her explanation, but she stopped when Lenny grabbed another piece of bacon and lifted it in a "cheers" gesture. He took a bite of it as he turned and walked away. Obviously, once the food had been touched, we couldn't put it back in the buffet pan, so it was a lost cause at that point. He had won the battle of the bacon.

The next morning, we had a different menu, and the campers were told they could take two links of sausage. Lenny was, once again, the first to break the rule, grabbing up four links in front of several of our staff. This time, he didn't wait for anyone to say anything; he simply held up his lanyard and wiggled it in the air in front of us before turning on his heel and disappearing into the breakfast crowd.

We finally stopped expecting him to follow the same rules as the "regular" campers and allowed Lenny to eat whatever he wanted. And though it was challenging, we also continued to tend to his cabin or make deliveries at his request, because that was easier than trying to explain that we weren't the Hilton with twenty-four-hour room service. (Everyone in my family remembers having to send staff out to his cabin several times, which was unheard of. No other speaker before or after him ever required "room service.")

I bring this up now to help you fully grasp the contrast that I observed shortly after Lenny's visit ended. Another familiar name showed up on the guest list as a group leader, and when I saw this person again, I was refreshed beyond words. Commander Dave was everything he had ever been and more. The very second he saw me operating the belay rope at the rock wall, he flew right back into his classic Royal Ranger exchange.

"Well, well. Look who it is, everyone! Joe Horn, the champion."

"Commander Dave!"

I gave him the side-clap of the century, truly and deeply touched to see him again but unable to take my hands off the rope lock for a full embrace.

"I see you've grown up to be a strong, able-bodied man of God, dedicated to His will and ready for service."

Dave picked up right where he had left off in my childhood. It was as if only a few days had passed since I'd seen him in class, and he was still mentoring me, helping to shape my faith. And he was every bit the hero to me in that moment as he'd ever been when I was a boy.

After a minute or two of casual conversation, I asked a question that had been prodding at my mind for years.

"Hey Dave, lemme ask you something," I began. "When I was a kid, you treated every single boy who wandered into Outpost 64 like they were your personal hero. I mean, a kid could come in off the streets with dirty hair and clothes, maybe even sporting some body odor, and by the time they left that same night, you made them feel like the class couldn't have happened without them. Man, these kids grew ten feet tall in an hour because of you! I watched it happen every week. I even watched some boys try really hard to make you mad, but it seemed like you were entirely incapable reacting in any way other than showing genuine love and concern."

Dave smiled, touched at my sentiment.

"How, though?" I shook my head. "*How* does a person function like that all the time? Why were you never mad? How could you just *keep* responding with patience and greeting every kid like they were superstars?"

As I cinched the slack in the belay, glanced at the climber above me, and pulled the lock at the post, Dave put his hands in his pockets and stared at the floor reflectively. I listened as he slowly began to share what had influenced his perspective on life…his *deepest* motivation.

In 1968, during the Vietnam War, Dave was a runner and machine-gun operator originally stationed at Fort Benning, Georgia. He was an outstanding marksman, well decorated, and well liked by his superiors. Although he witnessed miracle after miracle wherein his life was spared by minutes or inches—including once when a suicide bomber blew himself up just outside a hospital in Thailand—the most life-changing event for Dave was when he was stationed as a twenty-one-year-old overseer of the airport in Korat, Thailand. He was supposed to go out on a detail report, and as he was preparing to leave, a fellow soldier by the name of Raymond Foster approached him and said, "Dave, I'm gonna take your place on this one for ya."

Dave, as responsible as he was in his position, agreed to let his friend go in his stead. At some point during the trip, the driver of the vehicle his friend was in encountered an unexpected ravine, and the Jeep ran off the road. Dave received a call about a crash and dispatched a helicopter to respond to the scene, where it was confirmed that everyone in the accident had died…including Raymond Foster.

For days and days following this news, Dave cried brokenheartedly. It *should have been him* in that ravine. Yet, a man who didn't deserve to die had taken his place. Dave would spend the rest of his life ruminating over the implications of that trade. From that day forward, Dave swore, he would live every moment as a kind of memorial of his friend's sacrifice. Every second Dave was alive, it was because someone else had given him life. Dave promised to never squander a second of it.

By extension, because Dave loved Jesus Christ—another Man who had laid down His life so Dave might live—Dave radically committed his life to honoring the Lord, not just in ministerial duty, but with dedicated love for all at every turn. Life is too short and fragile, Dave acknowledged, and he felt the Holy Spirit say clearly to him, "You've *got to* start telling people about Jesus. You've *got to* spend the time you have left on this earth telling people about Jesus…"

I was captivated by Dave's story, and for the first time, I understood not only how he had loved the ragtag kids, but I also began to appreciate the layers of his worldview as they manifested into some of his familiar catchphrases, such as, "A Royal Ranger is ready for *anything*!" More than all else, however, I finally comprehended an underlying truth that had been nagging at my nerves about the men who stood in sharp contrast to Dave…

What motivates a person to step into the role of a minister?

Is it fame? Fortune? Two extra pieces of bacon?

Or is it loving radically for the sake of Christ so that the "Billys" of the world will inherit a place in the eternal Kingdom of God?

There just wasn't any question when it came to Commander Dave that his motive was in line with the "servant" Church that Christ came to build, and not with the Pharasaic Church that Christ came to tear down. In a sea of loud and pretentious super-preachers whose Pee-Wee-on-a-train style ministries eventually drove me to jump from the train car and question my role in ministry, there was Dave, as solid and as true as the day I saw him for the first time in Outpost 64. And shucks… If *Dave* could so faithfully serve in the Body of Christ as the most loving and supportive man—and if, by doing so, he could make the people around him feel the love of Christ so powerfully that they would remember that feeling for the rest of their lives (unlike emotionally charged altar experiences that left them doubting later)—then I could, too.

Seeing Commander Dave reminded me what it was all about. His short visit to camp that week helped me take a deep breath and feel reassured that the "big brother to all" role I am most comfortable in will result in more good for the Kingdom of God than any other I could try to squeeze into. Although I had already let go of the super-preacher idea, Reverend Lenny's visit, followed shortly after by Commander Dave's, was a clear message from the Lord—and now I was tuned in enough to receive it full blast: The Body is made up of many different parts, and trying to be a part you're not ordained for does more harm than good.

But it was crucial that, while the Lord was confirming my identity and role in His Kingdom work to be less sensational than I once thought, He also reminded me how supernaturally and sensationally He *can* use His people, and how He might gift them appropriately for those occasions. I needed to be shown this one more time, and it needed to be in no uncertain terms. Only then would I "get it." Only when I saw the miracle of "that day in Crane," balanced by all the things I had seen at the altar until now, would the message He wanted me to carry to the rest of you come to full clarity.

The episode that occurred in that tiny little church in Crane, Missouri—when Whitney, Alicia, and Debbie came to minister— was so unbelievable that even now, three years later, my family can hardly believe it happened. Every time the story is told, we still find ourselves shaking our heads, because up to this point we've all had solid training in the values of prudence, having been exposed to "spooky Pentecostalism" our whole lives. However, because one of our own—Donna—was at the center of the miracle this time, *and* because everything that happened lined up with the Word of God, there was no denying that the Lord was behind it.

Our church, when everyone was present, had a congregation of about twenty people since the church had recently closed down because of a community split and was now in the process of rebuilding. Pastor George and his wife, Margaret, had graciously stepped in to launch a ground-zero restart, and although the number of regular attendees was slowly increasing, there were many Sundays when attendance was only ten or so. On those Sundays, the worship team facing the pews involved over half of the congregation (sometimes only leaving two or three people in the seats). The worship team was made up of myself on guitar and lead vocals; Donna on harmony; James, Donna's husband, on bass; Nita, my mom, on drums; Liz, a college student, on bongos; and Cynthia, a fifteen-year old, who sang with a voice like a Celtic bell. (Though my mother was a regular attendee, Dad was unable to come with her to services because his radio, television, and news ministries required his presence.)

Nita, Donna, James, and I are all but two members (Stan Williams on rhythm guitar and Allie Anderson on keyboard) who make up the Christian band called Broken for Good (BFG) that you may have seen featured on episodes of SkyWatch Television. It was around this time that BFG released our song "Jonny," which was featured shortly thereafter on the home webpage of *Charisma Magazine*, so it stands to reason that if we were all going to the same church, we would all lead music if we were needed. And in this itty-bitty church, believe, me, we were needed desperately. However, as Donna has attested in sharing her testimony about this day, none of us—Mom, James, Donna, or myself—was on the church's stage to fulfill a personal dream or be Sunday-morning attention hogs. Quite the contrary, my family has received our share of attention due to the widespread recognition of my father's bestselling books and other media, so we really appreciate the *anonymity* that comes with attending an undersized church. (If attention or glory had been our goal, we easily could have plugged ourselves into some of the enormous churches nearby. We live in the Springfield area of Missouri, a *major* city within the appropriately named Bible Belt, so finding a place to show off in front of huge congregations clearly wasn't what we cared about when we formed this worship team.) As a result of loving the opportunity not to be in the limelight each week, Donna and I had started featuring Cynthia more and more on the vocals—as often as her stage fright would allow her to.

Singing during this particular service, however, was presenting an extreme challenge for Cynthia, because her father had passed away a few weeks before…

She had arrived at church with a classic "be strong" jawline that morning, determined to swallow down the pain of loss to get through another day, but I knew, based on the depth of sadness she wore externally, that there was more to her torment than her father's recent passing. Over the past several months, she and I had often traded "How ya doin'" banter as I was setting up my guitar and amp, and over time, she had started to share the details of her father's deterioration more openly with me and Donna. His death was not unexpected, and because of the pain he had been in during his latter weeks, Cynthia had come bravely to the stage in knowing that her dad was in a better place. This day, however, something seemed to be weighing on her extra heavily, and when I asked her how she was holding up, she got straight to the heartbreaking truth.

"Last night I had a dream that dad was back," she said. "He was telling me that he hadn't actually died after all—that it was all just a terrible nightmare, a bad dream, and that everything was going to be okay. He reassured me that he wasn't going anywhere anytime soon, and that he would be there for me when I needed him in the coming years."

Cynthia went on to tearfully describe how happy and secure she had felt hugging her dad, reaching out and touching him in her dream, *knowing* that it was real and feeling wave after wave of euphoric relief that she was with him again and that he was healthy and glad to be home. She simply *believed* that because he would never lie to her, she could trust his words and rest assured that he hadn't actually died.

When she had first awakened, she had felt an initial surge of joy as she prepared herself to run to the next room and fall into her father's arms again...but that sensation was followed by the heavy, harsh reality: her father was, in fact, gone. Dreaming that he was with her again and that everyone was content, then waking to find his empty chair was worse than if she hadn't dreamed anything at all. The tease was more than she could handle, and throughout our practice she was, understandably, a hair's breadth away from a breakdown.

By the time special musical guests Alicia and Whitney arrived on that Sunday, the congregation felt fuller than usual. These girls who had come to sing and minister to us looked to be in their early twenties. It was clear they were sisters, and they immediately struck me as sincere as I worked with them to adjust their microphones during setup. There was something different about them that made them stand out from most of the ministry groups I had seen. Their genuineness was piercing, unignorable, like an anointing they couldn't have hidden if they had wanted. Even Donna mentioned that when we were preparing to pray for the service in the back room minutes before worship, she noticed that "those girls who came here to sing today just seem authentic...*really* sweet people."

Worship began as normal, and when Alicia and Whitney went to the front of the sanctuary to begin their set, they acknowledged having the same sense about our congregation as we had about them. During their introductions, both shared that they were touched and honored to be in a church where they could feel the Holy Spirit in our midst. "You can always tell when you've come to a really *sincere* church," Alicia said. "There's a corporate exhortation for the presence of God that you can't put your finger on, but you can *feel* it. We feel that here."

Before they strummed their first chord or sang their first note, a palpable connection between everyone present had been solidified. The guests instantaneously felt like one of us.

Just prior to each song in their set, the girls explained the spiritual significance of and life lessons behind what the Lord had led them to compose. Their harmonies were amazing, and the musical compositions were beautiful, but the lyrics to the original songs they had written were projected on a screen behind them, and that was what really struck me (and several others around me, as tear-filled eyes and later testimonies would show). During one song after another, the hearts of these young ministers were bleeding out into the room with words that glorified our Savior and edified the Body of Christ from angles no other Christian band had done, in my experience. I could sense, powerfully so, the presence of the Holy Spirit in these songs, and I knew the Lord had big plans for Alicia and Whitney's future.

As the girls started to wrap up their presentation, a woman I had never seen began walking to the microphone.

"This is our spiritual mother, Debbie," Whitney said. "God speaks to her and uses her to speak into people's lives wherever she goes."

My gut twisted, and those classic walls of distrust and suspicion quickly shot up. Though it had seemed to me thus far that Alicia and Whitney were earnest, straightforward followers of Christ, something about the phrases "spiritual mother" and "speak into people's lives" caused me to pause. I couldn't force myself to tolerate yet another "prophet of God" telling me I'm supposed to sell my house and go to Africa or that I should "name and claim" a personal airplane and a million dollars because God wants me to be prosperous. As Whitney handed the microphone off to the woman, I took a deep breath, hoping she would at least put someone else in her crosshairs and leave me alone.

My prayers were answered, but not exactly how I'd hoped.

First, Debbie set her focus on my sister. I saw Donna shift in her pew as she returned the woman's gaze. Donna's expression was one I recognized well, as it was one she frequently plastered on her face in uncomfortable times. It's as blank as an expression can get, because she knows the "Mr. or Mrs. Whizzbang" drill: If you look *bored*, you'll get called out for being unspiritual during church. If you look *interested*, you'll be sent to a foreign country or given a ministry charge because you made the mistake of appearing receptive. If you look *worried*, you'll be told about hidden sin in front of everyone because the "worried" expression can only mean you're repentant. And if you *cry*, oh my goodness…it'll be a combination of all the above plus ten other things at least.

Donna and I had learned the hard way that false teachers, preachers, and ministers who run the Church like showmen understand how to "scan the crowd and pick the victims." (It's an art mastered by many cult leaders also, like Jim Jones, who was known for responding to cues in facial expressions and body language to garner maximum manipulation power over the crowds for years before the Jonestown Massacre of

1978 took the lives of 909 victims in Guyana.) But Donna and I have mastered a survival technique of our own: We understand how to *be in* the crowd and look just aloof enough that the ministers would be putting their own theatrics at risk by calling someone as unexciting as us to the stage.

As soon as Debbie's gaze fell on Donna, I thought, *Don't do it lady… Donna's not gonna roll with this. She won't respond. She won't come to the front. She'll walk out and embarrass you. Don't do it, don't do it, don't do it… Donna has zero appetite for being prophesied over by people she doesn't know. She's hiding—and healing—in a small church for a reason.*

Debbie held eye contact with Donna for a few more seconds before she turned her attention elsewhere. As if the victory was a result of my and Donna's expression technique, Donna risked a quick glance at me over her shoulder. I gave a hard blink and the slightest nod in recognition. Donna and I were probably out of the woods, and as small as our congregation was, that left only our spouses (who looked as unexcited as us), my mother, the pastor and his wife, and about seven others. Things would probably be alright if she stuck to the pastoral couple and the church in general, as I was hoping she would. The pastor and his wife were used to being put on the spot in this way.

But alas, no…

Debbie, from out of the blue, called *Cynthia,* of all people, to the front.

The alpha-male protector within me regarded this fragile teen as she obediently slipped into the aisle and made her way to Debbie's side, and I silently prayed that this woman would make it short and keep it kind. I couldn't bear watching Cynthia endure the public humiliation of being told she had "hidden sin in her life" on a day like this. Just imagining the horror of the "hidden sin" message being syncretized with this young girl's concepts about her father's death sobered me in an instant, and although I was cool as a cucumber on the outside, on the *inside* I was begging for God to bring wisdom and order to this moment. I knew all too well that sometimes it takes many true people of God many years to *undo* what pain or trauma one thoughtless "prophet" can inflict on a new or young believer when that "prophet" "ministers" from the flesh. Although I was devoted to reaching out to Cynthia later on if I needed to, I hoped the damage wouldn't be done in the first place.

I just couldn't stomach this fragile, impressionable girl having her heart strings pulled in confusing directions.

But just as soon as the dread took root in my gut, Debbie's words worked like a release latch, and I found myself challenged to open my mind. Although Debbie didn't speak about the death of Cynthia's father, she eloquently addressed the pain: "The Holy Spirit just wanted me to tell you that this thing with your father is going to be alright. The Heavenly Father loves you, and He wants you to know that you *are* strong enough to make it through this."

Wait a minute… I thought. *How could she possibly know about Cynthia's dad?*

"Sweetheart," Debbie went on to say, "you weren't two sentences into that first song you sang for worship this morning and you were just in tears up there. I saw that pain and knew I had to tell you in front of all these witnesses that the Lord has His hand on you. He's aware of your loss, He knows the hurt that you feel, and He wants you to know that you are His child. You *will always* have a Father. Nobody can change that. No shift in family dynamics on this earth is going to change that."

Huh… Well how about that.

I glanced at my wife, Katherine, and she looked as contemplative as I felt. I know my wife's facial expressions well enough to know what her doubt looks like, and she wasn't doubting *or* accepting at this point. She, like me, was processing thoughts that would require both mind and spirit to comprehend. Were we observing a *real* gift of the Spirit? One of the supernatural ones?

Cynthia was trying to hold herself together, but her chest jerked with silent sobs as Debbie continued her encouragement, telling Cynthia that the Lord had *huge* things planned for her future. Cynthia nodded cooperatively, then walked brusquely to the very back row of the sanctuary as soon as Debbie's words came to a close. As the rest of the church was looking toward Cynthia with concern, I was keeping my eye on Debbie.

Just as before, Debbie's focus returned swiftly back to Donna, and a few intense moments hung in the air between them.

No. Not her. Anyone but her, I went back to pleading in my mind. *It wouldn't matter if you knew every last secret of every person in here. If you call Donna out, she's gonna leave, and she might not ever come back. Lady, you don't even know how bad your timing would be if you were to make Donna the center of attention.*

Debbie had no way of knowing that Donna had only recently begun to attend church again. Although Donna's faith in Christ had always been solid, she had felt she needed a break for a while to focus on the Word away from the influences of others, and her consistent attendance at this little church in Crane was one of her final steps in what can only be described as "religious abuse rehab." To make matters even more precarious, one of the recent services at this church had involved a Pentecostal missionary couple who sang loudly in tongues over everything. (Their display was pure chaos without a breath; they even interrupted our own pastor explosively and repeatedly as he tried to pray for the offering, make announcements, and even introduce them as our guests.) When the missionary couple had given the altar call and Donna and her husband, James, hadn't gone to the front, the man and his wife had given them a stern stare-down, as if my sister and her husband were unspiritual elephants in the room. It took Donna a few weeks to come back after that, and when she did, it was only because she was rational enough not to blame our home pastor or congregants for how the guests had run the service. But if this Debbie woman, whom we had never seen before, suddenly arrived on the scene and started calling Donna to the front, it was likely to be my sister's last Sunday in attendance.

I looked at Debbie, then at Donna, and back at Debbie again. The congregants were still sharing reassuring nods and glances at Cynthia. I understood the delicacy of the moment, and my thoughts were flying.

Pass. Move on. Next person. Anyone but Donna. Leave that one alone.

Donna's expression was still a blank wall, yet it was "alive" enough not to be mistaken for boredom. Despite Debbie's unbelievable accuracy in describing Cynthia's situation, Donna held firm in her distanced countenance. She didn't appear belligerent, but she wasn't welcoming, either.

Awake, but not excited.

As invisible as humanly possible while being directly stared into.

Although the "staredown" only lasted a few seconds, I was glad when the majority of congregants once again quieted and turned their attention to Debbie, as it obligated her to make her next move. What a relief it was that her attention turned to Pastor George this time.

"You have been planting seeds of growth for a long time in this building," Debbie said. George nodded in affirmation. "And there has been a lot of talk throughout the years, especially recently, about how this church might be poised for expansion."

I nodded as well. It was true. We had *all* been talking about church growth in the last several months. We had even implemented new programs to serve families with children. George had brought a schoolteacher on staff to teach the kids' Bible curriculum, and she had launched at least a hundred brilliant ideas and counting from the moment she arrived, including "Kid Sunday": one service per month that was run entirely by the kids. Even though the congregation only had my little girls and Donna's kids as regulars, puppet shows, choreographed routines, and every kind of illustration imaginable had been put into effect just months before this day. George had also seen to the adults by purchasing a brand-new coffee maker and setting up a breakfast rotation program: every week, a group of women prepared breakfast for the whole church, so that anyone could come in from straight off the streets and get a hot, free meal. As the shepherd of this flock, Pastor George was doing all he could to see more people join us permanently.

On the other hand, we *were* a really small church…so Debbie's words were a safe blanket statement that just about anyone—with or without a Spirit-given gift—could have said, and it would have been true. I considered this "lucky guess" angle for a split second before she nailed it yet again.

"In the past," Debbie said to George, "this church faced some very challenging times, *big* transitions, and it was painful for you and your family."

"You got *that* right," George openly admitted. I knew he was thinking about a couple of years earlier when he had made the difficult decision to close the church because of feuding families. In the aftermath, everyone in George's family had lost dear friends.

"The Lord is pleased with those who honor Him and continue to work through the pain of ministry." Debbie's eyes flickered over to Donna again for a second, and then back to George.

Why do you keep looking at Donna? I pondered. *It's never gonna happen…*

By now, I was beginning to believe that Debbie was spiritually more legitimate than the fraudulent ministers we'd seen based on what I'd heard her say to the others. I had even made a mental note to tell Katherine later that the defensive shield that rose up in my gut when Debbie first started speaking dissolved almost as quickly as it had risen. But I still couldn't shake the thought that if the Lord really was communicating with Debbie, He would have told her by now that calling Donna to the front and making her the center of attention was the *last* thing on earth she would respond to.

Yet…something else was revealed in this exchange. Debbie wasn't scanning the room and focusing on Donna casually as she was looking for people whose lives she might speak into, she was zeroing in on

Donna *specifically*. Debbie seemed almost as distracted by Donna's presence as Donna was by Debbie's.

Debbie gestured to George's wife, Margaret, and descended into a heartfelt conclusion. "God will honor you in time for the work you've put into this place. You and your wife are faithful here. It's often that *steady* work for the Lord—the work that gets the least attention—that shows a person's true nature. Bless you for your service to the Lord here."

Most of the congregation was looking at George, who was humbly nodding and smiling at Margaret, as a couple quick whispers of reassurance were passed on to our pastor and his wife.

Debbie gave a last glance in Donna's direction, but I noticed a fresh resignation within the woman's countenance. Without hesitation, her eyes moved right past my sister. Donna noticed it, too, and her shoulders relaxed.

An elderly gal in the back was next. (Debbie got her attention by referring to "the lady in the back with the long hair" and then saying something about her having great strength in the community. That word was accurate also, because this matriarch is a pillar of the community in Crane and several surrounding cities. Debbie's words were received well.) Following that, Debbie handed the microphone back to Whitney. Together, the sweet musical sisters gave a closing prayer and dismissed us for the afternoon, making a quick announcement about CDs for sale on a table in the back of the room—and just like that, it was over.

Donna's relief was visible. She stood up, tossed her purse strap around her shoulder, and released a huge sigh. I smiled back at her, happy that she had escaped having to make a scene. I was curious about what Debbie might have said to her if given the chance (and I mostly wondered if she'd nail it again, since my sister has always been so complicated; you can't "guess your way through a word" for Donna), but at the end of the day, I knew that if the Lord had wanted to speak to Donna, He most likely wouldn't have orchestrated a public display with her at the center. It was probably all for the best that it was over so suddenly.

James and I headed to the stage as usual to pack up our instruments. Donna and Katherine went to the back to get the kids ready to leave. Mom hurriedly bought a CD from Alicia and Whitney before going to pick up Dad from his office at Defender Publishing for a Sunday afternoon date. Most of the congregation made their way out of the building as well, so the only people left were my family, Donna's family, George's family, and the guests who were packing up their CDs and business cards. James and Donna had driven separate vehicles that day, so as James was wrapping cords and organizing a haul to load into the back of his Suburban, Donna was trying to get the kids to put their shoes on, find their coats, grab their Sunday school papers—the usual after-church drill—alongside Katherine, who was about the same business.

As Donna got closer to the exit, Debbie slid out from the rest of the group and gently placed her hand on Donna's arm.

Oh no. Oh no! I thought as I saw Donna bristle at the woman's touch. *This is gonna be Donna's last service here if Debbie starts telling Donna that the Lord has a word for—*

"The Holy Spirit has a word for you, Honey," Debbie said boldly.

That's it. Nail in the coffin. We had a good run with Donna on the worship team, but it's over now.

Before Donna could respond, Debbie uttered literally the *only* words she could have said that would make the rest of us, *especially* Donna, stop and listen: "He told me, 'Do not call her out.' He told me that if I spoke to you in front of the church, you were going to get up and leave, so I left you alone before. Do you have a minute to speak privately?"

Donna blinked, slowly lowered her arm from Debbie's grasp, and turned like a mechanical doll to Katherine behind her. "Katherine, the lady wants to speak to me," Donna said as she gestured behind her shoulder at Debbie. For the first time in a while, Donna had an expression. She was dazed, disoriented.

It was *true*… For once, something personal "given by the Lord" and delivered to Donna through a human vessel was *true*. She absolutely

120

would have left, and no matter how skilled a "crowd-scanning shark" is, the fact that Donna was prepared to politely excuse herself from the building and drive home the instant Debbie called her name from the stage isn't a fact that could have been read from simply looking at Donna's face.

Yet I know Donna very well, and I knew what was going through her head as she stood near Debbie at this moment. Donna would chalk up a "word from God" coming from another person as a "lucky guess" up to the very end. Slowly, her expression went from baffled to skeptical as her eyes darted about the room, processing Debbie's words. Donna was preparing to reject anything Debbie was about to say. Then Donna looked at Katherine, who nodded with a "good luck" smile.

"Um…" Donna looked down at her redheaded son, who was glancing between Donna and Katherine anxiously, hoping that he would be allowed to run and play for a few more minutes. "Can you watch my kids, I guess?"

"Sure," Katherine nodded and quickly led the kids back into the snack area for a while.

Donna turned back to Debbie in with a demeanor I'd seen so many times: deep breath, stiff spine, chin up, eyes concentrated and emotionally detached, and hands grasping her purse for a quick escape when things got too bizarre.

"I'm Debbie." The woman's hand glided out between them.

"Donna," my sister said, offering her hand in cold obligation.

Debbie got straight to it: "While I was up there," she gestured to the stage, "the girl I saw looking back at me every time I looked at you…I just kept thinking to myself that you were in hiding. I knew before I went up to the front that I was going to say something to you. All morning I've known I was supposed to share with you some things the Lord wants you to hear, even when all I could see was the back of your head. The Holy Spirit told me that I would share with you based only on seeing you from behind. Then when I saw your face and made eye contact with you, I just kept thinking to myself that you were hiding. The girl in that pew has layers that are being stifled."

Donna remained stiff and silent. Debbie continued, her words gentle, as if she knew she was speaking to a cracked china doll precariously near the edge of a ten-foot ledge over stone ground—but she was also filled with confidence.

"I meet a lot of people, and I speak to them when I feel the Lord is asking me to. This thing here," Debbie gestured back and forth between them, "this is nothing new for me. But I feel that this particular meeting is a divine appointment for you, and maybe for both of us. You are hidden in plain sight. You're tucked away right here in Crane, and sometimes that feels uncomfortable for you, but you're being groomed right now for something bigger." Debbie paused for a moment and switched gears: "I don't know anything about your family, but I get the feeling they are all involved in things, doing what they do every day, and you're in a season of floating. You feel like you have no direction while everyone around you knows exactly where they're going."

Like lightning, the most recent—and loudest—of all Donna's concerns hit my memory, a cluster of feelings she had only shared with select family members:

"It's just this family…" Donna had said to me over coffee weeks earlier. "Everyone has 'a voice,' you know? Mom does her miniature horse thing, Dad is the illustrious 'Tom Horn' who has a billion books coming out all the time, you have this music thing you feel good about, and in the midst of it all, I have this nagging sensation I can't explain that I'm supposed to be doing something, or saying something. It's like I'm supposed to be working on this big…life project…for the Lord or whatever, but I have no idea what it is! He's stirring me to move, but I don't know in what direction!"

Donna had looked exhausted as she wrestled with trying to explain her newfound quandary. When I asked why she hadn't yet started another book, I almost regretted the question as she bounced back in anxiety: "What would I say if I were to write something on my own? I'm not passionate about anything in particular, and I don't have anything to say. I have been comfortable all my life just being in the back room in a support role, and if it were up to me, I would never change that, but now it's like the Lord is asking me to do something from within *myself*. I can't find 'my voice' in the world because I don't really *have* a voice. I've been hired to ghostwrite books for other people for so long my brain is scrambled when it comes to the idea that I would say something of my own. But I also suddenly feel so uncomfortable being silent—like every moment I'm alive, the Holy Spirit is poking me in the side, saying, 'Find your voice! Find your voice!' Argh! What am I supposed to do? Where is my voice? I hate this feeling!"

It had become difficult lately to talk with Donna about life, ministry, or the future without this subject coming up. She had been in a rut—we both knew it. Now, suddenly, a woman who had apparently come from out of nowhere knew it, too.

Debbie proved as much with what she said next: "I feel like the Lord is telling me that you're struggling to find your voice right now."

The words *precisely* matched what Donna had been saying in secret for months. Up to this point, I had been hanging out next to the instruments and fiddling with cords and guitars. Mostly, I had just been finding things for my hands to do so I could remain near Donna in case she needed an emergency response team to obnoxiously—yet seemingly obliviously—intervene in the conversation and provide an escape route if things went south. But after what Debbie said about struggling to find a voice, I saw the slightest movement of reassurance on Donna's end.

She nodded.

Mind you, it wasn't a big nod, and it wasn't a grand enough gesture to affirm whether Debbie was right. It could have easily been taken as a noncommittal, "I'm listening politely," response while Donna reserved the right to think Debbie was way off in her assessment. Nonetheless, to *me*, it was a big deal. *I* knew what it meant. Debbie was breaking through the wall somehow…

Well now… Maybe, just maybe, there's not an instant severance package on the other end of this conversation?

I abandoned the stage and moved nearer. Now that Debbie's words were hitting close to home, it would be even more devastating if the conversation suddenly turned into a lecture about disobedience or hidden sin. If Donna so much as gave me "the look"—another one of our code expressions signaling that she needs rescue from an uncomfortable social situation—I would be ready to get her out of there. We all had a busy afternoon planned, so it wouldn't be dishonest for me to butt in, give Donna a fellowship-clap on the shoulder, smile at Debbie, and insert some "Well, you guys ready to hit the road?" derailment.

James—who again, had taken a separate vehicle that morning—saw that the conversation wasn't going to go over well if one of their kids got bored in the snack area and decided to interrupt, so he thanked Katherine, discreetly gathered them from the back room, and slipped out. Katherine followed suit, and soon only George, Donna, Debbie, our guest group, and myself were hanging around. (With everyone else gone, I noticed a few more unfamiliar faces; others had come along with the girls. I would find out later that they were Jim, Alicia's husband, Joyce, the girls' grandmother, and Mary, Debbie's close friend. These names have since become intimately important to our family, as I will explain later.)

"You have been tucked away," Debbie was saying as I walked past and leaned against the back wall, "hidden for a time of training. God has placed you into an uncomfortable phase of *learning* so that when the time comes for you to *speak*—and He *will* give you that voice you feel is missing, Donna—you will speak with an authority you wouldn't have had otherwise. But He is raising you into a new place, Honey. A new place with fresh perspectives and new boldness. This year is going to blow your mind, and you won't be the same person when it's over. Not only are you going to be given direction and find your voice, you're going to change entire communities. You're going to radically challenge entire cultures. Yours is going to be *a voice of the nations*. There will be people who come to know the Lord based on the words that *you* say, and they wouldn't have come to know Him otherwise."

Debbie had said the words calmly, but I could tell they had landed on Donna with a deafening reverberation, like the gong outside a Chinese emperor's palace had been struck less than a foot away. Donna's skepticism began to melt into reverent fear and awe. Tears filled her eyes as she slipped her purse off of her shoulder and dropped it onto the pew beside her. In an attempt to hold together her emotions, she swallowed what I imagined was a stubborn lump in her throat, then folded her arms in front of her chest. She turned back to Debbie, stiffening her spine and tilting her chin, but everyone—including Donna, herself—knew her charade of indifference had just crumbled, exposing a surprisingly receptive layer underneath.

"The Holy Spirit wants you to know that you aren't going to be a *fluffy* Christian."

At that, Donna let out a sob, as yet another layer of her tough mask crumbled. Casual conversations taking place elsewhere throughout the room trailed off. To most people within earshot, that last comment would have seemed absurd. But those closest to Donna knew that her private prayer for the last ten years and counting had been, word for word, that God would not allow her to become a "fluffy Christian"—a term Donna had coined to represent the men and women in the Church of God who wanted to talk about feelings and emotions at the altar but who wouldn't carry out due diligence in seeking the Lord or His will. A "fluffy Christian" was, to Donna, the same as a "lifestyle Christian" who didn't really know God, but who attended church once a week for the social benefits or to fulfill family expectations. As such, Donna's deepest prayer was that God would never allow her to be a part of the "social club disease" that she felt was killing the zeal of the Body in her generation. The "fluffy" reference was silly, and it was the *least* orthodox adjective a person would use in a prayer...which was precisely why Donna and I knew Debbie's words were from the Lord. Only *He* could have given Debbie that word.

Pastor George looked at me with a raised brow. He didn't know Donna as well as I did, of course, but he knew her well enough to know she would rather run barefoot over a pile of nails than cry in front of people in a place where she felt as vulnerable as she had come to feel in church. I returned his gaze for a moment, but I couldn't offer an answer. I just maintained my distance and continued to observe.

Debbie paused for a moment. She appeared confused, trying to iron out a mystery.

"I don't know what it is, but I see you speaking in front of what looks like a bunch of camera equipment. Not like in front of the press or in a huge church, but something…something in the media. Maybe involving the Internet."

Donna Howell was not a personality the world knew *at all* at that time. She wouldn't have been recognized from any work she'd done through SkyWatch Television or Defender Publishing, as she had been serving behind the scenes as a researcher and ghostwriter up to this point. Nobody knew who she was, so nobody could have stalked her online and faked this odd, "I see camera equipment," line to awe a crowd. There was, as of yet, no way for a stranger to know that Donna was constantly surrounded by television studio cameras, the footage from which was uploaded daily into major media, including the Internet. Also, though Donna had nodded one time early on in Debbie's message, since that moment, Donna hadn't *even once* given Debbie any indication that she was correct. Debbie was on her own tracks with the Lord, and she was on a roll.

"Donna," she said, "I don't know if you're a writer, or if you even like to write, but I get this image in my head that you're a writer. Does the word 'Kindle' mean anything to you? I see just…just *mountains* of books surrounding you and more flowing out of you. Books with your name on them appearing in print and in something called a 'Kindle.'

Life-changing books that are going to set people free and force people to question how they've been living and how they've been ministering. These books, they're wrapped up, like in twine and packages, and they *all* need to go out. They *all* need to be released."

Donna's emotional walls were toppling down. Kicking off her sandals, she knelt to the floor and started crying openly. I stood watching in complete shock. I had seen so much in my life that hadn't been real that it had become impossible to move me—until now. There I stood, with no other choice but to believe the miracle I was witnessing and admit that supernatural gifts were still a part of the Body of Christ. Debbie was giving out one hard-hitter after another after another. Donna and I could hardly accept one revelation before another one was shoved into the atmosphere—and the disclosures were all matters that had only been discussed within the walls of a family member's home. I couldn't help but think of 2 Kings 6:12b: "Elisha, the prophet who is in Israel, tells the king of Israel the words that you speak in [the privacy of] your bedroom."

I looked over at Alicia—who, at this point, was simply the girl who had come to sing that morning; I couldn't even remember her name—and shook my head. Pointing to Debbie, I shrugged. "She has no idea," I said. "She simply has *no* idea what she's speaking into my sister's life right now."

George began to pray. Alicia, Whitney, Jim, Joyce, and Mary all stopped what they were doing at the merchandise table and joined in prayer, stretching their arms out to Donna. Everyone present knew that we were witnessing a supernatural event with eternal implications. Debbie sat down next to Donna and continued to speak, but she didn't touch her or try to comfort her by stroking her back or anything else. This was yet another powerful sign that God was directing her actions, because physical contact was another trigger that would have set Donna off and made her recoil in the moment when God was finally reaching her with answers for the first time.

"Honey, listen to me," Debbie said softly. "I don't want to tell you anything that isn't from the Lord. I'm not here to scare you or hurt you, and I have no agenda at all to try to impress anyone, but I feel we're not quite done yet. I believe the Holy Spirit has more to say. Think of the person you're listening to at home in your private time. Consider how large that person's audience is, the number of people who are hearing that person's message. Imagine that for a moment."

Debbie, once again, wouldn't have had any way of knowing it, but the person Donna was listening to in the evenings was Joyce Meyer, whose in-person audience numbered in the hundreds—if not thousands—every time she delivered a sermon. (Later, Donna noted that it was interesting that Debbie had a genderless way of referring to "the person" she was listening to. Debbie could have said "he" in reference to a well known preacher [most of whom are male], but she didn't assign what she was hearing from the Lord to a male, which would have been a logical mistake. This was another small sign among many that day that she was receiving her directions directly from the Lord.)

"Have you got that image in your head?" Debbie asked. "Are you imagining that number?" Donna didn't respond, so Debbie went on. "Double it. Triple it. Quadruple it. That's your future audience. We're talking about multitudes of people that you will reach and in a very short time. You are an atmospheric changer. When you step into a room, people will be challenged by you—and in positive ways—before you've said anything, just because of the reputation you will have built for yourself."

Donna finally let go completely. It was hard to hear Debbie's tranquil voice over the top of my sister's wailing; she was crying harder than I had ever seen her cry. A person just entering the church might have thought she'd been given news that her child had died based on how her entire body was wracking in sobs. Pastor George's prayers got louder, and many people around me were beginning to tear up also. To those of us who *knew* her, Donna wasn't emotional at all—at least not in front of others, so the intensity of this scene was shocking. It was a broken dam, and everyone was caught in the overflow.

"Yet I see a viral audience," Debbie continued. "Do those words resonate with you? A 'viral' audience? You're in front of cameras and you're speaking to the women of the nation. I don't know what the word is about the Internet where people are doing the shows, you know what I mean? Safe distribution, tucked away, hidden in plain sight, yet seen and heard all over the world. I don't know how to explain it. It's just a download of things that are kinda unfamiliar to me."

I knew what Debbie meant more than *she* did. SkyWatch Television and Defender Publishing represented potential audiences that numbered in the millions, especially in the coming years when my father, Tom Horn, would expand our networks. However, the writing, publishing, recording, and producing happened behind closed doors, away from the public.

"And the primary tools from which this enormous global ministry will take root are going to make themselves known to you within a year. Before a year from today, you will already see some of this that I'm speaking to you take place. I just know it, Donna. I see it in you. It's gonna change *generations* of thinkers."

Donna was wailing helplessly on the floor. So many false prophets in her life had called her out, put her down, and filled her young head with loads of nonsense, telling her she had hidden sin one minute and then trying to fly her to Africa to be a missionary the next… More than thirty years of religious abuse and manipulation bubbled to the surface as Debbie spoke about things she didn't even understand.

"Hey girls," Debbie said, turning to Alicia and Whitney. "I need some help over here."

The sisters headed over, slipped into the pew in front of Debbie, and hoisted up on their knees, leaning over the back.

"You girls sing something, please. I don't know what's happening here, but we are witnessing a historical event right now. I'm in over my head with this one. I don't know if I'm helping this woman or devastating her."

As Alicia and Whitney began to sing in harmony, Debbie leaned over and spoke even softer than before. "Honey, I wish I could tell you it gets easier. I wish I could tell you that you're just gonna go on home and make lunch and all these feelings of today will subside over time, and that you're going to go back to your normal routine, but it's just *not* gonna happen for you that way. This thing that you've been trying to avoid, this thing you've been attempting to shake off, it's not going to go away. These incidents that have been happening to you late at night when you're trying to sleep but you're being kept awake by visions and images in your head…these things are from the Lord and He's not willing to leave you alone."

Donna hadn't told anyone except me, Allie, Mom, Dad, and James about her nightly episodes, but I knew exactly what Debbie was referring to. Donna had explained to us in private that she had been "preaching in her head" while she was trying to sleep these last few months. Though she tossed, turned, and prayed for the Lord to clear her mind of these "sermons" and let her rest, every time she closed her eyes, she saw herself boldly proclaiming the Gospel to huge crowds. More than once, she had quoted Scripture in these imaginings, gotten up from bed to look up the verses, and discovered that she had accurately quoted obscure and unfamiliar passages. It was almost always the same story: Donna would start to nod off, drifting peacefully into the slumber state just before full-fledged sleep, and then she would see herself on a stage, preaching the Word of God. Despite attempts to shake it off by getting up and watching television, reading a novel, stuffing herself with food, or even taking Tylenol PM, the second her head hit the pillow and the house was quiet again, she would go straight back into the mental preaching scenarios. It wasn't unusual in those days for her to come to work like a zombie. When we asked her how she was feeling, she would report that she had been up until five o'clock in the morning "doing the preaching in the head deal again." If Debbie was correct, these nightly disturbances wouldn't cease until Donna entered the next phase of her calling.

"You have to quit wrestling God, Honey. You have to let God show you what He wants to do."

Something I hadn't felt in my heart since I was a boy came flooding back. A faith I hadn't had since childhood was pulling at me so strong in that moment, begging me to forget about all my scars and believe in the mission of God's people again. I had *never once* lost faith in God, but I had long since lost faith in the idea that His people would carry forth His gifts with reverent caution and respect. And there, standing a few feet away from my broken-yet-liberated sister in shambles, a flood of conviction took over all my cynicism. It was just like "that day when I was nine" all over again. You simply can't fake what occurred in that room. You can't make it happen in your own, human power. Debbie proved to me—to *all* of us—that the gifts of the Spirit are as alive today as ever, but that their greatest manifestation is when the focus is on the Lord and not on the show.

Feeling that she had done what she came to do, Debbie bowed her head and prayed for Donna. None of us really remember what her prayer was, but when the prayer ended, Donna proved that she wasn't interested in poetic finales or grand exits. She didn't even say "amen" as she stood. She silently grabbed her purse, and, without facing Debbie, walked to the exit of the church. Just before she left, she looked at Whitney.

"My husband bought your CD, right?"

"Yes," Whitney nodded. "He got a copy."

"Okay. Bye guys."

That was all there was to it.

Everyone released nervous chuckles as we watched Donna leave without another word. In fact, Donna hadn't said a word since she had asked my wife to watch her kids. The whole mind-boggling occurrence had taken place without my sister giving any response to anything that had come out of Debbie's mouth, except for that solitary, noncommittal nod early on. Donna had never told Debbie about SkyWatch,

Defender Publishing, or any of the media work we're involved in—so Debbie didn't know a thing about us—yet she had repeatedly described a company that exactly matched the description of what ours would soon become. I was floored, but in keeping with the speed of the day, I wasn't allowed even a minute to digest it all.

Before thirty seconds had passed, Debbie approached me with a look of concern.

"You're Donna's brother, right?"

"Yes, uh-huh. I'm Joe."

"Oh gosh, Joe. I really didn't mean to rattle your sister today," she said. "I didn't want to upset her. I kept looking at her while I was sharing with the others at the front. The Holy Spirit is the one who told me to speak to her in the first place. I knew that much just from seeing the back of her head behind her in the pews, but when I got to the stage, He said, 'Don't you dare address her in front of this church. If you do, she's gonna get up and walk out.' So I was waiting to talk to her afterward… and…and all this happened. I'm sorry if I—"

"No, no," I said in reassurance. "You have no idea how accurate that is, Debbie. You can't possibly understand what happened today. You don't know Donna, but trust me: She *would have* walked out. She probably wouldn't have been mean about it, but there's no doubt in my mind that she would have left the building. And don't feel the need to apologize. You can't fathom what you did today. None of us can."

I shook my head, tempted to pinch myself to see if I was awake. It still didn't feel real. "None of us can really know what happened to or for Donna today, but the girl who turned into a puddle on the floor? That wasn't Donna. You don't understand…you just *can't* understand. We were raised together, and I've seen how she is in times like these. She would no more cry and fall apart like that than jump off a cliff. I've never seen anything like it."

No words were strong enough to accurately paint the picture I was trying to describe to Debbie and the girls. Even now, I struggle in my attempts to express how numb and unresponsive Donna was at this time in her life, and how impossible it would have been for any human to pull that kind of response out of her, regardless of credentials or reputation. God, and God alone, had to be the explanation. He had to have been trying to reach her; that's the only rationale I could give the girls in front of me, and it was dramatically inefficient in helping them grasp how big this day had instantly become in my family's history. We would be talking about this for *years*.

"Well, I feel like I need to share something with you, also," Debbie said.

"Oh? What's that?"

"Yes, and there will be more in the future, but I don't think today is the right time for it all."

"Okay…" I blinked, unsure of how I was expected to respond to such an enigmatic statement.

"For today, I just want to share that I know you have a creative job. There are a lot of creative demands upon you at work."

Debbie's accuracy rating had been a hundred percent all morning, so by now I was no longer blown away by the fact that God had also communicated with her about my personal situation. Like Donna, I didn't stop Debbie long enough to tell her she was right; I just let her talk. I wasn't about to tell her that my gag job description at work had recently become "Creative Lab director of SkyWatch Television"—an endearing title assigned by the rest of the SkyWatch and Defender Publishing leadership teams. (A "Creative Lab" is an initial meeting we hold in every department while planning future releases or how a trailer or documentary film will play out, etc.) For years up to this point (and still occasionally at the time of this writing), it had been my responsibility to create promotional trailers, lay down voiceover work in a hundred different tones and accents, act out hundreds of roles for our media projects, and create and edit video footage for commercials, etc. My job always has demanded a *lot* of creativity from me. Because building Sky-

Watch TV and Defender Publishing has often required our core staff to "ride the bike before it's built," I've often been completely tapped out—overwhelmed in the art and imagination department because we simply needed more staff to help with my workload, and the ministry was growing faster than we could hire help. My brain has been fried more times than I can count, and it usually happens on the same weekend I'm expected to crank out a big, explosive DVD set or commercial, and so on. Debbie's comment that there were a lot of creative demands upon me was certainly true.

"Soon," Debbie said to me, "somebody is going to ask you to do something that makes you feel like you're starting all the way over again on a project that you feel passionate about, but it will be the *right* thing to do. Just be obedient when that door opens. Do whatever it is, even though it feels like it's going to take you all the way back to the beginning."

I nodded, hanging on her every word.

"There's more, Joe," Debbie shook her head, "but today is not the day. I feel I need to let you and your sister rest. We will speak again, though. There will be another opportunity to share with you."

Normally, I would take a promise like hers as seriously as a meaningless "let's do lunch"—a phrase that's really dropped into a conversation to *end* it. But, coming from this woman, I didn't doubt that the promise was delivered with intention. If Debbie said we'd speak again, then I was sure we would speak again.

In the meantime, however, it was well after one o'clock in the afternoon, and as much as I wanted to take a breather and discuss everything that had happened, I needed to eat lunch and reconnect with my wife. Reluctantly, I wrapped up casual conversations with George, Alicia, and Whitney and headed for home.

The rest of that story, as told over and over by several witnesses, goes as follows…

Donna, the *second* her car door shut behind her, fumbled shakily through her purse for her cell phone and dialed Mom's number.

"Hello?" came Mom's cheery voice.

"Mom? Are you with Dad?"

"Donna?!" Mom heard Donna's voice trembling, and since she knew her daughter wasn't an emotional person, she assumed something terrible had happened. "Are you okay? Is someone hurt?!"

"No. Everything is fine, and nobody's hurt. Is Dad somewhere by you?"

"Yes. He's right here. We're on a date. You need to talk to him?"

"Well, no. Kinda. Probably…I don't know, Mom. I don't know what to do."

"Take a deep breath," Mom said. "Tell me what's going on."

Donna took several deep breaths, but they didn't help. She was shaken to the core, and the deeper she breathed, the closer she got to another round of wracking sobs. "Uh… Okay. You remember that 'spiritual mother' woman who came up at the end of the service today?"

"Uh, yeah…" There was a pause on the other end of the line. Mom was disgusted. "Don't tell me… She did some big 'speak over you' thing after I left, didn't she?"

"Yes, but it's not what you think." Donna let out a sob and checked her rearview mirrors. There was no movement behind the glass panels of the church's main door leading to the parking lot, but she wasn't willing to take the chance that someone would emerge to check on her again, so she started her engine and drove aimlessly down the street. "Hang on. Let me get outta here."

"I could just… I mean… I'm just… *Really?*" Mom sighed heavily, not even attempting to disguise her aggravation. As our mother, she had been dealt a heavy dose as well over the years, always having to answer for, and then *fix*, the deeply-rooted "boo-boos" that had been inflicted upon her kiddos whenever the scam artists came to town. Additionally, Tom Horn's children were flaming targets for folks like that, and over time, many had made the mistake of thinking that if they looked super-spiritual to those closest to Tom, they would have the tools they needed to crawl into his inner circle. Whenever Mom was able to discern that ahead of time, she stepped in protectively, so it was clear she was beating herself up for leaving Donna behind when she had left right after the morning service.

"Mom, listen," Donna continued. "I feel like the woman at the well right now, telling her whole town that she met someone who 'knows everything about her.' This Debbie lady knew so much. She knew *so much*, Mom. And I never told her anything about me! I can't believe what she said! My voice, my prayers! All these things I... You there, Mom?"

"Hang on." Donna heard Mom's distant voice murmuring something on the other end of the line, so she quieted herself to listen through the wind and static: "...singing girls had a 'spiritual mother'...brought Cynthia to the front and talked to her...so now there's some woman telling Donna a buncha stuff. She's fine. Nobody's hurt, but she's pretty shaken up."

"Mmm, nah," Dad said in the background. It was a learned—and wise—teaching of Dad's that anytime a new "signs and wonders" personality came into town, the healthiest reaction we could ever have was one of guardedness. "It doesn't mean anything. Why is Donna all worked up?"

"I don't know," Mom said, stifling the Mama Bear anger that activated every time religious people threatened the safety or spiritual health of her cubs. "I'm still finding that out."

Donna toggled her blinker and made her way onto the highway headed for Springfield. "Mom, I know it sounds crazy, but *you know me*. You know that I wouldn't just freak out the first time a prophet comes to town naming and claiming and 'thus saith the Lord'-ing over everything, don't you?"

There was another brief pause as Mom considered the question. "I mean, yeah, I know that," she said. "I know you're not naïve, but I don't know a thing about this woman. What was her motive?"

"Mom, *please*, you're missing the point! It's not about *her*, okay? She said so many things! I just need to see Dad, and I don't want to be trying to talk above the volume of traffic over cellphones that go in and out of coverage zones. Can I *please* come see you guys?"

They didn't even need to discuss it. Mom gave Donna directions to the restaurant where Mom and Dad were headed for their date. Quickly, Donna called James to let him know where she was going, and that she had much to tell him when she got home. Ten minutes later, she arrived at the seafood place.

As she stepped into the restaurant, Donna scanned the dining room for familiar faces. Mom spotted her and waved her over. The closer Donna got, the more Mom could see her daughter's puffy, red, swollen face from all the crying she'd done in the last couple hours, and it fueled her frustration. She dropped her cheerful countenance and started shaking her head in a maternal, "what a shame" fashion. Dad went from having a smile of greeting to displaying an "I'm calling baloney" expression as he stood up from the circular booth and allowed Donna to scoot in between them.

"Let's get you something to drink first," Dad said. "Then you can tell us all about the mysteries of the universe as told by the chosen one this morning."

Sarcasm. One of our family's most prized defense mechanisms. When everything appears too absurd to be taken seriously, it's the gift that keeps us laughing.

Mom scoffed and slid a tall glass of ice water toward Donna. "What was this woman's motive? Did she know who our family was from before or something?"

"No, Mom." Donna took a quick sip and continued. "She doesn't know anything about our family. She still doesn't. We didn't say a word. You, me, Joe, James, and Katherine aren't on TV anyway." This was true at the time. Donna went on: "She couldn't have recognized *us*. Besides, even if she had stalked us for months and saw what little media I *have* done, that wouldn't explain how she knew some of the things she knew. She read my mail, Mom. I'm not kidding. I've met a kajillion 'prophets' and 'apostles' and 'mouthpieces of God' before—you know the routine—but I've never seen anything like this. I can't even process it." Donna stared at the table, visibly shaking from an adrenaline rush. "If she *does* have a motive—and I'm not saying she doesn't—then her motive is supported by God this time, because she knew things about me nobody could have known."

Mom softened and looked at Dad, reflectively. His stern skepticism remained.

"So what's the gist?" he asked. "You're living a life of sin or something? You flyin' to India? Something in the vast cosmos is creating a wall between you and God?"

Donna shook her head. "No, it's nothing like that. All she did was confirm who I am already, but then she started saying the most insane things about my voice in the future."

"Your *voice*?"

"Yeah. Um… Let me start at the beginning."

Over the next hour, Donna told Mom and Dad everything. She laid out every word of Debbie's that she could remember. Although Dad remained straight-faced until she was finished—of course, waiting for potential whammies before committing to a reaction—Mom was full of questions:

"You said the Holy Spirit was the one who told her not to call you to the front of the church?"

"That's what she said, yes."

"Did you tell her that you would have actually left?"

"No. I didn't say a word to her the entire time."

"What did she say you were supposed to *do* with your life going forward?"

"That's just it, Mom. She wasn't telling me what to do. She just said I was about to be loosed, that I was going to find my voice and my identity, and that I would be used by God to challenge entire cultures and change spiritual atmospheres."

When Donna came to the part of the story in which Debbie had told her about the "multitudes" that would be Donna's "future audience," Mom's jaw dropped and she became a believer.

"I knew it! I knew it! I've been telling you that same thing for months, and in those same *words* even!" Her eyes watered up as she lifted a hand to the air like an antenna to the Lord. "I just knew it…"

(Donna had heard those words from "Mama" many times, certainly. But just as a prophet is not without honor except in his hometown [Mark 6:4; Matthew 13:57], "Mama" is sometimes the last person her kids listen to. This part of Debbie's message was all Mom needed to hear.)

As Donna's account of the morning's events drew to a close, she noticed a change in Dad's countenance also.

"Then what happened?" he asked.

"Then…then I left. That's it. The whole story. I just got up and left. I asked if James had bought their CD, and then I walked to the car without another word. I called Mom and came here."

Dad *finally* relaxed the skeptical brow. Donna had recounted the entire occurrence and never delivered the whammy he had been expecting. The message from Debbie had checked out. But what Dad said next changed everything for all of us…

"I believe every word of it. I confirm it. It's all going to happen. I've seen this coming for a *long* time."

Donna looked at Mom, who appeared equally as shocked as Donna felt. Mom cupped her mouth and shook her head in disbelief. Donna started crying again.

"I mean it," Dad said. "Yeah. The whole thing is legit. I confirm it."

It was the first time in our family—*the first time ever*—that Dad had immediately confirmed and acknowledged the authority of a word from God as given through another human. Those of us who saw Debbie speaking to Donna assumed that Dad would "eventually come around" to believing that the woman's words were convincing, but none of us expected anything more than a gradual acceptance after a long season of observation. Dad's gut has always been the final word for us because his gift of discernment is off the charts, so when *he* says something is real, it becomes real for the rest of us. His authority on issues of the supernatural is so prevailing that his confirmation was actually the most powerful moment of the day—more influential and formidable than anything else that had been spoken. Had he doubted Debbie's words to Donna, Donna would have questioned them also, despite the words she said that logic (or stalking) could not explain.

Gifts of the Spirit are *real*.

And sometimes, they *are* sensational.

For a long time following that day in Crane, I waited for Debbie's word about me to come to pass. I repeated it in my mind a lot in the beginning: "Soon, somebody is going to ask you to do something that makes you feel like you're starting all the way over again on a project that you feel passionate about, but it's going to be the right thing to do." I believed that prediction could happen at any moment. In the meantime, our SkyWatch and Defender Publishing team kept in touch with Debbie and the girls. Debbie wanted to observe and support Donna in her upcoming activities. We learned early on that we had the same goals in ministry, and our paths kept crossing, so by the time this "starting-over" insight occurred, we were all close friends, but it happened when I least expected it (and after I had basically forgotten all about it).

I had launched a program on the SkyWatch airways called *Teens Rock*. It was a branch off of our central program targeted to a teen audience. Pictures of me pointing to the sky with a brotherly smile had started to appear throughout our promotional literature. In a way, I was just doing what I've been called to do with the giftings God has given me. I love to see the "Billys" of the world have a friend, and I love even more to address misconceptions that the Church has occasionally placed upon its youth regarding subjects like hidden sin and whether you're "holy enough" to be blessed with a gift even if you're not slain in the Spirit (or some equivalent) at the altar. I had plans to address all kinds of questions that Christian youth are asking today, and of all the creative projects I'd ever been involved with, this one had come from my own passions rather than simply being a job I had been hired to carry out. My "voice," you could say, was channeling into what I did for a living.

Within a week from the time I pitched the idea to Dad, I got the green light from every direction and had already held several Creative Lab meetings. This was slated to be my *magnum opus*, and we planned segments that would appeal to both genders (including a "Modest Fashion Modifications" runway feature that would show young girls how to transform the latest skimpy clothing trends into an appropriately modest wardrobe). We had plans for building a set that would allow dramatizations, human videos, stand-up comedy, and much more. What a show we were putting together!

It was going to help a *lot* of young people.

And it was my own creative idea.

One that I felt passionate about…

However, something from the very beginning felt "off track." I kept wanting the project to work the way I envisioned it, but after we recorded the first program, it was clear there was an inherent disconnect between our target audience and the audience we had spent the last decade fostering. As much as I wanted to have a positive "if you build it, they will come" approach, SkyWatch TV simply wasn't formatted to appeal to teens. It has always been more of an adult-centered research-and-discovery company. Teenagers had no reason to tune into our show at the nationally syndicated programming times and channels that we had established over the last few years, and I didn't see today's YouTube generation tuning into our networking, especially when each episode is a half hour. (At least when it involves young people, you can't compete with the ten-minutes-or-under style of online videos from a traditional, old-school television anymore, unless you're lucky enough to have formed a relationship with major networks that are already geared to that demographic.) On the other hand, we knew that the young-adult content we were producing would never keep the attention of SkyWatch TV's regular audience, so it was starting to feel like an *enormous* undertaking to convince our regulars that they needed to invest time in my new vision; I was proposing to "fix" a studio that wasn't broken, one might say.

As busy as I already was with my other duties and responsibilities as chief operating officer, the now full-time job of trying to force *Teens Rock* into the SkyWatch mold was overwhelming. I "just knew" that I was supposed to make it work, though, so I kept trying, finding myself drowning creatively under the weight of such a mismatched effort. It felt clumsy, but by golly, I was committed to making it work.

Then, one day as I was meeting with Dad about the company's future, I shared some of my concerns about *Teens Rock*, expecting him to tell me how to promote it in such a way that it would work for our audience. Later, he emailed me and said, "Joe, about *Teens Rock*: Perhaps think about letting that go completely. Move forward with some of the fresh ideas we discussed earlier. I realize this may make you feel like you're starting all the way over, back at the beginning, but I think it's the right thing to do."

I had long forgotten Debbie's original comments to me at the church that day when I was telling a coworker about the email of Dad's as an explanation for the sudden shift away from the show. My coworker had been told about Debbie's word for me back when it had happened, and he made the connection.

"Wait a second," he said suddenly. "You know what the end of your Dad's email reminds me of? Remember what Debbie said?"

The second the truth hit me, I knew, just like Debbie had said, that "it would be the right thing" to simply let go of my show idea and start over. Although that was a challenge, because I had been convinced I was doing the right thing, the experience was necessary for my growth in the company. Every television appearance I've made since that time has been smoother as a result of my having leadership in the *Teens Rock* project.

Once again, Debbie had nailed it.

I could tell about twenty additional stories that have proven to me and my family that Debbie has a God-given, incredible gift of speaking into peoples' lives. She hasn't rendered anyone quite as "undone" since she spoke to my sister that day in Crane, but it wouldn't be a stretch to say that she *frequently* shares unbelievable and life-changing truths with those around her. Debbie—as well as Whitney, Alicia, Jim, Mary, and Granny—has become a dear friend of the family. We support them—and vice versa—in every ministry project that we undertake.

As far as what ended up happening with Donna and her "voice of the nations," she has gone on to write two best-sellers, one of which—*The Handmaidens Conspiracy*—is challenging the entire Christian Church to reconsider its archaic stance on women in leadership positions within the Body, based on thorough, scholarly research and resources that have been in existence for the last two thousand years. Donna has also appeared in major media, and her voice has now been heard all over the world. Considering what she's up to these days with SkyWatch—and what projects she has down the pike—Debbie's words have only begun to come to fruition. Even if Donna were to stop doing what she's doing now, she would have already fulfilled Debbie's predictions. However, *without* Debbie's timely intervention and willingness to deliver God's message to Donna, Donna would no doubt still be working in the back room of our publishing house as a ghostwriter, specifically because that's precisely where she always wanted to be. But *with* Debbie's timely intervention and willingness to deliver God's message into Donna's life, there's no doubt in my mind that she will go in the bold direction she's headed right now, and that nothing will ever be able to stop her.

Survey says?

This is just the beginning.

Me at age three: About a year before I "joined the worship team" and had help tuning my guitar.

Displaying my fourth-grade class project. The year I experienced some of the heaviest bullying I had ever faced.

My fifth-grade school picture in Mrs. Phillips' class.

Mrs. Barbara Phillips

Ironically, though I couldn't hardly hack it in regular school, I was extremely adept in the martial arts. This is when I was about ten.

Family portrait from our 1987 church directory. Clockwise from left to right: Allie, Mom (Nita), me, Dad (Tom), and Donna.

Class clown: This is a seventh-grade yearbook picture taken before Bob Backstrom intervened. In case you're wondering, that wasn't an awkward-flash moment. I fully intended to display that ridiculous expression.

Uncharacteristically well behaved: I knew I couldn't get by with making a goofy face for my seventh-grade yearbook head shot that my parents would see.

Eighth grade: the year I was school mascot.

Mr. Bob Backstrom

Commander Dave, highly decorated with official Royal Ranger honors. As of 2019, he is still acting as Outpost 64 Ranger Commander.

Commander Dave with two of his Royal Rangers in 2006.

Dave and his wife, Linda, in 2018. Linda has supported Dave's ministry efforts for more than four decades.

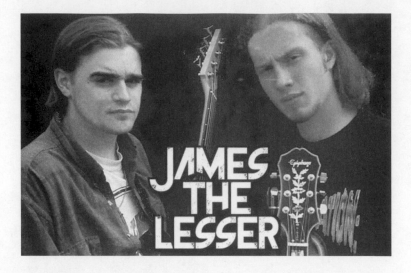

Jason Pumphrey (left) and I (right) in a 1997 promo picture of our Christian rock band, James the Lesser. Note my "mysterious rock star" face. This was my "Wizard of Awe" phase. Poor Jason endured a grand amount of judgmental tomfoolery in those days...

Jason and me, late 2018 when he flew out to surprise me on my birthday.

Our little worship team leading the song service at the church in Crane. From left: Mom (Nita); sister, Donna Howell; me; and my brother-in-law, James Howell.

Alicia (left) and Whitney (right), in a promotional photo for their album titled *Core*.

Whitney (left) and Alicia (right), singing in our church the day we met.

Debbie Short, from that infamous "Day in Crane."

Debbie (right) with her husband, Chuck. Both have since become dear friends and invaluable prayer partners with our family and ministry.

Promotional shot of me in my brief stint as the host of *Teens Rock*.

In keeping with Mrs. Phillips' fifth-grade prediction that I would grow up to be a musician, this is the cover for our Christian band's latest release: *Joe Horn and Broken for Good: Right Where You Stand.* From left: James Howell, Mom (Nita); me; Donna Howell; Stan Williams (our rhythm guitarist and close family friend); and older sister, Allie.

WHAT IS THE MESSAGE?

Joe Ardis on the set of "Jonny The Criminal"

WHAT IS THE MESSAGE?

Joe Ardis Horn of Skywatch TV on the set of "Jonny The Criminal"

Promotional posters of Joe Horn and Broken for Good, taken during the "Jonny Project"—a multimedia project aimed at taking the Gospel to prisoners all over the United States. The photos are stills from the music video, *Jonny Was a Criminal*, which was released on DVD alongside a passionate "Prodigal Son" sermon by Pastor Bruce Belin, who played our very own motorcyclist prisoner, "Jonny."

On the set of SkyWatch Television.

Me and my beautiful wife, Katherine (left), in the green room at the *Jim Bakker Show* studio, minutes before we recorded the network television episodes about my last book, *Timebomb*.

Me today.

CHAPTER SIX

More to the Gifts Than We Thought?

This book has been, to this point, a reflection on my life lessons and relationships, shared in the interest of providing powerful examples of some of the Holy Spirit-given gifts that we're about to delve deeper into. We'll transition now to a focus on the varying gifts of the Spirit, both the known and lesser-known, in hopes of assisting you readers in the process of recognizing—*and unlocking*—your own giftings.

Because whether you know it or not, you *do* possess heavenly giftings designed by God for use in His Kingdom work.

But is there more to the gifts of the Holy Spirit than we thought? Are we so used to our cultural and traditional concepts of the gifts that we don't see others that are clearly there, or that we misunderstand the gifts we have often heard about? Are we overlooking how the gifts are truly supposed to be employed as they are in the original languages and contexts of Scripture?

The first place to go is the Bible, of course, but not always only to the English translation. God's Word has a great number of things to say that we miss when we limit His message to our own language and inter-pretations. As anyone can guess, following the Lord's directive with our lives while we don't completely understand His directives to begin with can be confusing.

If you've ever tried to get to the bottom of what your gifting might be, you're probably thinking you'd be wealthy if you had a dollar for every time you were directed to 1 Corinthians 12:8–10. It's true that this passage is a terrific place to start. However, our modern Church is now so familiar with the passage's list of spiritual gifts that if you don't immediately feel a connection to it (especially as a new believer), you may begin to question whether you *have* a spiritual gifting at all. But the Bible is clear that the Holy Spirit equips *all* members of the priesthood for service, and He will not send a priest or priestess of His Church out to minister without the power needed to be efficient in that calling.

I believe that right now, we, as a corporate Church, need to do two things: 1) understand the gifts listed in 1 Corinthians 12:8–10 perhaps a little more deeply than we currently do; and 2) know, understand, and more widely acknowledge the *other* passages that speak about gifts with just as much attention as we give 1 Corinthians. Then, individually, we need to comprehend our own giftings and commit to sharing them in healthy ways.

I would like to dig straight into study, but two crucial points need to be made first…

Be Careful What You Say!

One thing that *really* bothers me—and it *should* bother anyone in the Church—is when cessationists say there can be no supernatural display, and then *every time* a supernatural display happens right in front of them, they say it's demonic or that a person somewhere in the mix is demon-possessed. Don't get me wrong: I understand that there is a time to call it when demonic activity is occurring. But what grieves me is when people have such a pattern of judgment that they don't consider the proof that the display might be *real*, and that it might originate from the Lord.

I sometimes wonder why some allow for "supernaturally demonic" occurrences but refuse to allow for "supernaturally holy" activities. Strange…

If there is no way that the enemy or his minions are benefitting from the spectacle—and if there is tangible evidence that positive change is happening for the sake of the Gospel or the Lord's name being glorified—then it is dangerous to gravitate to the claim that there is demonic activity.

In Mark 3, we read of how the scribes and Pharisees claimed that Jesus Christ was demon-possessed, because He was casting out demons, and the religious men couldn't fathom that Jesus' actions were empowered by God. This is the moment in the Scriptures where we land at the dreaded "blasphemy of the Holy Spirit" verse (Mark 3:29–30) that many Christians fear. I beseech you, readers, *please* be careful when you call out supernatural activity as being of demonic origin. I am, at times, the harshest skeptic of all, and I'm sure after reading about parts of my life, you can see why I have good reasons to be skeptical—but those who label everything they don't understand as "demonic" are making a *dangerous* move.

What We Will Not Be Discussing

In the coming pages, I've chosen to focus only on the "gifts" as distinct from "offices" or "titles." As this book is not a church leadership training program or a theological study on ecclesiastical titles, it would be a huge distraction to discuss the responsibilities of every role (apostle, pastor, preacher, teacher, evangelist, and so on), especially since the titles differ among denominations.

For instance: There is an ongoing debate about whether the gift of apostleship should be considered among the gifts of the Holy Spirit because Paul mentions apostleship as an office, but, depending on who you're talking to, that confuses "apostolic gifts" with "the modern office/title/authority of an apostle," and that's an enormous mess completely unrelated to this study.

My goal in writing this has never been to provide learning materials for men and women who already know they are called to be administrative leaders; it has been to show *every* man and woman of God that he or she is *already* a leader in the gifts that the Holy Spirit has assigned, and help them recognize the value that their contributions have in light of eternity.

With these things in mind, let's go deeper.

1 Corinthians 12:8–10

A little later, I want to come back to the beginning of 1 Corinthians 12, from the first to the seventh verses, because some of the biggest secrets regarding our giftings are stored there. But for now, let's look at the gifts as they're listed in the most popularly referenced section of the Word.

> For to one is given by the Spirit the word of wisdom; to another the word of knowledge by the same Spirit; To another faith by the same Spirit; to another the gifts of healing by the same Spirit; To another the working of miracles; to another prophecy; to another discerning of spirits; to another divers kinds of tongues; to another the interpretation of tongues. (1 Corinthians 12:8–10)

Here we find the first nine gifts to study:

1. The Word of Wisdom
2. The Word of Knowledge
3. Faith
4. Gifts of Healing
5. Working of Miracles
6. Prophecy
7. Discerning of Spirits
8. Tongues
9. Interpretation of Tongues

Some of these terms are self-explanatory and others cause quite a bit of confusion. This partly stems from the fact that the Church Body is split into denominations and sects. For example, some groups hold a cessationist view on some or many of the gifts, which means they believe gifts were given by the Holy Spirit *temporarily* to build and strengthen the early Christians in the first century. Since then, some denominations say, those gifts have ceased. (The gifts of tongues, interpreting tongues, prophecy, and miracles are often at the center of these debates. It is sad how much the Body fights about these issues.)

To readers who may have been expecting a lengthy theological explanation regarding which denominations believe what and the groups that are right or wrong, I hate to disappoint you, but that isn't the purpose of this book. I have zero intention of blasting any denomination's doctrines, both because I can't stand dissension in the Church that is *supposed to be* loving the lost instead of arguing amidst itself (James 4; 1 Corinthians 1:12; 3:4), and because it would require our focus to veer into interdenominational territories that I truly believe are about to become far less important anyway. (If you want to know *why* I believe that, read Donna Howell's book: *Radicals: Why Tomorrow Belongs to Post-Denominational Christians Infused with Supernatural Power*. Her approach shows the error of a Church dedicated to warring between factions.)

What I *can* do is: 1) tell you when I've seen unexplainable occurrences that defy human abilities; 2) offer some word-study insights; and 3) allow you to draw your own conclusions, based on your own convictions—not only regarding cessation, but also concerning the execution of the gift (since Paul did not describe them and there are varying interpretations on what he was referring to).

The Word of Wisdom and the Word of Knowledge: The difference between wisdom and knowledge is distinct, but the words have historically supported the same purposes. They are *related*, but not synonymous. Whereas knowledge is the obtained collection of data or facts (through study and research, for instance), wisdom is the ability to discern and/or judge right from wrong or true from false, and it's most commonly gained through life experience and maturity. An old adage says, "Knowledge is knowing that a tomato is a fruit, while wisdom is knowing not to put it in a fruit salad."

Wisdom is typically seen as the more desirable gift, yet neither of these gifts can exist without the other: Without knowledge, wisdom would have nothing to discern; without wisdom, knowledge's collection of data and facts could not be applied toward a useful purpose (not to mention, a person can be fooled with false information without the wisdom to discern; fake news, anyone?).

Some believe these gifts, in context of how the Holy Spirit equips them, are an overlap of a teaching ability only: They should not be viewed as anything supernatural when they are in use. One person studies and investigates, another wisely examines and discerns how to apply those studies and investigations. If these two work together (such as in church leadership), the teaching that pours forth from one or both of them will be sharpened by the Holy Spirit. While the intervention of the Holy Spirit is innately supernatural, the execution of these gifts in person appear to be instilled within the natural character of the men or women with the gifts.

Others, however, see these gifts as operating under a divine oratory revelation: The Lord speaks through the gifted to impart either: a) facts that could not have otherwise been known naturally (gift of knowledge); or b) the will of God over a matter of truth, the exposure of a wrong, discerning the right steps in tough situations, etc. (gift of wisdom). The former might be observed when, as an example, a woman stands up in the middle of a church service and says God told her that someone in their midst was diagnosed with a brain tumor last Thursday at 3:14 in the afternoon. That is a fact otherwise unknowable. (I have seen these displays many times. I haven't always been able to verify that the secret wasn't discovered through gossip or conversation before those kinds of services, but what I saw with Debbie that day in Crane was unexplainable.) The latter might be observed when, as another example, a man stands to give the Lord's will and council over an administrative issue that has been tearing the church apart in the last year, and proceeds to give advice so perfectly befitting the scenario that the wisdom displayed can only be of heavenly origin. (This, too, I have seen many times.)

There is some debate between denominations about whether Paul was referring to extremely wise and knowledgeable teachers, or whether he was describing a more sensational manifestation of these gifts. The problem with discounting the sensational side of things is that, just like myself, many have witnessed these gifts being used in more dramatic demonstrations—and no, as I addressed before, they can't always be traced to demonic origin.

But perhaps some greater insight lies within the Word itself.

Elsewhere in Paul's letter to the Corinthians—and this would be the *first* place to look, even before other Scriptures outside this letter, because it would be written to the same audience, by the same author, in response to the same circumstances, and therefore it's guaranteed to be the closest available context for exegetical comparison—Paul talked about a secret wisdom and knowledge of God:

Howbeit we speak wisdom among them that are perfect: yet not the wisdom of this world, nor of the princes of this world, that come to nought: But we speak the wisdom of God in a mystery, even the hidden wisdom, which God ordained before the world unto our glory: Which none of the princes of this world knew: for had they known it, they would not have crucified the Lord of glory.

But as it is written, "Eye hath not seen, nor ear heard, neither have entered into the heart of man, the things which God hath prepared for them that love him."

But God hath revealed them unto us by his Spirit: for the Spirit searcheth all things, yea, the deep things of God. For what man knoweth the things of a man, save the spirit of man which is in him? even so the things of God knoweth no man, but the Spirit of God. Now we have received, not the spirit of the world, but the spirit which is of God; that we might know the things that are freely given to us of God. Which things also we speak, not in the words which man's wisdom teacheth, but which the Holy Ghost teacheth; comparing spiritual things with spiritual. But the natural man receiveth not the things of the Spirit of God: for they are foolishness unto him: neither can he know them, because they are spiritually discerned. But he that is spiritual judgeth all things, yet he himself is judged of no man. For who hath known the mind of the Lord, that he may instruct him? but we have the mind of Christ. (1 Corinthians 2:6–16)

Here, Paul is clearly describing literal supernatural knowledge and wisdom—facts and discernments that mankind would not obtain through any means other than the Spirit of God. The same author, when he wrote to the church in Ephesus, said he prayed "that the God of our Lord Jesus Christ, the Father of glory, may give unto you the spirit of wisdom and revelation in the knowledge of him" (Ephesians 1:17).

The Greek words Paul used when he wrote "the word of wisdom" and "the word of knowledge" in 1 Corinthians 12:8 were *logos sophia* ("the word of wisdom") and *logos gnosis* ("the word of knowledge"). Both *sophia* and *gnosis* could mean either earthly or divine wisdom/knowledge depending on how it was used within the Bible.

Logos meant a few different things depending on the context (for instance, it could mean, at times, a meditation of the mind), but its primary use is as "speech" or "a word uttered by a living voice [which] embodies a conception or idea."[1] When compared to the previous verse in which Paul says the giftings of the Holy Spirit will be given to "profit withal" (to benefit others, not just edify the one gifted; 1 Corinthians 12:7), this could not therefore mean a word "from God only to the gifted one." This *logos* spoken word, in order to profit withal, must convey concepts or ideas from God to others, such as in an assembly or one on one—but the gift is to be shared, not hoarded for one's own secret benefit. (We will visit Paul's "profit withal" more later on.)

So whether one wishes to believe that Paul's words about the wisdom and knowledge gifts mean simply teaching or were referencing something more extraordinary, we know it involves the gifted believer opening his or her mouth and speaking to others for the gift to be in use. Barring complete cessation of these two gifts, they require people *of this generation and alive at this time* to be willing to speak boldly, when God says to speak.

Faith: Obviously, this gift doesn't simply refer to a belief in God, because that applies to every Christian. However, just as obviously, the word "faith" (Greek *pistis*: "credence; moral conviction of religious truth"[2]) denotes the act of believing in something. How then does "regular faith in God" differ from the "Holy-Spirit-infused *gift*-faith in God"?

It can be difficult to describe something Paul said two thousand years ago through language translations and across spans of cultures and mind-blowingly different circumstances, when the only thing he said about the gift of faith was that it is received "by the same Spirit" as all the others. However, classic commentators and scholars have brought not only unique perspective to this question, but also unity of logic, as many tend to agree. Survey says: It's simply the ability to trust in God's divine provision and intervention at all times and in every circumstance.

Some reflections do link the gift of faith with more supernatural endowments, such as having faith to move mountains (Matthew 17:19–20), but there appears to be an error of logic in that trail. The gift of miracles can't possibly work if the miraculously gifted member of the Body doesn't have faith that the miracle God is about to perform will work in the first place, so when it comes to miracles such as moving mountains (and other sensational demonstrations), that appears to fall under the gift of "miracles," not "faith." There would be no distinction between the two on the list otherwise.

But don't be quick to assume that the gift of faith (which could be reworded as the "gift of trusting God no matter what," if the classical commentaries are correct) is not a powerful gift. In fact, there are *times* when it just might shine as the brightest and most useful in the Body, as well as the gift that keeps the others going when corporate faith is threatened with stagnation. I love what *Barnes' Notes* says about this:

> Many of the most useful people in the church are distinguished mainly for their simple confidence in the promises of God; and often accomplish more by prayer and by their faith in God than others do who are distinguished for their wisdom and learning. Humble piety and reliance in the divine promises, and that measure of ardor, fearlessness, and zeal which result from such confidence; that belief that all obstacles must be and will be overcome that oppose the gospel; and that God will secure the advancement of his cause, will often do infinitely more in the promotion of his kingdom than the most splendid endowments of learning and talent.

Indeed, if a man were disposed to do good on the widest scale possible, to do the utmost that he possibly could in saving people, he would best accomplish it by seeking simple "faith" in God's aid and promises, and then under the influence of this, engage with ardor in doing what he could. Faith is one of the highest endowments of the Christian life.[3]

That might just be one of the most beautiful things I've ever read. Why? Because although it is not void of supernatural endowment and intervention from the Holy Spirit who gives the gift, it doesn't intrinsically rely on signs, wonders, and spectacular demonstrations in order to become what *Barnes'* so eloquently recognizes as tremendously useful and accomplishing—that gift which "will often do infinitely *more* in the promotion of [God's] kingdom"!

In my own life, I've witnessed the miraculous signs of God more often as a result of this gift than of any other, yet the one gifted is frequently the quietest, humblest person I know at any given time. In the past, it has bewildered me how *solid* some people's faith and trust in God is, regardless of every circumstance. I remember when my mother's best friend, Henrietta Stewart, was informed that my wife and I could not conceive. Doctors had run several tests and told us that it just wasn't going to happen. We wanted children so badly it was becoming an obsession. Katherine shed uncountable tears in those days, and she was personally crushed every time she heard of a young girl opting for an abortion. But Henrietta kept speaking to us with terms and phrases that sounded as if she didn't even know we had a problem. Her faith in God's ability to give us children was so grounded in confidence that I often didn't know how to respond when she would share her gift with me.

"We've tried everything," I would say. "Doctors have done all they can."

"Well, when these doctors have to deliver your children in the future, we'll all have a good laugh, won't we?" she would respond.

I believe God heard her prayers, because today we enjoy four beautiful children that "were never going to happen."

No doubt about it, Henrietta was unshakable. She sat day in and day out on her porch with a pot of tea, encouraging others to be faithful in their walk with God *and* in their own gifts until the day the Lord took her home. She was the epitome of the "accomplishing" people *Barnes'* described, and she—and so many others like her that I could name—have done more to promote the Kingdom of God than can be accounted for on this side of eternity.

If you are lucky enough to be given the gift of faith by the power of the Holy Spirit, own that with self-assurance.

Healing and Miracles: The Greek word translated "healing" in 1 Corinthians 12:9 is *iama*, and it means just what it sounds like: "a cure (the effect):—healing."[4] Likewise, the words "the working of miracles" (*energema dynamis*) mean just that. These gifts are self-explanatory and need very little analysis. Simply put, the Holy Spirit gives certain members of the Body the ability to be the conduits through which *God* cures an individual or performs a miracle over the forces of nature. It's a mistake to believe that the human host holds the healing power over sickness, mental illness, death, or the forces of nature. However, when physical healings and miracles have taken place in recent history in front of witnesses and in the name of Christ—*and when all glory has been given to God through whom the healing/miracle is possible*—the authority and authenticity of Christ, His Gospel message, and all of Scripture has been vividly displayed. It's pretty hard for nonbelievers to claim Christianity is nothing more than a creed or lifestyle when the Lord of Christianity is given credit for a healing or for defying everything we know is possible within the realms of earthly reality.

One confusing thought pops up in conversation now and again amidst believers: If Christ and His apostles after Him healed so many people in the New Testament, why doesn't this happen all the time now? Were the healings and miracles only for the first century?

As clichéd as the often-given answer sounds, it's still true: Miracles and healings happen *all the time* overseas today. Just ask a missionary. Just because our Western Christianity doesn't produce the results the same doctrines do for the destitute in Third-World regions, we shouldn't assume the gifts have ceased (especially in light of the medicines we have here that can now treat diseases and conditions that couldn't have been treated in New Testament times). Nor should we say that it's not a miracle when God heals someone over time, or when we pray for rain for our crops and "coincidentally" the rain falls. The healings and miracles reported in the New Testament happened amidst a people who were willing to recognize the healings and miracles for what they were. Today, we simply "get better" or "get lucky rain," less willing than our ancestors to credit God for something when the world of medicine or forces of nature gave no indication that something positive was about to occur. We're "blessing numb," to the point that any true miracle has to be ramped all the way up to a hundred for us to accept the hand of God where and when it takes place.

However (perhaps most importantly): If a Great Awakening is just around the corner like the *Final Fire* book postulates—and I think it *is*—then we are looking at a day when there might be a sharp increase of supernatural events such as healings and miracles in *every* territory. I believe "Western Christianity" is about to get a major facelift from being social clubs to becoming a people with a first-century passion for Christ, and those in the Body who believe they've been endowed with the gifts of healings and miracles need to prepare themselves *now*.

Get ready *now*, and *live ready* until that day arrives. Draw closer each day to the Savior and His beautiful character. Read His story repeatedly. Thank the Father over and over again for His amazing Son-gift to all. Press into the Holy Spirit like never before, asking Him to lead you and guide you in every conceivable way regarding your gift, because it's going to be astonishing and remarkable...but it is also going to be a momentous responsibility that you will need to be reliable and serious about while functioning within that calling.

Prophecy: Straight out of the gate, I have to tell you that the gift of prophecy doesn't *always* mean foretelling future events. The words "prophet" (noun) and "prophesy" (verb) both derive from the Greek *propheteuo.* This word covers many kinds of public exhortation categories, among which is "to teach, refute, reprove, admonish, comfort others."[5] (Note that several mainstream Christian denominations choose to see the "office of a prophet" as a different responsibility than the "gift of prophecy." The "office" of a prophet has all but ceased in Western Christianity.)

I can't count how many times I've heard Christians say things like, "You can tell if a prophet is a true prophet of God if what they say comes true when they said it would." But prophecy is more complicated than that. Jonah was a true prophet of God who outright told the Ninevites they would be (not "might be") destroyed in forty days. That didn't happen (Jonah 3:4, 10), yet we still identify Jonah as a true prophet because he delivered the word of God to the people and his message resulted in mass redemption. Isaiah was one of the *great* prophets, and when he said King Hezekiah was going to die (would "not recover" [NIV]), everything looked pretty certain and bleak until the king's prayers of repentance reversed his illness *and* delivered him from the hands of his Assyrian enemies (Isaiah 38:1, 5–60). Still, we don't consider Isaiah a false prophet just because his foretellings didn't go down the way he said. These are not the only biblical examples of this (consider also Huldah, who prophesied about the peaceful death of Josiah, who later died under a volley of arrows because he disobeyed God: 2 Kings 22; 2 Chronicles 35:20–21), yet there is no question that these prophets delivered the word God wanted them to deliver. Therefore, it's not accurate to view a prophet of the Lord only as one who fills the role of some kind of inspired fortuneteller.

I would like to suggest a redirect from the concept of "prophet" as "foreteller for God" and steer instead to "deliverer of the will and purposes of God." But then, if the "word of wisdom" and "word of knowledge" gifts are in essence giving a word from God to His people through the one gifted, how is the gift of prophecy different?

I admit that this is so closely related to the same concepts as the other two that it's easy to get confused. First, let's look at what the same writer said about prophecy elsewhere in the same letter: "But he that prophesieth speaketh unto men to edification, and exhortation, and comfort" (1 Corinthians 14:3). So far, we know that in the context of the letter to the Corinthian congregation, the Paul's emphasis was upon the corporate edification and lifting up the Body to positive places of growth and comfort. This would be a better angle to focus on than Old Testament prophets and their offices, since the directives of Paul follow the Great Commission of Christ and His Church, which is the Body we're currently a part of.

Now, let's look at what *Thayer's Greek Lexicon* says of the Greek word Paul used (*propheteia*) in his 12:10 reference to prophecy as a Holy-Spirit given gift: "prophecy, i.e., discourse emanating from divine inspiration and declaring the purposes of God, whether by reproving and admonishing the wicked, or comforting the afflicted, or revealing things hidden." Whereas *Thayer's does* go on to specify "especially by foretelling future events,"[6] it's clear that a modern prophet of the Lord in action today isn't limited to uttering words about what is coming.

But whether it's about the future or the present—and whether it's about knowledge or wisdom—a prophecy is, based on sources like *Thayer's* (and the opinion of several scholars who have tackled this subject), the utterance of God's will to the extent that the message given *could* go beyond our temporal and finite comprehensions and conditions, such as the deep mysteries of the Lord.

For example, earlier I said a person with the "word of knowledge" might know that someone was diagnosed with a brain tumor the previous

Thursday at 3:14 in the afternoon. That speaks of a truth that couldn't have been known unless the Holy Spirit told the one gifted with the "word of knowledge"; *however*, the nature of the message is temporal, and not at all mysterious: Doctors, here on planet earth and in the natural realm, communicated with a patient about a tumor on a specific date and time. It's a circumstance of our human condition. The same could be said about the other example I gave regarding the man who shared the "word of wisdom" in order to assist the church that was falling apart because of an administrative issue. Again, it's wisdom given from the Holy Spirit to the one gifted with the "word of wisdom," so in that regard, it is supernatural and mysterious, but at the end of the day, it's a subject related to our finite, earthly, temporal reality. Nothing in these examples is innately tied to the deep mysteries of the Lord or His grand purposes in the spiritual realm. A *prophecy*, on the other hand, is described by scholars like a hope from the Lord of some grand, otherworldly concept we wouldn't have otherwise even known to imagine—a message so far above our human circumstances that it is, by nature, transcendent and all but incomprehensible, like Abraham being told that he and his barren wife would have as many children as there were stars in the sky. Once again, *Barnes' Notes* has a flair for truncating and simplifying a complicated subject. The following is from *Barnes'* approach to Romans 12:16, but it is his focus on the description of "prophecy," as well as his seamless consolidation of New Testament uses, that brings clarification:

> The apostle [Paul] now proceeds to specify the different classes of gifts or endowments which Christians have, and to exhort them to discharge aright the duty which results from the rank or function which they held in the church. "The first is prophecy." This word properly means to predict future events, but it also means to declare the divine will; to interpret the purposes of God; or to make known in any way the truth of God, which is designed to influence people. Its first meaning is to

predict or foretell future events; but as those who did this were messengers of God, and as they commonly connected with such predictions, instructions, and exhortations in regard to the sins, and dangers, and duties of people, the word came to denote any who warned, or threatened, or in any way communicated the will of God; and even those who uttered devotional sentiments or praise. The name in the New Testament is commonly connected with teachers; Acts 13:1, "There were in the church at Antioch certain prophets, and teachers, as Barnabas, etc.;" Acts 15:32, "and Judas and Silas, being prophets themselves, etc.;" Acts 21:10, "a certain prophet named Agabus." In 1 Corinthians 12:28–29, prophets are mentioned as a class of teachers immediately after apostles, "And God hath set some in the church; first apostles, secondly prophets; thirdly teachers, etc."

The same class of persons is again mentioned in 1 Corinthians 14:29–32, 1 Corinthians 14:39. In this place they are spoken of as being under the influence of revelation, "Let the prophets speak two or three, and let the other judge. If anything be revealed to another that sitteth by, let the first hold his peace. And the spirits of the prophets are subject to the prophets;" 1 Corinthians 14:39, "Covet to prophesy, and forbid not to speak with tongues." In this place endowments are mentioned under the name of prophecy evidently in advance even of the power of speaking with tongues....

[But note the cautionary side of this gift, as Barnes' goes on to address:] They [prophets] had the power of using their prophetic gifts as we have the ordinary faculties of our minds, and of course of abusing them also. This abuse was apparent also in the case of those who had the power of speaking with tongues, 1 Corinthians 14:2, 1 Corinthians 14:4, 1 Corinthians 14:6, 1 Corinthians 14:11, etc.[7]

So just as with the gift of healing and miracles, the gift of prophecy is one the Church should not take lightly. Again, many cessationists believe these gifts are no longer given by the Holy Spirit for the Church today. Although I don't necessarily agree because I can't find sufficient biblical evidence to suggest a first-century cut-off of a gift given "to teach, refute, reprove, admonish, [and/or] comfort others"—which is what a prophet really is once you remove our Western, "fortuneteller for God only" concept—I can appreciate the care that should be taken when considering what and who a prophet would be today. Ultimately, *only* the Holy Spirit—not an earthly denominational credo—decides how to equip people for the cause of the Gospel, and above and beyond all of mankind's debates about cessation, the Church should agree that this is one gift we should *all* be extremely careful about. Those who claim to be prophets of the Lord but who utter messages that lift themselves above others or twist words or circumstances for their own gain are playing with fire. I've seen—over and over, as my stories throughout this book relate—the damage a false prophet can cause.

If you truly believe the Holy Spirit has equipped you with the gift of prophecy, pray first and foremost every day that He will guide you in that gift for His glory, and His alone. Seek continual humility and obedience, for yours might be a limelight gift, indeed.

Discerning of Spirits: Every follower of Christ has the ability to grow in personal discernment of good and evil (and the spirits thereof, such as demons, angels, etc.), and the longer we pour ourselves into the Word of God and draw closer to Him, the more we will, as Hebrews 5:13–14 states, develop and sharpen our personal discernment.

Unlike some of the sensational, attention-grabbing gifts that rely on personal revelations from the voice of God that nobody else could know, or on mysterious manifestations or demonstrations of power, this gift—compared to other internal biblical evidence—is based simply on knowing God…knowing Him well enough to instantly recognize when a sermon, a message, a doctrine, an event, or even a person comes along that conflicts with Him or His truth. Those with discerning spirits will retain so much truth of the Word that they will quickly recognize and distinguish whatever is contrary to it. The primary function of this gift relies on the ability to simply know when a source of information—such as doctrine—is of God. (That's not to say that the gifted one must have the entire Bible memorized, or any such extreme, but too many verses point to the clear benefits of Bible study to just chalk up this gift to "discernment by intuitive feelings.")

I can't think of a time more important than right now for members of the Body to be equipped with this gift developed to its fullest.

Let's look at a few other key verses regarding the function of this gift in a corporate setting. First, Paul, in a letter to Pastor Timothy of Ephesus, said, "Now the Spirit speaketh expressly, that in the latter times some shall depart from the faith, giving heed to seducing spirits, and doctrines of devils" (1 Timothy 4:1). In a follow-up letter, Paul wrote to Timothy again, saying, "For the time will come when they will not endure sound doctrine; but after their own lusts shall they heap to themselves teachers, having itching ears; And they shall turn away their ears from the truth, and shall be turned unto fables" (2 Timothy 4:3–4). The picture Paul is painting here sounds like one of a world with global teaching (think YouTube) where everyone can find an "authority" who will say whatever he or she wants to hear. Their ears will itch for fables, or "doctrines of devils," instead of for the sound doctrine, so long as the truth is twisted to conform to their own concepts and agendas (which sounds quite like a description of our current, American postmodernist "What *is* truth?" culture). Yet this same Pauline masterpiece urges us to "study to shew [ourselves] approved unto God, [as workmen] that needeth not to be ashamed, rightly dividing the word of truth" (2 Timothy 2:15).

If you believe you've been gifted with the discernment of spirits (or the ability to recognize dark influences/voices), keep your nose in the Word of God like the proudest nerd in the advanced class. Continue to ask the Holy Spirit to reveal Himself to you: His nature, His character,

His will, and His ways. Then, when the doctrines of devils are present, you will be able to discern.

What an important gift for today!

Tongues and the Interpretation of Tongues: The most talked-about of all these gifts (at least in my experience growing up—*everywhere* I went) are the final two, both relating to the events recorded in Acts 2. Opinions about this issue are at times in such stark contrast that it can be difficult to remain neutral: Often, when asked for our opinion on the matter, any response we give is wrong for *someone* in the room. Even silence on the subject can mean more than we want if the listeners are amped-up enough to read more into it. I've seen more division amidst the Body of Christ over this doctrinal/theological issue than over any other.

Some denominations take the cessationist view: The Holy Spirit inspired *xenoglossy* (from Greek *xenos* ["foreigner"] and *glossa* ["language"]; literally "foreign language"; when a person suddenly speaks an earthly, foreign language he or she hasn't learned through natural means) for the rapid growth of the first-century Church—but now that Christianity has been spread all over the world, the gift of tongues (and the interpretation thereof) is no longer needed and has ceased. Then, of course, some denominations believe the Holy Spirit inspired both *xenoglossy* and *glossolalia* (from Greek *glossa* ["language"] and *laleo* ["to talk"]; when a person speaks a divine language that is unknowable by any earthly culture; known in today's Church circles as "speaking in tongues" or "speaking in the prayer language")—and that both tongues and the interpretation thereof are alive in the Church today for the edification of all, and as a "sign to the unbelievers" (1 Corinthians 14:22).

Many books and articles have been dedicated to explaining the words of Paul on the issue of tongues and the theological and interpretational differences between denominational stances on the matter. I have my own opinions stemming from a lifetime of seeing evidence on *both* sides of the debate and involving the testimonies of people of both questionable and unquestionable integrity. However, I once again have no intention of turning this book into a hard stance on tongues and whether they belong in the Church today, primarily because it's not the purpose of this book. (Note, however, that neither *xenoglossy* nor *glossolalia* are found in Scripture. These compound words were formulated in recent centuries to distinguish between the interpretations of "holy" and "natural foreign" languages in the ongoing tongues debate. Perhaps this is just another reason we shouldn't be arguing about it?)

There are many approaches to what the gift of the "interpretation of tongues" always was in the Word. Some believe it was only a communicative gift, like *xenoglossy*, speaking in tongues, but opposite: A person could hear someone speaking in a foreign language—one he or she never had learned—and suddenly understand and be able to convey what the person said. The interpreter, along with the speaker, could use these gifts in conjunction and miraculously have a fluid conversation with everyone present in order to lead others to the Lord. Others believe that public, prophetic *glossolalia* utterances of tongues can be spoken aloud in services today as long as someone with the gift of interpretation translates the heavenly language into a message from the Holy Spirit to the congregation. Still others believe *glossolalia* tongues can be spoken both in private and in public, with or without an interpreter, for both corporate and personal edification in drawing nearer to God.

I personally believe some people have the gift of speaking in and/or interpreting tongues, but because of what I've seen in churches—including the abuse of that gift—I believe the authentic gift of tongues and interpretation of tongues is *always* used for the Lord's glory. Properly used, these actions are not disruptive, won't draw attention to the speaker or interpreter, and do not derail God's purposes. To simplify, I believe speaking and interpreting tongues as they are represented by Paul in 1 Corinthians 14 (his rebuke of the disorderly service) is a good example of how these gifts are to be used. Though many would agree with this assessment, there are likewise many others who would allow chaos if they thought it would launch or accompany revival excitement (which is counterproductive anyway, since revivals launched or accompanied by chaos do precisely what Paul described in verse 23: "If therefore the whole church be come together into one place, and all speak with tongues, and there come in those that are unlearned, or unbelievers, will they not say that ye are mad [crazy; insane; acting like lunatics]?").

However, the discussion requires balance. If we, while speaking in tongues, "pray with the spirit" or "pray with the soul" instead of just with our mind and thoughts like Paul clarifies (1 Corinthians 14:14), many young Christians of the future, tragically, would be praying *only* from intellect and logic, and never with the spirit or soul. Therefore, as a closing thought on this matter: I am concerned about the idea of certain subsections of the Body corporately abandoning the gifts of tongues and interpretation. I believe we are to embrace and use *all* the gifts the Holy Spirit has left for us. Unfortunately, due to the misuse of these two gifts—as well as because of numerous false teachings about them—there is a certain stigma attached to using them in the Church today. My prayer is that our younger generations will be better equipped and informed in this area tomorrow, and that they will operate in the fullest confidence.

1 Corinthians 12:28

As I stated earlier, so much of what is readily quoted today regarding the gifts of the Holy Spirit as given to the members of the Body comes back to 1 Corinthians 12:8–10. It isn't that Christians don't know about the rest of what's there, because many believers faithfully study the Word of God and understand that the list of gifts goes beyond those first nine. But when the subject has repeatedly come up in *my* life, no one has ever said a word about the rest of the gifts. The first of these "skipped-over" lists is in the same chapter even, just a little farther down, beginning in verse 28.

Sure, I knew that 1 Corinthians 12:28 addresses offices God has appointed, but I was an adult before I finally looked at that verse as being *within the same context* (how did I miss this?) as the list we just visited. There Paul is, talking about the varying gifts the Holy Spirit uses to equip the Body in 12:8–10, then he talks about the importance of all members of the Body working together in 12:11–27. He then comes *back* to list more gifts that "God hath set" in the Body for the same "profit withal" purposes (in context) as the previous list in 12:8–10: "And God hath set some in the church, first apostles, secondarily prophets, thirdly teachers, after that *miracles, then gifts of healings, helps, governments, diversities of tongues*" (1 Corinthians 12:28; emphasis added). We've already discussed miracles, healings, discernment, and tongues. (Please remember that I am focusing on "gifts" as distinct from "titles" or "offices," because my goal is to encourage those who may not know how important their contributions to the Church really are, and to help them realize their gifts can even be grander in the plan of the Lord.)

From this list, we have these two additional gifts to reflect upon:

1. Helps
2. Governments

Again, many have probably read this verse many times throughout their walk with God and, like me, though they may have absentmindedly acknowledged that the Holy Spirit has empowered a lot of beautiful wonders throughout Scripture, they don't land on this verse and let it breathe like the others we just discussed. The second they begin to wonder what their gift is, they go back to 1 Corinthians 12:8–10 and compare themselves to that limited section of Sciprture to see how they connect with any of the nine most popular gifts.

But wouldn't it be sad if people spent their whole lives waiting for the Holy Spirit to give them the gift of healing when, all the while, they were called into performing great ministry for the Lord in the Body's "governments"? Wouldn't it be demoralizing for believers to spend years finding their greatest joy in helping others, while simultaneously feeling guilty and unspiritual because they aren't uttering words of knowledge or wisdom?

Don't miss what the God-breathed Word might be telling you. Let's dig!

Helps: How many times have you heard sermons on the gift of tongues, healings, or miracles? Quite often! Now, how many times have you heard sermons on the gift of helps?

…I honestly don't think I've *ever* heard such a sermon. In fact, what on earth does that even *mean*?

The Greek word for "helps" here is *antilempsis* ("a laying hold of"[8]), which derives from *antilambano* ("middle voice" use of *lambano*): "to take hold of in turn, i.e. succor; also to participate:—help, partaker, support."[9] We can gain further insight from other instances of this word in Scripture:

- "I have coveted no man's silver, or gold, or apparel. Yea, ye yourselves know, that these hands have ministered unto my necessities, and to them that were with me. I have shewed you all things, how that so labouring ye ought to support [*antilambano*] the weak, and to remember the words of the Lord Jesus, how he said, 'It is more blessed to give than to receive'" (Acts 20:33–35). This verse is being spoken by Paul as he has assembled the leaders of Ephesus together for a meeting. The context ("silver, or gold, or apparel" followed by "blessed to give") emphasizes that the leaders of the Ephesian congregation should be assisting the poor and weak, both with their monies as well as with supplies for their other needs (clothing, food, etc.).
- "Let as many servants as are under the yoke count their own masters worthy of all honour, that the name of God and his doctrine be not blasphemed. And they that have believing

masters, let them not despise them, because they are brethren; but rather do them service, because they are faithful and beloved, partakers [*antilambano*] of the benefit. These things teach and exhort" (1 Timothy 6:1–2). Again, these are the words of Paul, in a personal letter to Pastor Timothy, this time directed to slaves in Timothy's Ephesian congregation. Paul is warning that even when a slave's master becomes a Christian—and therefore a spiritual "brother"—the slave isn't removed from his position as a servant. It honors God, Paul is saying here, for the slave to continue to treat his master with full respect and obedience—not *despite* the newfound spiritual brotherhood, but *because of* that relationship. In this instance, with *antilambano* translated as "partakers" (i.e., participants, contributors) and in reference to slave masters, Paul is emphasizing mutual support—the slave master supporting the slave and the slave supporting the slave master—but the context is within the boundaries of the subject "brethren." In other words, we should be willing to support back and forth mutually (or, as the definition of *antilambano* extends, "to take hold of in turn") and at all times as spiritual equals and brothers, regardless of our temporal relationships. Although the context applies to a master/slave relationship the likes of which we no longer see here in the United States, we can still apply the lesson of "full giving and receiving of support in all mutuality regardless of titles" to many situations, such as supervisors, administrators positions, etc. We, today's "slaves," are to serve our Christian supervisors (or equivalent) with integrity—not "despite" their position as spiritual equals, but "because of" spiritual reciprocity as fellow partakers in the work of the Lord.

So far, the gift of "helps" appears to represent the unique ability of offering support wherever it's needed—from feeding and clothing the weak to leading with integrity to participating in ministry. This gift describes a mature, deeply-rooted, radical support structure operating supernaturally, as instilled by the Holy Spirit and applying in any way it is needed.

However, it wouldn't be wise to assume that the gift of helping should be viewed as less important than any of the others just because the benefit the gift provides isn't specified in 1 Corinthians 12:28, or because of its association with humble tasks. Don't fall into the trap of believing this gift is generic, less rewarding, *or* that it lacks adventure. Many times, the greatest advances toward a goal—such as spreading the Gospel—originate from the passionate performance of duties that don't yet have a title, or whose description (like "helps") is so vast that the title remains vague. The gift might appear at its onset to be obscure, but don't discount the sheer strength the Word says this gift carries. Take a look at this last instance:

- "He hath helped [*antilambano*] his servant Israel, in remembrance of his mercy" (Luke 1:54). This verse is sung by Mary, who is praising the Lord for sending His Son (whom she is, at this moment, still carrying in her womb). In this context, the "help" emphasis is upon one who rescues.

Please don't miss what Scripture just revealed…because this is *huge*. God—*Himself*—is the "helper" in this verse. This particular context is *not* pointing to how God aids us in our daily lives or makes us more comfortable. In *this* framework, He personally displayed the gift of "helps" (*antilempsis/antilambano*) right here in the book of Luke, *when He sent the prophesied Messiah and saved an entire nation*. That Greek word, in reference to God rescuing all of Israel, is not a mistake. Nobody can say this use of *antilambano* is a divine "whoops." The Greek language includes many ways to say "help" or "assistance," and the careful historian (as Luke is called) could have used any of them, but he chose *antilambano*.

184

Let that sink in…

The Creator of the universe is not above demonstrating the gift of "helps" as He saves the whole world and every believer in it and crushes the wall separating Jew and Gentile forever.

Wow! Is that beautiful, or is that *beautiful*?

Yes, I would venture to say that the gift of "helps" might at times involve tasks that we, in our busy lives and limited spiritual comprehension, perceive as menial or unspectacular. But it simply *cannot* be regarded with condescension or contempt, and it must never be viewed as a gift of "favor-doings," lest we discount the spiritual, emotional, nurturing side of Spirit-led assistance as well. Our culture today sees the word "helps" as one woman offering to help another carry in a few groceries. But think about it: When we're in trouble, what's the *first* word that comes to mind? "Help!" When we call out that word, everyone knows we're not asking for someone to carry our groceries. *Antilempsis* translates to "laying hold of" something in a supportive way. This is a *rescue* we're talking about! It's a matter of survival. It's not a "making something more convenient" gift; it's a "Church can't survive without it" gift. There is an aggressiveness, an excitement, an *action* behind the assistance provided, and the recipient of the help (whether an individual or a church) is in trouble the minute that help is absent.

We do a disservice to the Lord and His act of saving all of mankind through Christ in His own moment of "helps" when we sneer at a gift such as this. One with the Holy-Spirit-infused gift of "helps" might be just who the Lord ordained to be the greatest witness for some people who otherwise wouldn't be reached through any other gift. Those who have been hurt by religious people in the past, for example, might not want to hear a word of wisdom or a prophecy, nor would they be impressed by a dazzling sermon, but they might pause to speak with a member of the Body who has the reputation of simply being helpful at all times. One with the gift of "helps" might be seen cleaning the church toilets some afternoon, but in the light of eternity and in the supernatural realm, that person's gentle and humble gift may have the Spirit-directed power to break down walls that separate and suffocate the lost, spread the salve of amity, and rescue lonely souls who no longer believe in the concepts of family.

Man... I feel *thrilled* at the notion that someone reading this book who has been deemed a helper by the Spirit will employ the gift to its fullest potential and watch as the harvest rolls in past the Kingdom gate.

If you believe you've been given the gift of helps: You mean *so much* more, and your gift is so much bigger, than you can fathom. If you continue to thrive in your use of your gift, if you continue to seek the will of the Spirit with every helpful step you take in His service, you *will* see people enter heaven as a result of what *you* do and say. How can I be so sure? Because that's precisely what the gifts of the Holy Spirit are designed to do.

Bless you, and thank you for your service.

Governments: The most frequent assumption about the gift of governments is that it is given to the pastor (or deacon, or presbyter, etc.) who governs his church. That might be accurate in some cases (*if* the pastor is serving in the position God has directed him), but that isn't the only definition that suits a person with the gift of governments. Nor is it accurate to say that it's all about organizational abilities or secretarial skills like scheduling and recordkeeping, as many do when this gift appears in the more contemporary terminology as "gift of administration." Sure, those descriptions speak of excellent, *necessary* skills and positions that every church body needs, and far be it from me to suggest that the gift of governments doesn't include these skills, but that is only going far enough to inspect the pretty skin of the apple when the gift hides in the core.

The Greek word for "governments" in this verse is *kybernesis*, and although it translates to "government," it derives from the Latin "to steer" or "to pilot,"[10] like the helmsman of a ship. This is likely the reason many scholars throughout time have concluded that this gift refers to a church leader, because these are the people who *steer* or *pilot* the church.

Understand, however, that since the account of the Fall of mankind in the Garden of Eden, there have been some leaders who steer others in the *wrong* direction. This would certainly be true of a malicious and proud pastor who comes into a church to infiltrate, conquer, and divide those over whom he isn't in complete control...and this is a scenario I've witnessed several times. Behavior like that doesn't come from a Holy Spirit anointing. But to the trusting congregants who assume the church leaders have been placed there by God to fulfill their "governments" gifting just because they have a title and an office, it can be *at the very least* peculiar when the leaders' true colors are exposed. People are left wondering what to think of those whom the "Holy Spirit" appointed. Wearing a leadership name tag doesn't automatically make someone an inheritor of the gift of governments—any more than standing in the White House makes someone the president. By that logic, not every person with the gift of governments has to be an officially and publicly designated administrator.

Remember, we're talking about a *gift* here, not a title. Paul listed titles and offices in quite a few places—including earlier in this same verse—but he listed "governments" within the context of gifts: "And God hath set some in the church, first apostles [office at the time; some believe it's an ecclesiastical title now], secondarily prophets [potentially office at the time; many claim the title now], thirdly teachers [office and title, both then and now; but note that this title is distinct from the gift of teaching, which will be addressed shortly], after that [the "after that" here could read "and now shifting to"] miracles [gift], then gifts of healings [gift], helps [gift], governments [gift], diversities of tongues [gift]" (1 Corinthians 12:28). (If you're confused as to why the words "then gifts of" appear after the first gift is mentioned, instead of prior to all of them, it appears that way in 1 Corinthians 12:8–10 also. Both times, the gift of healing is introduced with the word "gifts," plural, and some of the classical commentators believe that is a reference to more than one kind of healing, i.e., physical and mental. In any case, the first gift on this list is that of miracles, just as Paul referenced earlier in the same chapter.)

Government for a megachurch can be huge and complicated, with many offices, roles, bylaw and policy writers, meetings, committees, and boards. It can *also* be, for a small church, two guys and their wives who go on a camping trip together twice a year to scribble down church property repair lists on a notepad while they're roasting hot dogs. The members of one of these groups look impressive and organized, and the members of the other look like they'd be a lot of fun to hang out with. So do the leaders of the polished church have the steering wheel in their hands? Or do the good ol' boys hold the wheel? Which group is led by one who has the gift?

The gift of governments might be given to *all* the people in these two groups…or it might be given to *none* of them, as the Holy Spirit sees fit to gift. The focus should never be upon a label or title, or upon appearances, but upon *the function of successful steering* (directing, leading) within the context of *government*—and because of its nature as a Holy Spirit gifting, the gift takes the form of the ultimate will of God, or it wouldn't be given to begin with. If a church is perpetually going in the wrong direction—let's say, for example, that it's tolerating heresy—then the helmsman of that ship *does not have the gift of governments*. The steering wheel is not in his hands, though he wears the tie and the name tag, because the Spirit will not leave the wheel in the hands of a captain who steers his ship and all its people away from God.

I approached the study of this gift from this angle not to suggest that any current leaders should be dethroned for lack of proof that they have the gift, nor because anybody needs to question established authorities for the sake of the Spirit. I simply see too many sources in my research that give a pat, cop-out explanatoin of this gift: "What's the gift of governments? Oh, that's an easy one. It's your pastor!" These approach the title as if it *is* the gift, and it's not quite that easy. A title or office should be given because of the gifting—never the other way around. I hope that all current official leadership positions of a church are filled with folks who have the gift of governments, but I can almost guarantee that not everyone with the gift holds an official title, because that is nothing more than forcing the Holy Spirit to bend to our own "certificates, degrees, and papers" game.

A paper doesn't choose the leaders, the Spirit does.

The subject shouldn't be viewed as complicated, either. The gift of government isn't terribly enigmatic, because leadership qualities tend to pop out when they're needed most, and sometimes only when the boat is beginning to get lost at sea does the Spirit-appointed helmsmen step forward—with or without a man-appointed title.

Who has the influence to pilot an entire church and all its members in an organized way—resulting in a well-balanced congregation whose core motives and goals are flowing efficiently in the Gospel-spreading direction the Spirit leads? Honestly, it may not be who you think. It might be that little old woman on the back row who is doing far more governing with her sweet humility and broad smiles than anyone else. Who can take the wheel of a ship during the most turbulent of church-splitting storms and guide the boat and all its sailors back toward peacefulness and agreeability? It might just be that young man who can't even spell his own name, but whose scorecard in the collaborative reconciliation department makes him a spiritual force to be reckoned with.

And perhaps most importantly for the sake of the Gospel: Who has the ability to look across the faces of a congregation and see not just attendees, but fellow ministers, each with unique leadership abilities in his or her own area of gifting? Who can reach out and make that little girl feel like a lion whose roar won't be silenced by bullies, that elderly man feel like the world's most important mentor who is never too old to advise, or that Millennial woman feel like her voice is important enough that she doesn't have to resort to aggressive social or political activities to be heard?

To inspire all of this in others, and inspire it in the *right* direction—the direction the Holy Spirit leads—is to display the gift of governments. It is *those* people who should be governing the Church Body. It's so much more than a title.

If you're already in a leadership position, examine your governing style. Does it point to Jesus Christ and Him crucified in all that you do, and in every piloting move you make as helmsman of the ship? Would you be ready to stand before the Holy Spirit at this moment and say wholeheartedly that you did your absolute best in that endeavor?

If you believe you've been given the gift of governments, pray that the *Spirit* will be the true guide of your ship, and that He will work through you to steer His people in the right direction. Pray for the right support around you, and prepare yourself for what might be one of the biggest growth seasons the Christian Church Body has ever experienced. If you *are* a leader, you *will* be challenged, and it won't always be easy. But if you're in it for the right reasons, your faithfulness accomplishments will be rewarding beyond measure.

Romans 12:6–8

We will conclude this look at the gifts with the gifts of grace that can be found in the book just before 1 Corinthians. The book of Romans is, according to many scholars and Bible students, Paul's greatest work. It is his longest letter, as well as the most theologically reflective, and it eventually led to the split between Catholics and Protestants during the Reformation.

Paul begins this portion of Scripture the same way he did in 1 Corinthians: by explaining the humility and mutuality the Body should have as a network. He then lists the gifts:

> For I say, through the grace given unto me, to every man that is among you, not to think of himself more highly than he ought

to think; but to think soberly, according as God hath dealt to every man the measure of faith. For as we have many members in one body, and all members have not the same office: So we, being many, are one body in Christ, and every one members one of another.

Having then gifts differing according to the grace that is given to us, whether prophecy, let us prophesy according to the proportion of faith; Or ministry, let us wait on our ministering: or he that teacheth, on teaching; Or he that exhorteth, on exhortation: he that giveth, let him do it with simplicity; he that ruleth, with diligence; he that sheweth mercy, with cheerfulness. (Romans 12:3–8)

From this excerpt, seven gifts are listed:

1. Prophecy
2. Ministry
3. Teaching (as a gift, not an office)
4. Exhortation
5. Giving
6. Ruling
7. Mercy

We've already covered the gift of prophecy, which derives from the same Greek word here as it did in 1 Corinthians, and it was used in the same context. As such, we don't need to revisit that gift here. Many believe the others are twin gifts corresponding to those that appear in 1 Corinthians. I believe that, though they can be similar, Paul chose different words in Romans than he did in 1 Corinthians, so they technically aren't identical.

Ministry: The Greek word here is *diakonia*, which means "service, ministering, esp. of those who execute the commands of others; of those who by the command of God proclaim and promote religion among men."[11] The root word is *diakonos*, which translates "deacon."

In the book of Acts, we read the following narrative:

> And in those days, when the number of the disciples was multiplied, there arose a murmuring of the Grecians against the Hebrews, because their widows were neglected in the daily ministration [*diakonia*]. Then the twelve called the multitude of the disciples unto them, and said, "It is not reason that we should leave the word of God, and serve [*diakoneo*; verb form of *diakonia*] tables. Wherefore, brethren, look ye out among you seven men of honest report, full of the Holy Ghost and wisdom, whom we may appoint over this business. But we will give ourselves continually to prayer, and to the ministry [*diakonia*] of the word." And the saying pleased the whole multitude. (Acts 6:1–5a)

The gift of ministry can be a confusing concept: On one hand, it clearly describes a *servant* (the word *diakonia* means "service"), while on the other, it describes a leader (minister, deacon). Whittled down to its most basic form, a *diakonos* in ancient Greece was a person who waited on tables while others were eating. That person might be paid for his or her service in wealthier homes (or given free lodging and food as compensation), but in lower-income households, *diakonia* referred to service carried out by the woman of the home. It is around this time in Acts, during the first century of the Christian Church, when *diakonos* started to become known as a leadership title in religious settings after the women were depended upon to head up certain community relief endeavors.

So which is it? Is *diakonia* a leader or a servant?

To illustrate that it's *both*, consider the hierarchy of domestic servants in a wealthy Victorian home: Under the butler were the following ranks, in order: coachman, first footman, second footman, and hall-boy. Under the housekeeper was the head housemaid, housemaid, and laundry maid. Under the cook was the kitchen maid, dairy maid, and scullery maid. Under the governess was the head nurse and the under nurse. (The valet and the lady's maid were in a category of their own.) In this historical arrangement, the butler, housekeeper, cook, and governess were the top leaders in the servant-staff hierarchy. They were at the top of the command chain, and their wages were considerably higher than that of the others. *All* of these positions, however, including the top four, were servant positions under the master and the mistress of the house, either of whom could issue an order to any one at any time regardless of the servant's rank in the hierarchy.

In ministry, we give men and women labels reflecting the authority they need to function in their area of giftedness, but every minister, regardless of rank, is still a servant to the Master. To this day, when we hear the words, "that man is a minister," we link that word to an authoritative position such as "pastor" or "presbyter," and we imagine that he has framed credentials displayed on a wall in an office somewhere. But when we hear, "that man is ministering to those people," we think of a humanitarian type of service, like feeding the poor or praying fervently for addicts on the street. All connect for a synergized goal. (Speaking of "synergized," the Greek word *synergos* was also used to recognize many key early-Church leaders. When studied at length, it, too, refers to both a leader and a servant.)

So, when Paul speaks of ministry/service as a Holy-Spirit-led gift, he is alluding to a unique ability to fill in the *service* gaps wherever needed. In application, the gift could be leading at times and following at others, but it *always relates to the act of serving other people*—in such a way as to show *internal leadership qualities by setting a good example*, regardless of hierarchical rank.

Recently, Donna was a guest on the *Jim Bakker Show*, and Debbie came to watch. After the taping, Donna explained to the security guards that she would like to have her lunch in the public cafeteria so that Debbie could join her. Instead, they humbly and graciously insisted that Debbie be escorted to the private greenroom and given the same treatment (and free lunch) as Donna. After all agreed to the plan, Donna, Debbie, and Katherine (who had traveled with Donna) were served in the manner one would expect at a fine restaurant: their drinks were promptly refilled and they received frequent, attentive offers of anything they needed. The individuals tending to the three woman were members of *Jim Bakker's family*! Any of them could be considered a celebrity by today's standards, yet *several* "lowered" themselves to serve not only my sister and my wife, but also Debbie, a woman they had never met, as if she were royalty, Acts 6-style.

Once a student of Scripture dips a little deeper into the study of Christ's concepts of about ministry and service, however, the beauty of this leading-by-serving concept gets *real*…

In Mark and Matthew, Jesus repeatedly states that the greatest of all leaders must be the greatest of all servants: "And he sat down, and called the twelve, and saith unto them, 'If any man desire to be first, the same shall be last of all, and servant of all [*diakonos*]'" (Mark 9:35); "And whosoever of you will be the chiefest, shall be servant [*doulos*; synonym of *diakonos*, but also means "slave" or "bondservant"] of all" (Mark 10:44); "But it shall not be so among you: but whosoever will be great among you, let him be your minister [*diakonos*]" (Matthew 20:26).

In Luke 22:25–27, Christ was answering the question about who among His followers was the greatest: "And he said unto them, 'The kings of the Gentiles exercise lordship over them; and they that exercise authority upon them are called benefactors. But ye shall not be so: but he that is greatest among you, let him be as the younger; and he that is chief, as he that doth serve [*diakoneo*]. For whether is greater, he that sitteth at meat, or he that serveth [*diakoneo*]? is not he that sitteth at meat? but I am among you as he that serveth [*diakoneo*]."

Here, Christ described His role to His disciples as a table servant, but when we read John chapter 13, we see Him *literally* serving His followers at the table of the Last Supper…just after He personally washed Peter's feet.

Yet again, we have God, Himself, operating in one of the gifts that we humans tend to overlook as a "lesser" installment. The gift of ministry or of serving is no laughing matter. Jesus, God in human form, became a table waiter—not because nobody else was willing, but because He knew the importance of setting a good example of service so that *the rest of the world and every Christian in it throughout time* would have that imagery in mind when we're tempted to view servanthood as a lowly position.

If you've been endowed with the gift of ministry/service, praise the Lord for it. You have that much more in common with the King who served you first.

Teaching and Exhortation: Like the gift of ministry—which, based on the office of *diakonos*, frequently comes with a leadership title—teaching often lands a person in a ranked position within church walls. Scholars and classical commentators link this reference to teaching as a gift that is almost always associated with a class of commissioned workers within the Church Body—and whereas there are different words that describe the offices through which teaching is executed (preachers, pastors, and exhorters), many involve the act of teaching. However, like the gift of government, many people have been given the *office* of teacher (*didaskalos*), even though they don't have the gift of teaching (*didaskalia*), so it's important not to assume that every "teacher" at a church has the gift of teaching.

The definition of exhortation, on the other hand, is a little different in modern times than it was at the time this passage was written. Today, "exhortation" is simply a form of encouragement, and it is covered by teachers (whether they are preachers behind the pulpit, pastoral figures in person, etc.), but in New Testament times, there were official exhorters. Although the gift definitely remains, the office does not. Several classical commentators acknowledge this historical shift, while noting the contemporary value of the gift:

[*Ellicott's Commentary for English Readers*:] It will be observed that in the apostolic writings, the one idea of "preaching" is divided into its several branches, "speaking with tongues," "prophesying" (which appears to have had reference to the more recondite portions or relations of the faith), "teaching," "exhortation." This last form of address, corresponding perhaps rather to our word "encouragement," would be especially needed in the troubled circumstances of the early Church....

[*Meyer's NT Commentary*:] [T]here are no longer mentioned such as possess [exhortation] for a definite function [office] in the church, but such as possess it generally for the activity of public usefulness in the social Christian life....

[*Barnes' Notes on the Bible*:] He that exhorteth—This word properly denotes one who urges to the practical duties of religion, in distinction from one who teaches its doctrines. One who presents the warnings and the promises of God to excite men to the discharge of their duty. It is clear that there were persons who were recognised as engaging especially in this duty, and who were known by this appellation, as distinguished from prophets and teachers. How long this was continued, there is no means of ascertaining; but it cannot be doubted that it may still be expedient, in many times and places, to have persons designated to this work. In most churches this duty is now blended with the other functions of the ministry.[12]

So, in the New Testament, teachers, preachers, prophets, and exhorters (as well as a few other titles scattered about Scripture) approached the delivery of God's Word and will from different methodologies based on what the Spirit empowered them to do, but they were united in the goal of spreading the Gospel with their words. Therefore, although teaching (delivering facts) differed from exhortation (passionately urging and encouraging), the subject that poured from the mouth of both naturally overlapped. Both were their own office in ancient times, whereas now, as *Barnes'* points out, the exhortation is blended with teaching.

Don't take that to mean that the gifts, as given by the Holy Spirit, have merged just because the offices have. Though one person can certainly have both gifts, each is still distinct. A brilliant professor with fascinating discourse outlines may never be any more encouraging to his audience than a safety pin; contrarily, someone on a street corner may not be able to retain facts by memory or articulate like a teacher, but when that person's tongue gets moving, exciting things might happen that are life-changing for everyone around.

Specific to exhortation, there is a need to understand not only the Greek word used in Romans 12:8, but also to note its associations, in order to understand its power. "Exhortation" is from the Greek feminine noun *paraklesis*, "a calling near, summons…encouragement; consolation, comfort, solace; that which affords comfort or refreshment, thus of the Messianic salvation (so the Rabbis call the Messiah the consoler, the comforter); persuasive discourse, stirring address, instructive, admonitory, conciliatory, powerful hortatory discourse."[13] By itself, it's a beautiful word, but its meaning gets even sweeter with the knowledge that another form of the word is the masculine noun *parakletos*, which is the "Comforter" Jesus promised to send—the Holy Spirit, Himself, giver of the gifts, the ultimate exhorter!

Before I researched exhortation for this portion of the book, I knew it was a form of teaching that sounded comforting and encouraging. But my jaw dropped when I saw *paraklesis*, because I've always known who the Paraclete was. That is so exciting and picturesque to me, someone who so closely relates to this gift.

Before we move on, we need to bring one vital element about teaching to the forefront. The Greek word *didaskalia* doesn't just mean "teaching," it also means "instructing."[14]

Sure, these two words are synonymous; they *can* have the same meaning, depending on their use in a sentence. However, there is a distinct yet subtle difference at their core: You can *teach* about anything by delivering information to a listener/student; all that is required of the student is to receive the information. *Instructing* is the act of providing tools for the listener/student to complete a certain set of tasks; the student is required to take action according to a charge. It's the difference between "telling someone things" and "telling someone what to do about things"—and the true, New Testament Greek *didaskalia* gift requires both.

I've seen many men and women of God stand and share knowledge about interesting subjects, but when it hasn't inspired me to do something with that knowledge—or when it hasn't prompted me to change the way I'm already doing something—I've sometimes questioned the value of that teaching, and have hoped that someone else in the assembly gained from it.

Believers who are genuinely empowered with the Holy-Spirit-infused gift of teaching—regardless of their office in a church building—will understand that instruction is part of the package, and they will present their teaching as a call for action or change. If they cannot accomplish this with fervor on their own, it *could* be that they need to partner with someone who has the gift of exhortation. Where teaching and instructing together say, "This is what the issue is and what you have to do about it," exhortation comes along, takes the hand of the student, and says, "I'll go with you and help you get there."

And why not bring that practice back? The early Church did that very thing, the classical commentators consider it a loss that it was discontinued, and those who have been given the gift of exhortation today are likely trying to find an outlet for their gift. Imagine a church where you get the best teaching you've heard in a while, and then, when you think it's over, an exhorter comes in like a town crier with a "you can do it" charge from the King. What an impact that could make!

I hope to see more partnering of gifts in the future of the Church. The gift network that God designed is so powerful when multiple giftings come together toward the same cause...

One last thought for both teachers and exhorters: If you believe you've been given one of these gifts, you must *also* understand that it comes with the responsibility of making sure you know that what you're teaching/exhorting is *correct*: "My brethren, be not many masters [*didaskalos*; the "be not many" translates today to "not many of you should be"], knowing that we shall receive the greater condemnation [other translations say "we will be judged with harsher strictness"]" (James 3:1). If the facts you're sharing are incorrect, then the instruction you give others will be erroneous—and, so, too, will the direction in which you send them.

The gifts of teaching and of exhortation are essential to the Body. Christians would have died off in the first century without the operation of these two gifts. They're the heartbeat of the thriving Church, but they also require us to honestly and open-mindedly *learn* before we teach/exhort, so that we can show ourselves approved, dividing the Word of God correctly (2 Timothy 2:15).

Giving: Yes, this means exactly what it says: giving. Yes, it means giving earthly items—not, say, giving knowledge or anything else that's intangible. And yes, the word used in this passage is a wide and general application of the Greek *metadidomi*, "to share…[or] impart,"[15] so money is only a tiny part of that.

If giving is merely the act of taking something we have and putting it into the possession of another, why does the Holy Spirit need to be involved? This sounds more like a biblical command to give than a "gift" to give…

The secret to understanding the concept of giving as a *gift* is in the words "he that giveth, let him do it with simplicity." "Simplicity" is from the Greek *haplotes*, a small word that means many beautiful things: "sincerity, mental honesty; the virtue of one who is free from pretence and hypocrisy; not self seeking, openness of heart manifesting itself by generousity…the virtue of one who is free from pretence…openness of heart manifesting itself by benefactions, liberality."[16]

It's human nature for us to want to give for the sake of personal gain, not for the sake of virtue. In selfishness exists a constant, greedy question whenever money or other possessions are relinquished—one that wonders what personal blessings from God that offering will buy, or how many compliments and accolades we will earn by donating that car... I could make the list longer, but you get the idea.

The literal application of this gift is very simple: The gifted one is a natural giver, handing out his or her own wealth or possessions freely for the sake of others so that God is glorified. The *only* way *haplotes*-style giving is even possible is through the Holy Spirit, which is as true a gift as any. But before we assume that the gift of giving is only endowed upon those who have much wealth or material possessions, keep in mind the lesson of the widow's offering from Mark 12:41–44:

> And Jesus sat over against the treasury, and beheld how the people cast money into the treasury: and many that were rich cast in much. And there came a certain poor widow, and she threw in two mites, which make a farthing. And he called unto him his disciples, and saith unto them, "Verily I say unto you, That this poor widow hath cast more in, than all they which have cast into the treasury: For all they did cast in of their abundance; but she of her want did cast in all that she had, even all her living."

If the widow's offering meant so much to Christ because of her attitude and faith in giving merely "two mites," then we know the Holy Spirit doesn't limit His gift of giving to those who are affluent. Those who have this gift can be recognized not by the amount they give, but by the attitude with which they give.

If you've been blessed with the gift of giving, thank you for the lives you've changed in eternity through your charitable deeds.

Ruling: Many take the Holy Spirit-led gift of ruling to be identical to the gift of governments, but I have a hard time allowing for that, since the Greek word it's translated from is *not* the same. As stated earlier, the gift of governments is related to one's ability to influence people to go in the right direction (*kybernesis*: "steer"; "pilot"), like a helmsman. A person with the gift to rule—Greek *proistemi*, "to stand before, i.e. (in rank) to preside, or (by implication) to practise: maintain, be over, rule"[17]—describes someone who chooses when to set sail and whom the shipmates will be. In other words, this referes to a *captain* of the ship, if you will, who manages people and announces decisions to the rest of the crew after consulting with his advisors (such as the helmsman).

Paul's words were "he that ruleth, with diligence" (Romans 12:8). The English word "diligence" inspires thoughts of someone who is careful, persistent, trustworthy, competent, and conscientious. When I hear "diligent," I think "tenacious" and "meticulous"—someone you can put in charge of a task, knowing it will get done the way it's supposed to. Although these are all pretty words that paint a person with grand imagery, believe it or not, the Greek word *spoude*, translated "diligent" here, first and foremost means "haste."[18]

"He that ruleth, with *speed*."

Pretty neat, huh?

The verb form of *spoude* is *speudo*, and it means "to 'speed'…i.e. urge on (diligently or earnestly);…(make, with) haste unto."[19] Yet *speudo* is not like the Greek *propetes* ("rash"; "reckless"), which suggests a clumsy, tripping speed. The Church doesn't need any more leaders who take flying leaps into unwise territory because they don't know where their next step is going to land… The kind of speed in *speudo* reads like those who are so confident in their steps that they need not wait around for others to do things for them. They grab the bull by the horns and *run* to get things done, fully assured that their followers are watching every step they take. This kind of speed, added to the carefulness suggested by the Greek, does translate to "diligent," it's just farther down on the list (of translational words, not of priorities).

I have already said this twice (once in the section on the gift of governments, and again in the section on the gifts of teaching and exhortation), but the following needs to be emphasized about this gift: Because the leadership of a church relies on mankind to elect and promote—and those man-made decisions may not always be within the will of God—not all men and women on a staff board will be truly endowed with the Holy Spirit's gift of ruling…and not all men and women with the gift of ruling will be appointed leaders on a staff board. We can't assume that the person standing on the highest rung of leadership in any church is there because the Holy Spirit put that person there. It would be wonderful if we *could* assume that, but beginning in the book of Genesis, we see a story of God's people having terrible rulers along with the good ones. Understand that the gift is an internal ability as endowed through the Holy Spirit. At times, there are those who have the gift of ruling without serving on a staff at all. Or, they *might* be an elder, according to the Word elsewhere (1 Timothy 5:17), which only further shows that modern titles within a church don't always represent a person's true gifting.

A person with the gift of ruling is a person others follow.

Jesus Christ was clear when He said that we will know what kind of people we're dealing with based on the kind of fruit their choices and lifestyles produce (Matthew 7:15–20). A leader of leaders, one who is sincerely led by a Holy-Spirit-infused gifting, will be the greatest servant of all, like Christ was.

A "leader" is only a leader if followers trail behind that person voluntarily.

Anyone else is a dictator, and the Holy Spirit doesn't endow the gift of dictatorship.

Christ was the supreme leader, and because of His compassion and gentility as the servant to all, two thousand years after His death and ascension, people from all over the world are still following Him—and many are willing to risk their very lives in His service.

Although there will only ever be one Jesus Messiah—and no one else will ever come close to leaving the legacy He did—*every* Christian should live as closely as possible to the example He set in His life.

Mercy: In the same way the gift of governments has often been considered as identical to the gift of ruling, this gift has at times been thought of as the same as the gift of "helps." But again, the words' s meanings aren't identical. Synonymous? Sure. Working toward the same goal? Obviously. But exactly the same? Not even close. They are equal in their motivation to assist, but the gift of mercy is extremely specific.

As discussed before, the Greek words behind what describes one with the gift of "helps" should be seen as one who responds to a call for help, or a rescuer. The Greek word for "mercy" (*eleeo*) can be applied several different ways, but it is primarily humanitarian within this context. There is the beautiful and emotional side to mercy, which is synonymous with forgiveness and clemency, and the Greek word *does* cover that also, but at the time Paul was writing about the gifts, the concept of mercy within had been redefined because of Christ. In Christ's example, mercy wasn't just a feeling or emotion about someone, it was an active, physical intervention. Consider Matthew 20:29–34:

And as they departed from Jericho, a great multitude followed him. And, behold, two blind men sitting by the way side, when they heard that Jesus passed by, cried out, saying, "Have mercy [*eleeo*] on us, O Lord, thou son of David." And the multitude rebuked them, because they should hold their peace: but they cried the more, saying, "Have mercy [*eleeo*] on us, O Lord, thou son of David." And Jesus stood still, and called them, and said, "What will ye that I shall do unto you?" They say unto him, "Lord, that our eyes may be opened." So Jesus had compassion on them, and touched their eyes: and immediately their eyes received sight, and they followed him.

When Christ and the word "mercy" were in close proximity, people were set free and lives were changed forever. The first definitions of *eleeo*, based on an outline of biblical use in particular, lists the following in this order: "to have mercy on; to help one afflicted or seeking aid; to help the afflicted, to bring help to the wretched; to experience mercy."[20] After the literal translation of "have mercy on," the biblical use outline goes straight into definitions that we view today as humanitarian work.

Think of how important charity and benevolence to others are in Christ's description of the Final Judgment:

When the Son of man shall come in his glory, and all the holy angels with him, then shall he sit upon the throne of his glory: And before him shall be gathered all nations: and he shall separate them one from another, as a shepherd divideth his sheep from the goats: And he shall set the sheep on his right hand, but the goats on the left.

Then shall the King say unto them on his right hand, "Come, ye blessed of my Father, inherit the kingdom prepared for you from the foundation of the world: For I was an hungred, and ye gave me meat: I was thirsty, and ye gave me drink: I was a stranger, and ye took me in: Naked, and ye clothed me: I was sick, and ye visited me: I was in prison, and ye came unto me."

Then shall the righteous answer him, saying, "Lord, when saw we thee an hungred, and fed thee? or thirsty, and gave thee drink? When saw we thee a stranger, and took thee in? or naked, and clothed thee? Or when saw we thee sick, or in prison, and came unto thee?"

And the King shall answer and say unto them, "Verily I say unto you, Inasmuch as ye have done it unto one of the least of these my brethren, ye have done it unto me." (Matthew 25:31–40)

Every time people with the gift of mercy clothe someone, feed the hungry, visit the sick or incarcerated, or give a drink to the thirsty, they are marking themselves as sheep who earnestly follow the Shepherd.

I never met the woman, but I guarantee that Mother Teresa had the gift of mercy.

To be motivated to alleviate the misery and pain of people who are destitute…and to know that it's the Holy Spirit who has instilled that inability to ignore the sorrow of others—that nagging, needling sensation that says you aren't even capable of doing nothing while others grieve. An intrinsic drive to put every need you have on hold until someone else has been clothed, fed, and cared for. The Holy Spirit leading you and taking you places you wouldn't have known to go, meeting people who have nothing and nobody, showing them physical mercy so they will be that much closer to eternal mercy, grasping the character and nature of a compassionate Father *through the works you do!*

Wow. Just wow. God is so good. He is so, *so* good.

Think about how this works in the literal sense for a moment: Jesus Christ showed us mercy in a way nobody else ever could, and then He ascended and sent the Holy Spirit to gift some of us with that same inherent thirst for bringing relief to others. The *same* God who healed the blind man now endows the gift of mercy. It wasn't enough to let Jesus bring merciful compassion; God is so unbelievably good in His nature that He continued that ministry through *us.* He is so good!

Words fail at trying to define the mysteries of God's ceaseless provisions. Thank You, Lord, for empowering us mere humans with even a fraction of Your character and image.

If you have the Spirit-led gift of mercy and are operating in it faithfully: Bless you for every drink, every meal, every piece of clothing, every visit, and every stranger you've sheltered. As you have done it unto the least, you have done it for Christ. I'll see you at the pearly gates.

Other Gifts?

First Corinthians and Romans aren't the only biblical sources of information about what the Holy Spirit empowers believers to do. Although passages in other books may not use the word "gift" as it relates to post-Pentecost indwellings, they relate that the Holy Spirit is constantly guiding us and "gifting" us with His supervision and counsel. For instance, consider the following:

- "But ye shall receive power, after that the Holy Ghost is come upon you: and ye shall be witnesses unto me both in Jerusalem, and in all Judaea, and in Samaria, and unto the uttermost part of the earth" (Acts 1:8).
- "And we are his witnesses of these things; and so is also the Holy Ghost, whom God hath given to them that obey him" (Acts 5:32).
- "Having therefore obtained help of God, I continue unto this day, witnessing both to small and great, saying none other things than those which the prophets and Moses did say should come" (Acts 26:22).
- "This is he that came by water and blood, even Jesus Christ; not by water only, but by water and blood. And it is the Spirit that beareth witness, because the Spirit is truth" (1 John 5:6).

Each of these verses recognizes that through the Holy Spirit, we witness to others, and our message is effective and world-changing. This might be viewed as the "gift of bearing witness," or something of that nature. Though this isn't considered a "gift of the Holy Spirit"—because witnessing is a universal Christian duty, not an individual affair—it is a gift to be an effective witness. To put it another way: The Holy Spirit gives specific gifts to certain individuals within the Body, and that's what makes the Body parts unique, yet operative in union. But to *all Chris-*

tians, the Holy Spirit—the Supreme Encourager—gives tools in abundance so that we can accomplish anything through Him, so long as our goal is to carry out His will. In a way, those tools are "gifts," though they are in a separate class from those we just studied.

That said, don't hesitate to ask the Holy Spirit to equip you in *any* work you do for the Lord, whether your passions fit the descriptions of these listed gifts or not. He will empower you with whatever skillset you need to move forward in His work.

CHAPTER SEVEN

Unlocking Your Gifts

At this moment, an Internet search just displayed probably a hundred articles on the "nine" gifts of the Spirit. We have to go *far* out of our way to find information about the rest of the gifts, yet, to the Lord and the optimal functioning of His Body, the other gifts are as essential as those listed in 1 Corinthians 12:8–10. Many people aren't even *aware* that there are more than nine gifts. Just last week, I was talking with an associate I met through SkyWatch—an intelligent, well-educated, theologically astute Einstein of a guy. When I mentioned that I was working on this book about spiritual gifts—both the popular nine as well as the rest—he responded, "Seriously? There are *other* gifts? I mean, I know about the tongues and the prophecy and so on, but what else is there?" I mentioned the gift of mercy, describing the humanitarian function within the Body, and it blew his mind. "No way! That makes *so* much sense! I've always seen these Mother-Teresa types and marveled at how they seem so naturally and inwardly driven to help people all over the world. I knew the Holy Spirit was behind those kinds of people, but I didn't realize until just now that they're actually functioning within a specific Body member gift. You get so used to hearing people in the

Church talk about prophesying and speaking in tongues that you don't think to scour the rest of Scripture for other places that identify literal Holy-Spirit giftings! What *else* is there?"

If someone as sharp as this associate has read the Bible fifty times or more and never made the connection, then I can only assume that at least *thousands* of Christians likewise don't know about the wonderful other gifts the Spirit has provided. Some people might already be operating in their gift, but because they may not recognize it as such, they may not understand they could be taking their gift so much farther in the specific ways the Word has defined. (Or worse, they may be functioning beautifully in a biblical gift and, without knowing that, feel they were never gifted like those around them.)

Let's go back to 1 Corinthians 12 for a few minutes, this time focusing on verses 1–7, and look at the distribution of the gifts. I'm working with the KJV; quotes are Paul's, and follow-up comments are mine:

1. "Now concerning spiritual gifts, brethren, I would not have you ignorant." This could be reworded, "I would not have you misinformed." (You will see why as we move forward.)
2. "Ye know that ye were Gentiles, carried away unto these dumb [as in "mute"] idols, even as ye were led." The Corinthians had been drawn into false religions.
3. "Wherefore I give you to understand, that no man speaking by the Spirit of God calleth Jesus accursed: and that no man can say that Jesus is the Lord, but by the Holy Ghost." Paul is describing the link between Christ and the Comforter here. The ESV renders it this way: "Therefore I want you to understand that no one speaking in the Spirit of God ever says 'Jesus is accursed!' and no one can say 'Jesus is Lord' except in the Holy Spirit." To us today, this is self-explanatory, but it was revelatory to the Corinthians, who had previously followed pagan ways.

The next several verses appear redundant, *until* we understand what drove Paul to write. We will read them first, then reflect on the bigger picture.

4. "Now there are diversities of gifts, but the same Spirit." There are lots of gifts, but they all come from the same Holy Spirit, who equips these in believers.
5. "And there are differences of administrations, but the same Lord." There are various ways of serving and many offices to be held by members of the Body, but we will all be working together for the same Lord, who is the originator of our gifts.
6. "And there are diversities of operations, but it is the same God which worketh all in all." There are many activities that the Holy Spirit can inspire believers to carry out, but no matter what, it is the same Holy Spirit for all believers, and all Spirit-given gifts come from the same God.
7. "But the manifestation of the Spirit is given to every man to profit withal." In other words, the Spirit empowers all believers for the profit of every person, for the common good of the Christian Church, and for the carrying out of the Great Commission.

Let's pause to reflect on the beauty of Paul's description here. If we digest these verses fully, we can see the power of the living Word in these verses.

First, some background information: Corinth was a hub for travelers in its day, and the religious climate was principally pagan. Although there were certainly settlers in Corinth, the history of this ancient city paints a picture that portrays a revolving door of chaotic voices as merchants and craftsman popped in and out, all with their own religious convictions. In addition, those living in the area relied on open-minded syncretism, or harmony between almost all world religions at the time, because travelers were influenced by many religions globally and arrived in Corinth as self-appointed experts. Perhaps put more simply, most people in this area cherry-picked what they liked from several religions and the rituals of the gods and mixed them into a giant theological mess—*then* they would travel to Corinth, sell their goods, and float about the city to "enlighten" everyone of what they "knew."

In earlier portions of Scripture, Paul had cracked down on the believers in Corinth for dividing into "camps" according to what teacher or theologian they followed: "For while one saith, I am of Paul; and another, I am of Apollos" (1 Corinthians 3:4). This kind of confusion is not only evident in Paul's letters to Corinthians addressing false teachings and chaos in the church there, it's also seen in extrabiblical historical accounts. For example, one fairly well-known summary appears in Frederick William Farrar's book, *The Life and Work of St. Paul*, published posthumously after Farrar had served as a chaplain to royalty. He was also a graduate of Cambridge's Trinity University and the archdeacon of Westminster. He described what Corinth looked like when Paul arrived: "It was into the midst of this mongrel and heterogeneous population of Greek adventurers and Roman bourgeois, with a tainting infusion of Phoenicians—this mass of Jews, ex-soldiers, philosophers, merchants, sailors, freedmen, slaves, trades-people, hucksters, and agents of every form of vice—a colony 'without aristocracy, without traditions, without well-established citizens'—that the toil-worn Jewish wanderer [Paul] made his way."[21]

The church Paul had planted by this time had become filled with confused congregants who still held to the idea that they would be empowered not only by the Holy Spirit/Comforter that this Jesus Messiah promised to send, but also by their many pagan gods. And, because syncretism was simply the way of the Corinthians, it was no doubt confusing when Paul arrived on the scene and said that true followers of Christ would no longer look to their pagan gods for blessings, giftings, or empowerment of any kind. The synagogue in Corinth had to put the smack-down on hundreds of years of firmly established interreligious tolerance and suddenly accept that all earthly powers and gifts carried out in the name of Jesus originated in and through the Holy Spirit *only*, and that they were *only* given to serve His purposes in, through, and for Jesus Christ. That's why Paul said what seems like the same thing four times and from four different angles.

However, now that we have a better understanding of the refutation/argument Paul was working from in 1 Corinthians 12—and therefore we understand that he was executing a countercultural whammy in his letter wherein *every word* would have been rich with fresh ideas—we should take a second look at the big picture of what Paul was trying to drive home to the *original* audience, in the same context, so that we can draw the richest application from it today.

In verse 1, it is made clear that we should not be ignorant of what gifts the Holy Spirit gives, and secondarily (by extension of broad context within the letter), we are urged not to be led astray by warped theology or misinformation about these gifts. Paul goes on in verses 2–3 to address pagan backgrounds and show the link between Christ and the Spirit, then he refutes pagan ideologies by stating four times where gifts come from and who they are supposed to serve: diverse gifts but the same Spirit (v. 4); diverse administrations but the same Lord (v. 5); diverse operations but the same God (v. 6); and finally, diverse manifestations of the Spirit to bolster the sake of the Messiah for the common good (v. 7).

By now, we have an abundantly clear picture of *who these gifts are coming from* and *whom they are to serve*. But it is extremely important to note that in verses 6 and 7, Paul was also stating *whom the recipients of these gifts would be* and the *evidence of their transfer*.

The word "all" from verse 6, in reference to those who will be given gifts, is from the Greek word *pas*, which not only means "all," but also "every." Within this use, one meaning cannot be divorced from the other. *Pas* is an adjective that describes both an individual as well as a corporate entity. The Body in this context doesn't refer to all humans on the earth, but to a collection of individual believers in the Christian faith, otherwise known in close proximity here as the "brethren" (12:1). More specifically, the word *pas* encompasses "each, every, any, all, the whole, everyone, all things, everything" on an individual level and the "some of all types" collectively and corporately.[22] The verse must never be read to say, "*Of those* that God decided to gift or empower, *they* all were gifted or empowered by the same God." In order to reflect the original intent of the author, it must be read: "*Every believer* was empowered and gifted by the same God." If you or someone you know has been under the impression that only *some* believers are gifted by the Holy Spirit, rest assured that in the priesthood of all believers, everyone is gifted. (This is certainly not the only time Paul uses words that involve *every believer* as a fellow inheritor of the Holy Spirit gifting amidst the Body, but I chose this verse because of its proximity to the 1 Corinthians 12:8–10 reference.)

The word "manifestation" in verse 7 is translated from the Greek noun *phanerosis*, which is further derived from the root verb *phaneroo*: "to make manifest or visible or known what has been hidden or unknown."[23] As such, in Greek, *phanerosis* translates as "exhibition."[24] Interestingly, we get our modern word "manifest" from the twelfth-century, Old French word of the same spelling, meaning, "evident, palpable." By the time it became a common English word in the late fourteenth century—a couple hundred years before KJV translators chose it as an English stand-in for *phanerosis*—it meant "clearly revealed."[25] Throughout the ages, over spans of varying cultures and languages, the reference remains the same. Now remember how it comes about in verse 7: "the manifestation of the Spirit is given to every man." The "every man" here is from *hekastos* ("each, every"[26]), synonymous to *pas* ("all; every").

There's no way around it: The Holy Spirit equips every follower of Christ—that means *you!*—with a gift, and He reveals it in such a way that it's "made visible," "exhibited," "evident and palpable," and "clearly revealed" *to you*!

God is not hiding from you. If you believe in Jesus Christ, then the Holy Spirit has already equipped you with a gift to serve, and although this verse doesn't say *when* the act of *phanerosis* (manifestation) will occur, it promises that it *will* eventually become known…

…after a certain qualifier/caveat has been satisfied.

Yes, there *is* a requirement.

O, but doth the Word of God ever fall short in its boundlessness revelations!?

The answer to that question is a resounding "no!" The Word is alive (Hebrews 4:12), the Word is God (John 1:1), and the Word will *never* stop breathing life into its readers because it is God-breathed and eternally useful for teaching (2 Timothy 3:16). But I digress…

Scholars and students of hermeneutics already know where I'm going with this "caveat." As is often the way in these passages, a biblical promise can't always be claimed in and of itself. Many times (and I would risk suggesting *every time*), these promises must be weighed against the "concentric circles of context."

If you drop a pebble in a lake, circular ripples flow outward from the site of the first splash. As the water slowly returns to stillness, the central site of the disturbance continues to move, creating more and more rings waving outward until they finally disappear. The "concentric circles of context"—an exegesis and hermeneutics principle—states that when attempting to draw the true meaning from a verse, the closest "ripples" (verses) immediately surrounding the verse matter most.

One example of this is found in James 4:2: "Ye have not because ye ask not." I could launch into a real diatribe here about the scores of prosperity preachers who have told enormous crowds that they "have not" that car or house they want because they "ask not" for that car or house. Taken alone, this verse indicates that we believers can get any crazy thing we want simply by asking for it—but that discounts the principle of concentric circles of context. Why? Because if you allow the "pebble" of James 4:2 to "ripple out" to the verses in closest proximity, you'll see that *the very next verse* explains that we won't get what we're asking for if we're planning to "consume it upon [our] lusts." To understand what *that* means, look at the verses farther out. Once we see that a chief theme of James' epistle is asking for wisdom and keeping the peace between believers, we'll understand that we shouldn't be asking for cars or houses, but for *wisdom* from the Lord, who gives it freely without holding back (James 1:5). However, sometimes this grievance occurs even when the perceived promise is *within the same verse* as the first clues! The first half of James 4:2 says, "Ye lust, and have not: ye kill, and desire to have, and cannot obtain: ye fight and war." Readers might not know what's being discussed here, but they can *at least* conclude that the verse isn't in any way leading to a promise of material prosperity, cars, houses, or any other such nonsense.

So, sometimes the concentric-circles-of-context principle doesn't need to rely on going outside of a single verse, as is the case with Paul's "manifestation" caveat. However, without paying attention to the other half of the verse, believers may not know there's a stipulation waiting to be satisfied before the gifts can be revealed.

Observe carefully what is said in 1 Corinthians 12:7, the *whole verse*: "But the manifestation of the Spirit is given to every man to profit withal." It's not just "given to every man," period. It's "given to every man *to profit withal.*" If the apparent gifting doesn't "profit withal," then it doesn't qualify as the *phanerosis* "exhibition"/"manifestation"/"revelation" of the Holy Spirit in one's life.

Therefore, "profit withal" becomes a significant context key. The phrase means precisely what it sounds like, from the Greek word *symphero*, "to bear together (contribute)… advantage:—be better for, bring together, be expedient (for), be good, (be) profit(-able for)."[27]

Pause…

Please don't miss what the Word of God says here. This is so much bigger than you might initially be thinking. Open your mind and reflect upon how the gifts of the Holy Spirit are inseparably joined to what is herein identified as a community purpose.

I know it sounds too obvious to appreciate at first, but let it sink in. Really let the beauty of *symphero* in all its simplicity penetrate your concepts of the modern, idiosyncratic, "*I* think; *I* feel; *I* believe; *my* opinion is" culture we belong to, and draw your mind into another day, another era, when following the Messiah meant that your gifts were never going to belong to you in the first place.

The only reason the Holy Spirit would ever reveal what your gift is and empower it to its fullest fruition within you is for you to acknowledge that your gift only equips you to more effectively give yourself away!

It's not "*your* gift." It never was. It's *His* gift to give, it exists to "profit withal" for *His* name's sake, and until it *fully becomes that in your life*, it will not genuinely become "manifest."

Let this simple but powerful "profit withal" qualifier tear down the walls of expectations, wants, needs, desires, feelings, thoughts, opinions, and comforts. Tune out the static from the channel called "preconceived ideas" or "cultural imprinting" and let the living Word of God breathe for a minute.

Are you still trying to uncover the Holy Spirit's gift in your life?

Ask yourself this question, and be honest with your answer: When was the last time you *truly, deeply* prayed the following prayerful questions in your own words between you and God?: "Lord, what gift might I have been given that will show others what You look like through the things I do? What unique patterns of behavior have you hard-wired me with that will constantly trace back to You and Your character whenever the lost are watching? What talent have You instilled within me that is so powerfully beneficial for others—a talent that blesses those around me so profoundly—that people can't help but want to crawl into the arms of the same Father, Messiah, and Comforter who gave me these gifts?"

Have you ever asked the Lord to make your life become wholly a prayer to Him? Have you ever asked Him to exercise His sovereign will and unfathomable leadership over everything you are and all that you own? Have you *completely* given yourself away to God? Are you so enamored with the idea of knowing God and His plans for you that all other earthly pursuits feel like ridiculous, counterfeit imitations of the heavenly realm you anticipate on the other side of this life? Are you so committed to the Lord that you would throw every temporal gain available during this lifetime into the nearest bonfire, just to bring another person with you past the gates and into the presence of the smiling Messiah?

Which do you seek first: The Lord? Or the gift?

Do you seek the gifts of the Holy Spirit because you want to display power moves like some kind of wizard-for-God? Or do you seek the gifts of the Holy Spirit because you love the Lord and His people *so much* that you want to be the best "you" that you can be for the Gospel's sake?

When you look around and see lost people, are you, in your core, motivated by dabbling with different spiritual "cool, shiny toys" that you can hold over others or use as God's "authority stamps" in winning a debate? Or are you crying on the inside, begging the Lord to transform you into someone who can walk into their midst, introduce them to Someone they've never seen before, and "profit withal," "for the common good" (ESV; NASB)?

Understand this: We *honor* God when we use the gifts He gives us in the way that He wants them used. But if we seek a gift for our own glory, exaltation, fame, success, stardom, celebrity status, or money, we *dishonor* God. We can't act surprised that we don't know what our Spirit-infused gifts are while our motives are only aligned to self-profit.

I pray that we are all in this for the right reasons.

And…I pray that we are all in this *together*. The Body only works when the members are functioning in union.

That brings me to my final thought on the matter.

That the World May Believe

I love it when I'm just minding my own business and all of a sudden a verse I've read a thousand times reveals a new and huge truth I've always scanned right over. Such was the case last year when I heard a sermon on the High Priestly Prayer of Christ recorded in John 17. After the sermon, when I went to my own Bible to reflect on the heart of Christ in that intense hour, I short-circuited.

As those who spend time in the Word may remember, Christ prayed for His disciples as He was preparing for His own arrest and death. His selfless words were charged with immense love for those who would remain in the world behind Him to continue the work He began. But there is a moment in His prayer that we, the Church, simply *are not* fully grasping…and if we ever did, it would change the world forever.

Christ's prayer begins with a focus on the mission He came to complete and the follow-up assignment of the apostles to develop the early Church after His ascension. Then, in verse 20, Jesus shifts His appeal to the Father by praying for *us*. Note the central, profound union He describes:

> Neither pray I for these [the apostles] alone, but for them also which shall believe on me through their word [every believer after the apostles, which is us]; That they all may be one; as thou, Father, art in me, and I in thee, that they also may be one in us: that the world may believe that thou hast sent me. And the glory which thou gavest me I have given them; that they may be one, even as we are one: I in them, and thou in me, that they may be made perfect in one; and that the world may know that thou hast sent me, and hast loved them, as thou hast loved me. (John 17:20–23)

We are to be one…just as Jesus and the Father are one?

"One" to the point that we are "made perfect"?

…Meaning that Christ wants us fellow Christians to be a unit with the same familial cohesion He had with His own Father?

Perfect?

When that concept hit me, I had to stop for a few minutes and allow the rapid brain bullets to shoot around in my head without anything else happening, lest I risk a ricochet and injure myself. My thoughts were out of control, because Jesus was asking the Father for something I didn't even think was possible for humans. We're fallen and wicked. We're finite and limited. We're immature and petty and selfish and completely incapable of banding "as one" to the point that we are "made perfect" even long enough to get through a Christmas season without arguing over pagan trees and commercialization, let alone make the world—

Then it occurred to me: Even more important than Christ's appeal for us to come together as one was the incalculable and limitless outcome of our unity upon the *globe*!

Trek with me:

That we may be one… One central unit, like a special ops team in the military, so familiar with our fellow soldiers, their individual skills, and the protocol we follow that we are a single, unstoppable force. We might be made up of many members, but we have only one goal in the Great Commission.

Even as Jesus and the Father are one, that we may be *made perfect*… A literal and complete perfection, so flawlessly joined in a network without weak links in the chain that our relationship is beautiful and seamless enough to compare with that of the Creator of the universe and His only Son.

Then the *world* may know and believe in Jesus? Not just the people in Judea or Samaria…not just the Jews…not just Muslims today. So that the *world* may know?

I can't be making this up. It's *right there* in John!

It's like walking through your parlor every day for thirty years, knowing there's a copy of Leonardo da Vinci's Mona Lisa on the wall… then one day standing close enough to its brush strokes to realize it's the original, valued at $620 million.

How could I have been *so close* to this epiphany every time I've read the Gospel of John, and never realized the enormity of this truth? How had this treasure been in my possession all this time?

The comparative adverb *kathos*, translated "as" and "even as" in these verses, is defined: "according as, just as, even as, in proportion as, in the degree that; since, seeing that, agreeably to the fact that."[28] No matter which of these definitions we choose, they add up to the same calculation:

**Christians + perfect unity like Jesus had with the Father =
the world believing in Christ.**

The verb *teleioo*, translated "perfect" in the string "that they may be made perfect in one," is defined: "to make perfect, complete, to carry through completely, to accomplish, finish, bring to an end; to complete (perfect), add what is yet wanting in order to render a thing full, to be found perfect."[29] Many of these definitions describe not only a relational perfection or whole unit, but also the completion of something like a promise or covenant—a joining of forces not just for harmony, but for *finale*. Again, pick whichever definition you like. It's *still* going to calculate:

**Christians + perfect unity like Jesus had with the Father =
the world believing in Christ.**

The verb *pisteuo*, translated "may believe" is defined: "to have faith (in, upon, or with respect to, a person or thing), i.e. credit; by implication, to entrust (especially one's spiritual well-being to Christ)."[30] Which do you prefer? They all render:

**Christians + perfect unity like Jesus had with the Father =
the world believing in Christ.**

When was the last time you heard someone give a testimony that
said, "I attended a church one day and I saw *so much unity*—the love,
friendship, cohesion between these people who said they were that way
because of Christ—that I knew I *had* to have what they had." How long
has it been since you've heard a nonbeliever say, "I'm ready to accept
Christ, not because my salvation comes with a bunch of free stuff, but
because when I walked into that room full of Christians, I saw *perfect
oneness*, and I knew that in order to be that way, they had to know the
truth." Have you ever heard a conversion testimony about the day someone saw a harmonious accord that was *so strong* between Christ's people
that His love was proved through them in an instant, trumping the
effects of every other earthly religion?

This moment in Christ's prayer says so much and so little at the
same time. Note that it's simply by coming together as one that we
accomplish everything Christianity stands for. It's not by winning theological debates, proselytizing, scheduling revival meetings, or running
Jericho marches on church property. And, as crucial as the gifts are—I
just spent an entire chapter trying to show that—it's not even through
the sensational utilities of the Body's giftings that the whole world will
know; it's purely and simply through *unification* of His children together
for a common cause!

As. A. Family.

So close that when you call a brother "brother," you mean it authen-
tically—adopting the transcendent, spiritual-realm definition that mutes
our common biological understanding of what it means to be kinfolk.

I beseech you, readers, do not let the depth and beauty of this biblical
concept sweep straight through you. Don't allow our culture's marginal-
ization of this beautiful passage—and the intensity of its promises—to
influence your reception of it. Don't be like some Christians who, when

hearing a simple truth in a postmodern age, overanalyze and therefore dilute the almighty power and provision already provided. Pray about this Scripture for a while. Ask the Lord to intervene and show you how deep the rabbit hole of mystery goes on this "familial unit made perfect" concept. Ask Him to reveal beyond the deepest reaches of your finite imagination what the world could look like—what this bleak, hopeless, broken world we live in *would* look like—if all Body members truly loved one another in the interest of mirroring the closeness of Jesus' relationship with the Father.

If you spend time consulting the Almighty God on this issue, you will come to a mind-blowing conclusion that this verse holds the key to the entire Great Commission. We can't show love to the lost if we fight amidst ourselves. We can't disciple new believers if the only family they have to come into is one that squabbles over the nonessentials. And even when someone becomes a Christian as a result of a sensational display of God's hand in a Holy Spirit gifting, we can't expect their awe to carry them into a relationship with Jesus long-term if our brothers and sisters are showing pettiness toward each other.

Imagine a world where all Christians have perfect (or even *nearly* perfect) unity—even to the point that denominations peacefully agree to let go of peripheral doctrinal differences. Can you imagine a post-denominational world where following Christ doesn't involve one tongues-or-no-tongues fight or the battle between the pre-, post-, and mid-Tribulation crowds? It's hard to imagine that now, for sure, but try. Take your thoughts there for a second and *try* to envision the proverbial grasping of Christian hands across every race, culture, and age range—from countries all over the globe and in every language—escalating to one universal power under the supreme authority of Christ, Himself.

It would be a force grand enough "that the world may believe" that the Father has sent the Son for the redemption of all.

The *world*…

That's huge.

Individual Value in the Body

In 2017, Defender Publishing released my father's autobiography: *The Boy from El Mirage: A Memoir of Odd Beginnings, Unexpected Miracles, and Why I Have No Idea How I Wound Up Where I Am*. In its introduction, I stumbled upon what I believe to be one of the most inspiring and convincingly articulated descriptions of the value of every person's role in the service of God—*especially* those that don't come in grandiose, sparkly, sensational, and attention-grabbing packages:

> As most of us know, Moses was born during a time when the pharaoh of Egypt had enslaved all the Hebrews, beat them mercilessly, and forced them to carry out hard labor in the sweltering sun. He then ordered that all male Hebrew babies were to be drowned because he felt threatened by the growing population, and believed that they were becoming strong enough to wage war against him. Moses' mother, Jochebed, hid her newborn from the Egyptians for a few months, but when she realized she wouldn't be able to keep him hidden any longer, she made a basket, covered it in pitch, and sent her baby down the river. When the pharaoh's daughter saw him drifting along, she drew him out, named him Moses, and raised him in the presence of Egyptian royalty. As an adult, Moses fled from the death penalty to the desert after he killed an Egyptian soldier for beating a Hebrew man. Arriving in Midian, he met and married Zipporah, and became a shepherd for his father-in-law's herd. One day in the desert amongst the sheep, he saw a burning bush. The Angel of the Lord spoke to him from the bush, telling Moses to return to the people he had left behind, speak to the pharaoh, and tell him he must release the Hebrew nation out of bondage. Equipped with supernatural signs and wonders, Moses obeys despite his

fear, and alongside his older Hebrew brother Aaron, they carry out the task God gave them. When the pharaoh refuses to release the people, ten plagues from heaven result in misery for the Egyptians, and eventually pharaoh agrees to let the people go. Changing his mind later, the pharaoh sends his armies to track down the Hebrews. Moses reaches the edge of a sea, cries out to the Lord with the marching armies behind them, and the Lord instructs Moses to part the waters by holding up his staff over the sea. The waters part, and the Hebrews cross through to the other side. Pharaoh's men followed them into the bed of the sea, and then the waters crashed down upon them, drowning the Egyptians in the same way they had drowned the Hebrew's young. Once freed, the people trek to Mt. Sinai, where the law, as well as the Ten Commandments written by the hand of God on stone tablets, are given to the nation of Israel.

In this story, Moses is the most visible hero. He was not, however, the *only* hero.

Many are aware that Moses was intended to be killed just after he was born because of the pharaoh's decree to throw all male babes into the Nile River. But a more overlooked part of the narrative is that Moses was never supposed to be born in the first place, as the pharaoh had instructed the midwives of the Hebrew people to perform a crude type of early abortion on every male child:

> And the king of Egypt spake to the Hebrew midwives, of which the name of the one was Shiphrah, and the name of the other Puah: And he said, "When ye do the office of a midwife to the Hebrew women, and see them upon the stools; if it be a son, then ye shall kill him: but if it be a daughter, then she shall live." (Exodus 2:15–16)

As we read along in the story, we see the hand of God upon Moses' life and the lives of the other Hebrew boys play out from the beginning:

> But the midwives feared God, and did not as the king of Egypt commanded them, but saved the men children alive.... Therefore God dealt well with the midwives: and the people multiplied, and waxed very mighty. (Exodus 2:17–20)

This order to kill babies from the birthing stool was given, and disobeyed, long enough before the birth of Moses that the people had "multiplied" and became "mighty" by the time Jochebed of the Levites gave birth to Moses. We will never know the number of male children that were born in this interim, nor will we know how many were allowed to grow into manhood or teen years prior to the pharaoh's next murderous rampage, but we know that because of Shiphrah's and Puah's one historic decision, a nation was able to multiply, and at least for a time, babies were allowed to live. Not only was Moses saved from the unscrupulous murder order, but so, too, were scores of others whose personal story, if written, would have made an incredible and fascinating memoir.

I can see the modernized title now: *Babe in the Hands of Pharaoh: The True Story of One Life Saved by Shiphrah*. One might wonder today what amazing tales of triumph and victory would have trailed such a soul had they been given access to an Internet blog site. Or perhaps: *Wrath of Pharaoh, Wrath of God: Puah's Account of Obedience Toward God and Against Egypt*. Imagine the inspiring moments we might learn about these women and their professions had they access to update their Facebook profiles just after this era of unspeakable tension when they made their decision—*that one historical decision that changed the course of the world*—to follow God instead of the pharaoh. What a ministry they may have had! And here's another: *Jochebed and the Basket Baby: How One Woman's Choice to Relinquish Her Child Ultimately Led to Freedom for All of Israel.* Talk about a serious drama. A tale of woe, faithfulness, surrender, and reunion would have followed if Jochebed had been given instructions on how to build a Kindle book through Amazon. People who have children of their own almost can't fathom the heartbreak this woman would have felt the moment she placed her sweet baby boy into that pitch-and-slime-covered basket of bulrushes and sent him down the Nile River to what might have been a cruel, violent, or miserable end. Nor can they fully comprehend the joy she would have experienced when she was brought to the pharaoh's daughter a short while later to be nurse to the very baby she let go!

So many, *many* stories that were never wholly shared out of just one biblical narrative, only silenced by the limited means of documentation at that time. Everyone has a story. There is no time like the present to live it to the fullest.

Certainly, if the midwives had made the wrong decision and went along with the abortion plan, or if Jochebed had allowed the Egyptian soldiers to take her child, another Moses could still have been born simply because God is all-powerful and could have made a way. However, that alternate story, too, likely would have involved someone willing to make the right decision and *be used by God* to bring it about. Someone had to make the right determination with willpower and resolve. Everyone remembers Moses, but without Shiphrah, Puah, and Jochebed, *or* others God might have chosen to use, there would have never been a Moses. The choices we make on a day to day basis in this life are important, no matter how old we are, what family we came from, how much money we have, how many degrees are behind our names, how many people we know, or how charismatic our personalities are. Maybe we are born to be the next David or Moses and free entire nations from enemies or slavery. Maybe we are born to be the next Mary Magdalene, Shiphrah, Puah, or Jochebed and make the right decision at the right time that sets a new standard of radical obedience to God for future generations. Maybe we are born to be the…unspecified children born unto Hebrew women during the pharaoh's reign of terror whose story is never published but whose [tiniest, uncelebrated actions] alters the patterns of the planet forever.

But one thing is for sure: We are *born to be*.

Not one of us is a mistake, and from the womb, each of us is known by God and given a purpose by Him. In this, we never need doubt.[31]

As my father so brilliantly pointed out, the Shiphrahs, Puahs, and Jochebeds are *crucial to the function of God's people*. His greatest plans can only be carried out when *all* players report to the field with equal willingness, and it shouldn't be assumed—in fact it's unbiblical to even think—that Moses' heavenly glory or honor is above that of his mother or her midwives, and that same concept applies today.

"Uncomely" Parts of the Body? Not Exactly…

In this post-New-Testament epoch when the Body of Christ is made up of many members (with no one being more important than another), Paul says the supportive roles should be given a specific kind of honor, glory, and protection—some respected classical Bible commentaries also say "attention"—that the sensational parts do not receive.

Pause. *Where* exactly does Paul say that?

That conclusion requires looking a little deeper at the context of 1 Corinthians 12, particularly at verse 23: "And those members of the body, which we think to be less honourable, upon these we bestow more abundant honour; and our uncomely parts have more abundant comeliness." Some who want to misconstrue this verse might recap this by saying Paul is asserting that some unsightly folks in the fold will be given dirty jobs, and it will be up to everyone else to give them a pat on the head and make them feel pretty. Others who want to read more into this verse than we should, in order to make the supporting roles *more* important than those of everyone else, might suggest that the supporting positions should be lifted to a higher social status or praised more than the others. When we hear "we bestow more abundant honour," we might imagine one person receiving all the gold medals while the rest only get silver or bronze. Even the word "bestow" in our time sounds like it's leading to a gift or a favor delivered by someone down on one knee or laying prostrate before a king—and that's not accurate in this context.

To really bring this light, let's look at two key words in the Greek, in the order they play out in the verse:

- The word *dokeo*, in English here as "which we think," literally translates "to be of opinion";[32] Paul is addressing the self-absorbed *opinions* of the Corinthian church members who had begun to treat certain, more visible members of the body with more admiration, like we treat celebrities today, and regarded everyone else as marginal, based on who had what Holy Spirit-given giftings. How can I be sure that "we think" here refers to a negative, narrow-minded opinion and not to a healthy corporate credo we should all adopt? It relies on concentric circles of context spreading out a little wider: As far as which gift was seen as the most sensational and worthy of being elevated, it's clear from 1 Corinthians chapters 12, 13, and 14, *all together*, that the

Corinthians were in a steep, speak-in-tongues competition. Their tongues-wars had become chaotic to the point that the entire congregation would come across to a nonbeliever as completely mad (meaning "crazy" or "out of their minds"; 1 Corinthians 14:23). The take-home thought from this: Paul is not identifying *any* roles within Christ's corporate Body as shameful or ugly ("less honorable"; "uncomely"), nor is he suggesting there would be an appropriate circumstance for that kind of branding. He is identifying an attitude problem ("which we *think*"; "to be of opinion") that results in support roles being viewed as unappealing or less important. If anything, Paul's words here should be seen as a gentle rebuke followed by a confident redirect.

- The word *peritithemi*, translated here as "bestow," literally means "to put on" (such as a piece of clothing; see Matthew 27:28), or to "surround" with something protective (such as a hedge or fence; see Matthew 21:33).[33] (This is not "Joe Horn theology," as you will soon see; this "clothing" and "fence" aspect of the verse has been widely acknowledged by scholars and cited in classical commentaries for hundreds of years, but its meaning gets lost in today's culture.) Paul isn't saying we should give those in support roles the biggest trophies or the loudest applause; he is saying we should *clothe* them in something. It's a figurative and poetic way of commanding that these supporting roles, whom the narrow-minded Corinthian Christians *opine* to be "less honorable" or "uncomely" (detestable, unappealing), must be under a metaphorical covering—one that should be *provided by the rest of the Body*. Paul said "*we* bestow," not "God will bestow," so this is one of those verses that requires action from *us*, fellow Christians. But what is this clothing?

Some might assume that *peritithemi* represents a support role being *hidden under* the clothing that has been "put on" because of the context of body parts. We wear clothing, not fences, so the protective aspect of "surround" when compared to the application of "hedge" or "fence" initially looks absurd…until we consider how much our bodies are protected when we put on clothing: We have a shielding layer (hedge of protection) between our skin and the wind, cold, heat, bug bites, etc. (all of which Paul would have been familiar with while traveling by foot throughout the ancient world during his missionary journeys); more importantly, clothing protects us from nonphysical factors like *shame*, because without clothes we would be nude and feel completely exposed. Paul is *in no way* suggesting that people in support roles should be shamefully hidden away, since the surrounding verses—as well as his references of clothing in *honor*, which is the opposite of shame—dismiss that as a possibility.

Contrarily, when we consider both the culture at the time of Paul's writings and the internal evidence within Scripture, we see that a person's clothing had the potential of identifying him or her with honor, glory, and even royalty…and *sometimes* it could mean all three of those things, like the "glory" or "splendor" of King Solomon, the richest human ruler in the ancient world, when he was compared to the "clothed" lilies (as referenced in Matthew 6:29). In biblical times, if the garment of a man was his glory, and if it reflected his standing with the Lord (such as being clothed in "salvation" in Isaiah 61:10), then to be "bestowed" (clothed; surrounded protectively) with clothing so handsome that it brings "abundant honor" would be a great reward, and that would place upon the seemingly "uncomely" parts all the more "abundant comeliness."

Do you see what just happened? It's all there in one verse. Those "ugly" support roles suddenly became quite beautiful… Paul's clothing analogy shouldn't be related to shame, but to *privileged distinction*. It relates more appropriately to "badge of honor" in our culture's lingo today than "hide it; it's ugly."

However, though Paul isn't suggesting certain people should be hidden for shame, he is allowing the natural cause and effect of "putting on" clothing to mean that body parts under garments are naturally more concealed (more protected; less visible) than others. Paul is acknowledging that some, because of their giftings, are in the limelight, while others are more anonymous, and *neither position is bad. Both* are a natural result of being members of the same Body that intrinsically *cannot* be made up of members who all have the same giftings, or else, Paul says, we amount to nothing more than a giant eyeball (1 Corinthians 12:17).

But we, as Christians, should always be willing to go out of our way to give supporting members of the Body the attention, care, honor, glory, and protection they need to function optimally.

As an example: We don't necessarily think about our knees every moment of the day, but if they begin to hurt from our negligence of their care, we begin to think about them constantly and take protective measures about them, fitting them with the right kind of clothing or braces, etc., because even though we don't think of "knees" as our most glorious body parts, if we ever had to live *without* them, we would be crippled. The best way to sustain optimal health, then, is to think *preventatively*, giving our knees proper care before pain from negligence can set in.

Before we move on, note how closely the classic *Barnes' Notes on the Bible* commentary follows this interpretation as well. I've included what it says about the following verse (12:24):

> We bestow more abundant honour—Margin, "Put on." The words rendered "abundant honor" here, refer to clothing. We bestow upon them more attention and honor then we do on the face that is deemed comely, and that is not covered and adorned as the other parts of the body are.
>
> More abundant comeliness—We adorn and decorate the body with frivilous apparel. Those parts which decency requires

us to conceal [which, in the 1830s—the time *Barnes' Notes* volumes were published—meant generally everything except hands and face, not necessarily anything of an adult nature, as proven by his next statement about further "adorning" these parts] we not only cover, but we endeavor as far as we can to adorn them. The face in the mean time we leave uncovered. The idea is, that, in like manner, we should not despise or disregard those members of the church who are of lower rank, or who are less favored than others with spiritual endowments.

For our comely parts—The face, etc. "Have no need." No need of clothing or ornament. [Why would they have no need for clothing or ornament that establishes honor? Because they are in the limelight already and are receiving honor publicly.]

But God hath tempered the body together—Literally, "mingled" or mixed; that is, has made to coalesce, or strictly and closely joined. He has formed a strict union; he has made one part dependent on another, and necessary to the harmony and proper action of another. Every part is useful, and all are suited to the harmonious action of the whole. God has so arranged it, in order to produce harmony and equality in the body, that those parts which are less comely by nature should be more adorned and guarded by apparel.

Having given more abundant honour—By making it necessary that we should labor in order to procure for it the needful clothing; thus making it more the object of our attention and care. We thus bestow more abundant honor upon those parts of the body which a suitable protection from cold, and heat, and storms, and the sense of comeliness, requires us to clothe and conceal. The "more abundant honor," therefore, refers to the greater attention, labor, and care which we bestow on those parts of the body. (emphasis added)[34]

Had you ever thought that the Shiphrahs, Puahs, and Jochebeds were supposed to receive greater attention, labor, and care than the Moses?

If you're a Body member in a limelight position, *don't forget or take for granted the value of those who support you, for they are to be labored over and clothed in glory for the King, who said the last will be first and the first will be last (Matthew 19:30; 20:16)!*

If you're a Body member in a concealed role, *don't forget or take for granted how valuable and crucial you are in what God has called you to do, for you are worthy of being loved, cared for, and clothed in glory as you use your life to serve the King!*

Devoting this kind of thoughtfulness to the more concealed Body parts is also necessary for personal development and identity as each of us grows in the Lord. How will a woman know what part she is to carry out in the Body if she's never given the attention needed to identify or nurture her Holy Spirit giftings? Worse, what if a self-absorbed Christian—like those in Corinth to whom Paul wrote this letter—makes another believer who is young in the faith feel he isn't important? That "mouth" may be silenced forever because he thought he was an "elbow."

Barring a miracle of God, Christians who truly believe their value is "only marginal" will rise to "only marginal" levels in *whatever* they've been called to do, whether from a more concealed position or a limelight position. We can't go about letting our knees think they're fingers. Nor can we allow our shoulders to be *weak* because some other Body member told them they weren't as crucial to the Commission as the ears. Our loudest, most visible members should be *that much more motivated to serve those under them.*

That is the message of Paul's letter!

It is *also* the message of Christ, Himself: "But Jesus called them to him, and saith unto them…whosoever will be great among you, shall be your minister: And whosoever of you will be the chiefest, shall be servant of all. For even the Son of man came not to be ministered unto, but to minister, and to give his life a ransom for many" (Mark 10:42–45).

How far beyond Paul's grievance we have stepped—and how careless we have become about Christ's words—when our modern Corinthian opinions inflate us to the point that we stroll in, steal bacon, and fling lanyards in the faces of young kitchen servers who may, as a result, feel like the clothing (attention; honor) they were draped in by their family members was cheap.

YOU...For Such a Time As This

We need heroes and leaders more right now than ever before—and what a tragedy it is if we have skewed concepts about what heroes really are...

What a tragedy it is if the only Body parts we clothe in heroic honor are the loudest ones, while the supportive parts we're commanded to drape in abundant beauty are withering and suffering from "ministry burnout"...

...And what a tragedy it is if the Moseses of tomorrow reject the orders of burning bushes, refusing to come into the fullness of their role as great leaders of God's people because they think they are only valuable as the foot that propels the body in the direction another part designates.

Let's think about that for a minute. I've spent quite a bit of time discussing how valuable and honored our supporting roles should be, and what a high priority they should have when it comes to showing them attention, protection, care, and gratitude. *I've also spent most of the pages of this book making the point that a "hero" isn't just the loud and visible Body members; it's those who live their God-ordained giftings—whatever those may be—to the fullest of what God has called them to do.* But how do leaders become leaders? What presses them, ready or not, into the limelight? Can out-front leaders miss what God is telling them because they're confused about their role?

Is it possible that a Body member everyone else *thinks* plays a supporting role has been called by God to be a great leader?

That was true for Moses.

It's also been true of many of our more recent leaders.

I remember discussions occurring around the lunch table every day at SkyWatch regarding the cultural symptoms pointing to the next Great Awakening while we were preparing to release our January 2017 title, *Final Fire: Is the Next Great Awakening Right around the Corner?* As I listened to the banter, I soaked up the information, learning much about the history of our Church, the men and women who refused to remain stagnant in their comfy lifestyles while heretical grievances were taking place all around them, and the *jaw-dropping, incredible* movements of God that followed their choice to act. I heard inspiring, true tales about some leaders in the Great Awakenings who were a decade younger than me and who drew an audience of thousands every time they spoke, each sermon one step closer to igniting entire nations into a passionate return to Christ. As I learned more about these people and their willingness to take action—as well as the social, political, and religious climates they were reacting to—it became very clear, very fast, that *we, today*, are at the cusp of another Great Awakening…

Yet, this next movement might not even be limited to a Great Awakening; it *just might* be a colossal reformation of the Church unlike anything we've seen in five hundred years since the time of Martin Luther, although the motives and causes would be unique to what we're facing today: a momentous split between the "Country Club Social Church" and the next generation of on-fire believers who will stop at nothing to take the Gospel everywhere—even *outside* the church walls—to ensure that the entire globe knows who this Jesus is and what He did for the sake of their eternity. This next generation of leaders could very possibly choose to focus so centrally upon Christ and Him crucified that the mere mention of throwing another member of their own spiritual Body under the bus for personal gain is unthinkable; there just might be a love running so deeply from within that *all* believers will become indistinguishable in their hearts from those with biological family ties.

They may have a passion for the lost so unquenchable that no lifestyle, physical appearance, or confrontation from unbelievers will stop them from risking even their own lives to show compassion.

Doesn't that concept excite you? Doesn't it make you want to get ready—no, *live ready always*—for the opportunity to get personally involved in increasing the number of eternal saints? Does the notion of *even one person* entering the Kingdom of God to sit by you and feast in your corner *forever* as a result of your actions today make you want to run to the throne in prayer and beg the Lord to put you in that person's life so much faster?

Get involved in a conversation regarding the "who's who" of the Great Awakenings. It will make you feel like you can conquer the world. Not *one* of the leaders called by God to do great things was any more talented or qualified than you, dear reader. They were all just men and women, parts of the Body, willing to do the Lord's work—and the Lord responded to their willingness. Some of the names we remember, the legacies behind the grandest movements of God in modern history, couldn't have accomplished what they did without the stepping stones laid out by those who had gone before.

Important to keep in mind: Our giftings don't need to wait for us to be at church to launch into effect. We are first and foremost called to provide for our own (1 Timothy 5:8)! The Church needs to start teaching that we should have our gifts in full operation even while we're at home around our families! Imagine my story—the relevant parts of which you've already read—without my "priestly" father at home who *clearly* has the gifts of ruling and of governments (you should see how well he governs SkyWatch Television!). Every Reverend Scam-Artist I ever crossed paths with might have conned me. I could have spent the rest of my life convinced I was supposed to be some Reverend Grand Wizard. And what about my mom? Without her unnervingly accurate "Spidey-sense," I know for certain I would have gone down a very dark path. Her gift of discernment was *wildly* active in keeping me from dating girls who were no good and hanging out with the wrong crowds. Mom was so close to the Lord that anytime anything "not of God" came onto the scene, she zeroed in on it with her maternal crosshairs and brought me to safety. Her gift of helps, exhortation, and the word of wisdom (not to mention a never-ending loop of patience that outlives every other person's fuse that I have ever known) kept me sheltered, nurtured, and secure. My *greatest* heroes of all—the grandest champions in my life—are my family. They all used their gifts at home.

Everyone should be using their gifts at home and everywhere else they go. It's essential for the shaping of the Body. We need heroes in the Church today, and no parts can be excluded.

Every Moses has his Shiphrahs, Puahs, and Jochebeds.

For instance, when we think of the Protestant Reformation, we think of Martin Luther, right? For good reason! But he certainly was not alone in his endeavors, and those who paved the paths for him will never be erased from history. Although I knew what the Protestant Reformation was when the *Final Fire* book conversations were happening around me at work, learning about it again as a mature adult opened my eyes to ideas I had never really paid attention to, and I saw that shift in Church history differently, as it originated hundreds of years prior to the birth of Martin Luther. What Luther did was enormous and necessary, but it was inspired by *those who had gone before him.*

Consider the following:

- Bible translator and theologian John Wycliffe (1324–1384) of Oxford University threw aside his reputation with the established Church to write about and spread the then-scandalous idea that a relationship with God should be *personal*: Men and women should feel free to pray, read the Bible, and pursue the Lord apart from the supervision of a priest. Although he died shortly after having a stroke and his body was buried traditionally upon death, Wycliffe was posthumously declared a heretic about thirty years later. His remains were declared unfit to rest in consecrated ground and thereafter his body was exhumed and burned.

- Czech priest Jan Hus (1369–1415)—foremost spearhead of the Bohemian Reformation (a Protestant Reformation forerunner event)—was so inspired by the writings of Wycliffe that he saw to the translation of Wycliffe's most controversial materials into the languages of his locals. For this, Hus was excommunicated from the Church. Afterward, refusing to be stopped, Hus began "free preaching" (preaching in unconventional areas, like the streets or parks), directly challenging the Church's sale of indulgences (which, simply put, was the Church promising less severe punishment in the afterlife in exchange for more money from believers in this life; it was a crude form of prosperity gospel in the earlier days). This angered Roman authorities, who placed a strict interdict upon the entire city of Prague that *no citizens* were allowed to participate in communion or be buried in church cemeteries until Hus conceded to silence. Hus, with consideration of his home city, went into hiding, but that didn't stop him from circulating his writings all over the territory through discreet channels while hidden away. The people were *so* hungry to hear his message (primarily centered around the concept that the Bible and Jesus Christ, not clergymen or Roman hierarchy, were the supreme authority over Christians, and that the Church needed to be cleansed from the inside out from manipulative corruption such as indulgences), that his writings quickly spread to Hungary, Poland, Austria, and outward. When he was burned at the stake, screaming forgiveness for his enemies as he died in flames, civil unrest exploded across the lands in a bloody series of battles known as the Hussite Wars: factions of Wycliffe/Hus followers defending their "Christ as the Head" faith to the point of death. Clashes surrounding personal religious freedoms escalated, accumulating uncountable deaths, until the Council of Basle met to negotiate a compromise.

These were the two men who went *before* Martin Luther, and *neither* had glorious endings. Without Wycliffe and Hus tearing down strongholds, weakening Church hierarchy, and planting seeds of reform within the minds of earlier believers, Luther's radical ideas might have been desperately out of time and therefore destined for failure.

Luther was so stirred by the writings of Hus that he, too, took on world-governing religious sources at the core (principally those in Rome), refusing to be still and accept the teachings of the Church he found flawed, such as: earning salvation and grace of God through rituals and/or purchasing indulgences; relying on a priest as mediator between man and God; and spending all of one's time on religious ceremony to secure one's eternal destiny, whilst ignoring the lost who have yet to hear or understand the Gospel. Luther, who had earlier been an obsessively pious friar and later a priest, caused an even greater uproar against the Church than Wycliffe and Hus. His famously celebrated *Ninety-Five Theses*—said to have been nailed to the door of the All Saints Church in Wittenberg—was perhaps the boldest contributing element of the Protestant Reformation, as it was a detailed list of protestations against the functions, operations, and theologies of the Roman Catholic Church. Over and over, despite opposition from the world's mightiest religious forces, Luther drove his central ideology of *sole fide*—that it is "by faith *alone*" (Romans 3–5) not by works, that a man can and will be saved; and that it is by the grace of the sovereign Savior, our "Head," and not by purchasing earthly favor with religious leaders, that we can inherit the Kingdom of God.

Luther was repeatedly summoned by religious leaders for councils, debates, and hearings, and each time he was ordered to recant his theology, he publicly refused, claiming that the papacy could not and should not be the ultimate authority over man, nor should the pope have the final word on scriptural interpretations. This "heresy" earned Luther a reputation of being the new Jan Hus—and that association was a *major* turning point in his mission of religious liberty. Whereas he had been brave and intense before, now he was an all-encompassing, all-consuming brushfire of passion, setting ablaze every ground he trod with a crackling flame of revolution. Every bold, countercultural move he made from that point forward was carried out with tenacity, and even when he was forced to face the Church in court hearings before the most threatening names within Roman Catholicism and told to recant or face the potentially fatal consequences, he stood firm in what he believed God wanted him to say…just like Hus and Wycliffe.

Thus, the split between Catholics and Protestants was set in stone, and the Reformation heralded a new dawn for the Body of Christ.

This is not a book on the history of the Christian Church—and I certainly don't want to paint Martin Luther as a saint (he made a lot of mistakes alongside his many good deeds)—so I will stop here, but do you see the pattern forming? Luther wouldn't have led the Protestant Reformation in the same unstoppable and fearless ways without the inspiration of Jan Hus' Bohemian Reformation. Jan Hus wouldn't have led the Bohemian Reformation without the inspiration of John Wycliffe. These names may draw less attention, but they are solid in the history books, and their honor and glory will *never* be forgotten…even though they were not present when the true fruits of their labors became a harvest of unthinkable numbers who found freedom because of the historical events they set into motion.

If someone wanted to view Wycliffe and Hus with a "glass half empty" approach, they could be seen as the quieter voices whose lives and legacies ended in tragedy, debasement, and shame from religion. Their lives of hard work could be seen as coming to a close without the kind of Hollywood romance or poetic justice our world has largely come to expect from dedicated soldiers behind a greater-good cause. From the *heavenly* perspective, however—the only one that should ever count for a true Christian—the boldness of thes two men started a movement that, upon completion, freed *billions* to enter a deeper level of knowing God as a true lover of souls and worshipping Him the way we do today.

That's not even considering how many lives beyond Luther's were touched by their writings; nearly *all* the trailblazers of the Great Awakenings were stirred by these men! Yet it doesn't end there. *Oh* how it doesn't end there!…

If only we had space, I could write another fifty pages describing the ways Wycliffe, Hus, and Luther paved the way for First Great Awakening groundbreaker Jonathan Edwards (from whom came some of the earliest concepts of "life group" meetings and youth groups), and how that pattern never stops: Edwards motivated George Whitefield (the celebrated theatrical "open air" preacher who heavily influenced early concepts of outdoor camp meetings and tent revivals), John Wesley, and Charles Wesley (credited as the founders of the Methodist Church), all three of whose assistance in the First Great Awakening was crucial. By the late eighteenth century, the innovative passions and ideas of these four men stirred much of the world to adopt the same practices with fervor and deep prayer for the Lord's anointing, and soon five more important men came on the scene: William and John McGee, William Hodge, John Rankin, and James McGready, who brought the South to its knees in the Second Great Awakening during an unprecedented, interdenominational uniting of believers unlike anything documented before or since—Baptists, Presbyterians, and Methodists banded together with the earliest Pentecostals as if they were a single denomination in the same Great Commission (which is *precisely* what we should be doing now, instead of engaging in interdenominational doctrine wars)! The McGee brothers, Hodge, Rankin, and McGready were unmistakably inspiring forerunners of the men and women who came after them, many of whom ended up as some of the greatest ministers in American history, such as: pioneering circuit-rider Francis Asbury; Harry Hosier, nicknamed "Black Harry" for being the first African-

American man to boldly and successfully preach to a white audience; Richard Allen, founder of the African Methodist Episcopal Church (the first independently black denomination on US soil); Lorenzo Dow, known for bringing enormous crowds to repentance, and whose book was at one point second *only* to the Holy Bible in sales; Methodist revivalist Peter Cartwright, who reportedly converted and personally baptized more than twelve thousand new believers; Charles Grandison Finney, whose teachings were so highly respected that he was posthumously inaugurated into the "Preachers of the Great Awakenings" list; and Seventh-Day Adventist Church founder, Ellen Gould White. All of *these* names (and many others) carried Christianity throughout the States and helped pave the way for the Third Great Awakening, which brought us, among hundreds of other ministers, my personal favorite of all time: Dwight Lyman Moody (frequently "D. L. Moody"), who, to bring this full circle, found himself repeatedly drawn to the sermons of nearly all the Great Awakening and Reformation leaders, especially George Whitefield.

Dwight Moody… There's something about the way he is described in historical accounts that stirs people. His character flies off the page with such unassuming sincerity, almost as if you can *hear* a good ol' boy chuckle and *feel* a pat on the shoulder when you close your eyes and imagine him standing there. I love how he's remembered in certain sections of *Final Fire*:

It didn't matter for a moment that Moody was new flesh in a murky and industrialized city like Chicago. Whenever he observed someone struggling, wherever an alienated soul was wandering, an outstretched hand was thrust into view, one that traced upwards to the smiling, cheeky face of a new best friend. If one held a different opinion than Moody—on any subject, religion or otherwise—it was with a sincere nod and a handshake that the matter was settled, allowance paved for both sides to agree to disagree, all the while holding steadfast to a harmonious and refreshing bond.[35]

That book goes on to describe Moody as having visited the filthiest and most dangerous slums with "a cheerful beam upon his features so wide one might think he had wedged a clothes hanger in his mouth."[36]

What I love most about Moody, and most relevant to this book's message, is what he was centrally known for while he lived: He was a nice guy.

Yes, you read that correctly. The illustrious, renowned preacher at the core of the Third Great Awakening was known for being just a regular Joe.

He couldn't even read for most of his life, and he never learned to write as astutely as his ministerial peers (he had help writing his sermons and letters), so he didn't succeed by being well educated or attending fancy seminaries. In fact, he was never even ordained!

Why didn't God call a man with a couple of doctorate degrees from a Bible college and impressive ministerial credentials to carry out Moody's tasks?

Because God chose Moody.

We can't attribute all Moody accomplished to the notion that he was prepared to be a preacher or that he was perfectly within his element to deliver a sermon and respond to the masses through some innate talent, because we know it's the opposite: He was *intensely* intimidated by the idea of preparing sermons and addressing huge crowds. I laugh out loud when I think about the time he preached what he thought was an uninspired and drab sermon, yet when he gave the invitation for the assembly to receive Christ, *hundreds* responded. He thought the people in the audience were getting up to leave, but when they stood there waiting, he assumed they were confused and gave the invitation a second time, this time directing them to file into the back room for prayer if they wanted to receive Christ. The throngs followed Moody into the back room and worked to set up extra seating. Moody, still convinced the people didn't understand, give the invitation a *third time*, instructing all who wanted to receive Christ to stand. When everyone in the building stood, he panicked, told everyone to go home and return the next day to talk to the church's regular leadership, and then left. The leadership contacted him the following day with the message that the entire church was flooded with responders, so he returned to assist them in prayer. Going against his comfort and facing his fear, he forced himself to continue his ministry there until every last person had been tended to…which took a full ten days! Imagine that—a Great Awakening preacher who chickens out on his own altar call!

Why didn't God choose a man who couldn't wait to be the center of attention in front of giant gatherings—one who could have handled these unpredictable situations like a pro, instead of a nervous, country-bumpkin shoe salesman?

Because God chose Moody.

Moody certainly wasn't an articulate speaker, according to those who heard him in person. The collected research from *Final Fire* summarizes:

> Of particular fascination is the fact that he *never did* mature into a great spokesman. Moody's speaking attire was mundane, his vocal intonations unpolished, his strings of words too simple to come from a minister. He pounded no pulpits. He frightened no one with the stirring of fear. His speeches were no more than a regular expository of Scripture. His presence was childlike and unassuming and unvaryingly *regular*…. [V]ery little else can be said about his style that would have drawn such numbers other than, perhaps, the will of God, Himself.[37]

One humorous description comes from an important social reformer and aristocratic connection Moody made in his later years named Lord Shaftesbury. He wrote that Moody was a "simple, unlettered" man with "no theological training" who simply *refused* to identify with any kind of denomination as he led crowds of thousands "totally without skill in delivery." He admitted that Moody's oh-so-ordinary ministry was carried out "without an approach to the fanatical, or even the enthusiastic…[seeking] neither to terrify nor to puff up; eschew controversy, and natter no passions." Shaftesbury goes on to describe how intelligent, rich men who would normally have every social cause to feel superior to Moody believe, upon meeting him, that he is untouchably above them: "So it is, nevertheless, thousands of all degrees in station and mental culture bow before [Moody]." And the best part of Lord Shaftesbury's portrayal: "Are we not right in believing—time will show—that *God has chosen the foolish things of the world to confound the wise?*" (emphasis in the original).[38] (Note that the word "foolish" here should not be viewed as Lord Shaftesbury calling Moody a fool. By choosing to quote directly from 1 Corinthians 1:27 in this way, Shaftesbury was making a point about Moody's humble peculiarity and the fact that education and social status are never requirements in God's ultimate plan.)

Why didn't God pick a person who uttered words like a magnificent Christian Shakespeare, bringing every attribute of Christology to life with poetry so beautiful or exhortations so robust that his messages would flow like a river of gold from his lips straight to the hearts of the listeners?

Because God chose Moody.

Nobody could understand why Moody became such an enormous name at the time, or why "thousands, then tens of thousands, then hundreds of thousands of people were coming to accept Christ through the Gospel as spoken by the humble war chaplain and relief worker…. Even the Royal Opera House of London seating five thousand proved only capable of housing one-fourth the numbers that were typical of some of Moody's smaller congregations. Before long, newsstands had little else to report about besides the miraculous outpourings of the Spirit wherever Moody went, and Moody-endorsed publications were in nearly every home."[39] The man was so many things to so many people—both genders, all ages, and every nationality—and yet the descriptions recorded by those who knew him are almost all written from the perspective of people who were baffled. The thoughtful accounts read as if those remembering their encounters with him are put on the spot to provide accolades about his oratory delivery skills, his boundless intelligence, or perhaps his dashing looks…and then they fall flat with yet another equivalent to: "He's just a really, *really* nice guy."

But as God was asking Moody to follow His grand design—*and as Moody was responding with a humble "Yes, Lord" to every leading (regardless of his comfort or feelings)*—"this unordained, nondenominational, misspelling and nearly illiterate, mid-thirties Tom Sawyer was leading every territory from one European border to another to its knees."[40]

All God needs is a "Yes, Lord" to do wonders with the lives of His people…wonders so grand that people, like Lord Shaftesbury (and every other person who observed Moody in action), are mystified and speechless.

Why?

Because God.

Period.

He only needs a "Yes."

A couple of my fears are that people a) don't know they've been called, and b) don't know how to respond to the call.

To begin my response to that, I would like to clarify a major theological conundrum that has kept many in the past from action. To do this, I will borrow an excerpt from Donna's *Handmaidens Conspiracy* book (brackets Donna's):

The word "minister" today typically refers to someone in the clergy of a church. A vocabulary study of the word, however, reveals: "When you minister to someone, you take care of them. All…meanings of minister—both as a noun and as a verb—

contain a grain of the original Latin [*ministrare*] meaning, 'servant.'" So the idea that a minister is one who preaches or leads a congregation is a Western-religion idea. If you are a Christian, *you are called to be a minister*, whatever servant position in life that means for you.

Second Timothy 1:8–9 says, "Be not thou therefore ashamed of the testimony of our Lord, nor of me [Paul] his prisoner: but be thou partaker of the afflictions of the gospel [be ready to be made uncomfortable and face resistance for the sake of the Gospel] according to the power of God; Who hath saved us, and *called us* with an holy calling, not according to our works, but according to his own purpose and grace, which was given us in Christ Jesus before the world began" (emphasis added). God has called *us*, the collective Body made up of *all believers*, with all parts intact. Romans 8:29–30, again the words of Paul, says, "For whom he [God the Father] did foreknow, he also did predestinate to be conformed to the image of his Son…. Moreover whom he did predestinate, them he also *called*" (emphasis added).

Some confuse Matthew 22:14 ("For many are called, but few are chosen") to mean that some are called into ministry (smaller audience), some are chosen into greatness as God's elect (larger audience), and then there's a third group of people who believe in Christ, but aren't called or chosen into ministry of any kind…. However, this verse follows Christ's Parable of the Wedding Feast, which dealt with the heavy Jews-and-Gentiles issue and salvation, and once properly understood (once the pop culture and Western-religion concepts are removed), it's clear that only *two* groups are being referred to: a) the many who hear the Gospel, and b) those who choose to believe in Christ and live their lives accordingly.

From a hindsight view, these two categories can potentially converge into a people who have both heard the Gospel *and* subsequently decided to live for Christ, assuming both are met positively through such a decision. Some will belong to the first category (those who hear the Gospel message), but not the second (those who choose to believe and live their lives accordingly), because they will reject the message. This interpretation is unanimous amongst the early Church Fathers. The classic *Pulpit Commentary* says as much: "All the Jews had first been called; then all the Gentiles; many were they who obeyed not the call; and of those who did come in, many were not of the inner election, of those, that is, *whose life and character were worthy of the Christian name*, showing the graces of faith, holiness, and love." Even the historian, Origen, said:

> If any one will observe the populous congregations, and inquire how many there are who live a better kind of life, and are being transformed in the renewing of their mind [those who live like Christians]; and how many who are careless in their conversation and conformed to this world [the lost who reject the Gospel openly, or the lost who pretend to be Christians but whose lifestyles oppose true Christianity], he will perceive the use of this voice of our Saviour's, "Many are called, but few chosen;" and in another place it has been said, "Many will seek to enter in, and shall not be able" (Luke 13:24); and, "Strive earnestly to enter in by the narrow gate; for few there be that find it" (Matthew 7:13, 14).

Therefore, we must regard Matthew 22:14 as an isolated warning following the Parable of the Wedding Feast. Its references to the "called" and "chosen" stand apart from 2 Timothy 1:8–9 and Romans 8:29–30, which speak to the believer who *has already heard the Gospel message and decided to live for Christ.*

There is no unrecorded "third category" of believers who are not called or chosen, but who live ordinary, non-ministerial lives. Any true follower of Christ who has the Holy Spirit in his or her heart *has already been called* as a minister (servant) of God, according to these verses in Romans and 2 Timothy. It does *not* mean that every true follower of Christ has to fulfill the role of a preacher. But whatever your calling is, "whatsoever ye do, do it heartily, as to the Lord" (Colossians 3:23).[41]

There is no such thing as: "I'm a Christian, and lately I've been feeling like the Holy Spirit is calling me into ministry." Again, if you are a Christian and you already have the Holy Spirit in your heart, you've *already been* called into ministry. The *second* you accept Christ and dedicate yourself to becoming His disciple, you're all-hands-on-deck for the Great Commission, and your life will in some way impact the Kingdom of God. That's precisely what "ministry" means to the Body of Christ.

Consider the priesthood of the believers: Peter, the esteemed bishop of Antioch, said in his first epistle (2:5, 9–10): "Ye [Greek *autos*, "himself, herself, themselves; he, she,"[42] referring to *all believers*] also, as lively stones, are built up a spiritual house, an holy *priesthood*, to offer up spiritual sacrifices, acceptable to God by Jesus Christ. But ye are a chosen generation, a royal *priesthood*, an holy nation, a peculiar people; that ye should shew forth the praises of him who hath called you out of darkness into his marvellous light; Which in time past were not a people, but are now the people of God: which had not obtained mercy, but now have obtained mercy" (emphasis added).

In case you missed it, YOU, dear fellow Christian, have already been initiated into this "priesthood." The English word "priesthood" in these passages comes from the Greek word *hierateuma*: "the office of a priest; the order or body of priests."[43]

Now it's just a matter of where and how He wants you to serve, with what gifts…and whether you will answer that calling of yours with bold-ness and tenacity.

Who are the leaders? Who are the heroes? Who are the immovable, stable, mighty men and women of strength and valor who will hap-pily throw every social or material gain to the wayside in the interest of pointing the world back to Christ and His eternal saving grace? Who are the radical John Wycliffe frontrunners, those John-the-Baptist-like Jan Hus trailblazers, who stop at *nothing—ever*—to challenge the stagnant Church of Religious Robes? Who are the Dwight Moodys (ministry, mercy) of this generation who will "Yes, Lord" their way into the full-ness of their calling because they trust God can make a Great Awakening preacher out of a regular "nice guy"? Who are the Debbie Shorts (word of knowledge, word of wisdom) who seek God *so closely* that they rec-ognize His voice over all others, showing they can deliver His words to people who need so desperately to hear them? Who are the Commander Dave Hoards (helps, exhortation, giving) who literally raise the heroes for the next generation? Who are the Mrs. Barbara Phillipses (teaching, exhortation) who inspire the "lost-cause delinquents" to realize their true potential and value? Who are the Bob Backstroms (governments, ruling) who will intervene to make ministers by channeling peoples' intrinsic character attributes into positive outlets?

You are already called. You're already initiated into the order. Own that with confidence, and don't let anyone rob you of the assurance that, as a member of the spiritual Body of Christ, you're as important as any other member (1 Corinthians 12:12–27).

If you're laboring for the Gospel of Christ—whether in official min-istry or a secular vocation, and regardless of the size and reach—don't assume you've missed your calling. Never feel that what you've been called to do isn't big enough or sensational enough. Don't make the mis-take of believing what the world indoctrinates us to believe—that small is unimportant and big is the only way—because if it's where God put you, you're precisely where you need to be. If you feel constantly prodded toward roles you perceive to be "grand," maybe the Holy Spirit is nudging you to pray about new avenues. So dream *big*, but let God be in charge of the increase.

The heartbeat of the Church depends on *all* the gifts, including those the Body may "opine" to be "uncomely" (like the Corinthians were guilty of). But there are *no* uncomely parts. You may be in the position to answer to the never-ending list of duties in a thankless and seemingly invisible position. You may be out there grinding it out just to take your life and your responsibilities to the next apparent "underdog" level. It may seem like you do *so many things* and you're busy all the time, but at the end of the day, you can't really even say what you accomplished. But know this: If you are operating in the fullness of your gift, as empowered and endowed through the Holy Spirit, you may not even know that yours is the voice that *is already* changing cities, communities, and the world. You are *gifted…*

You are *called…*

You were placed on the earth for such a time as this…

Go.

Notes

1. "Strong's G3056," *Blue Letter Bible*, last accessed April 23, 2018, https://www.blueletterbible.org/lang/lexicon/lexicon. cfm?Strongs=G3056&t=KJV.

2. "Strong's G4102," *Blue Letter Bible*, last accessed April 23, 2018, https://www.blueletterbible.org/lang/lexicon/lexicon. cfm?Strongs=G4102&t=KJV.

3. *Barnes' Notes*, "1 Corinthians 12," *BibleHub*, last accessed April 24, 2018, https://biblehub.com/commentaries/barnes/1_ corinthians/12.htm.

4. "Strong's G2386," *Blue Letter Bible*, last accessed April 23, 2018, https://www.blueletterbible.org/lang/lexicon/lexicon. cfm?Strongs=G2386&t=KJV.

5. "Strong's G4395," *Blue Letter Bible*, last accessed April 24, 2018, https://www.blueletterbible.org/lang/lexicon/lexicon. cfm?Strongs=G4395&t=KJV.

6. Under the "Thayer's Greek Lexicon" heading at: "Strong's G4394," *Blue Letter Bible*, last accessed April 23, 2018, https://www.blueletterbible.org/lang/lexicon/lexicon. cfm?Strongs=G4394&t=KJV.

7. *Barnes' Notes on the Bible*, "Romans 12:6," *BibleHub*, last accessed April 24, 2018, http://biblehub.com/commentaries/barnes/romans/12.htm.

8. "Strong's G484," *Blue Letter Bible*, last accessed April 24, 2018, https://www.blueletterbible.org/lang/lexicon/lexicon.cfm?Strongs=G484&t=KJV.

9. "Strong's G482," *Blue Letter Bible*, last accessed April 24, 2018, https://www.blueletterbible.org/lang/lexicon/lexicon.cfm?strongs=G482&t=KJV.

10. "Strong's G2941," *Blue Letter Bible*, last accessed April 24, 2018, https://www.blueletterbible.org/lang/lexicon/lexicon.cfm?Strongs=G2941&t=KJV.

11. Under the "Outline of Biblical Usage" heading at: "Strong's G1248," *Blue Letter Bible*, last accessed April 23, 2018, https://www.blueletterbible.org/lang/lexicon/lexicon.cfm?Strongs=G1248&t=KJV.

12. "Romans 12:8," *BibleHub*, last accessed April 26, 2018, http://biblehub.com/commentaries/romans/12-8.htm.

13. Under the "Outline of Biblical Usage" heading at: "Strong's G3874," *Blue Letter Bible*, last accessed April 23, 2018, https://www.blueletterbible.org/lang/lexicon/lexicon.cfm?Strongs=G3874&t=KJV.

14. "Strong's G1319," *Blue Letter Bible*, last accessed April 24, 2018, https://www.blueletterbible.org/lang/lexicon/lexicon.cfm?Strongs=G1319&t=KJV.

15. "Strong's G3330," *Blue Letter Bible*, last accessed April 24, 2018, https://www.blueletterbible.org/lang/lexicon/lexicon.cfm?Strongs=G3330&t=KJV.

16. Under the "Outline of Biblical Usage" heading and the "Thayer's Greek Lexicon" heading at: "Strong's G572," *Blue Letter Bible*, last accessed April 23, 2018, https://www.blueletterbible.org/lang/lexicon/lexicon.cfm?Strongs=G572&t=KJV.

17. "Strong's G4291," *Blue Letter Bible*, last accessed April 24, 2018, https://www.blueletterbible.org/lang/lexicon/lexicon. cfm?Strongs=G4291&t=KJV.

18. "Strong's G4710," *Blue Letter Bible*, last accessed April 24, 2018, https://www.blueletterbible.org/lang/lexicon/lexicon. cfm?Strongs=G4710&t=KJV.

19. "Strong's G4692," *Blue Letter Bible*, last accessed April 24, 2018, https://www.blueletterbible.org/lang/lexicon/lexicon. cfm?strongs=G4692&t=KJV.

20. "Strong's G1653," *Blue Letter Bible*, last accessed April 24, 2018, https://www.blueletterbible.org/lang/lexicon/lexicon. cfm?Strongs=G1653&t=KJV.

21. Frederick William Farrar, *The Life and Work of St. Paul* (London, Paris, New York: Cassell & Company; 1885), 315.

22. Under the "Outline of Biblical Usage" heading at: "Strong's G3956," *Blue Letter Bible*, last accessed April 23, 2018, https://www.blueletterbible.org/lang/lexicon/lexicon. cfm?Strongs=G3956&t=KJV.

23. Under the "Outline of Biblical Usage" heading at: "Strong's G5319," *Blue Letter Bible*, last accessed April 23, 2018, https:// www.blueletterbible.org/lang/lexicon/lexicon.cfm?Strongs=G5319.

24. "Strong's G5321," *Blue Letter Bible*, last accessed April 23, 2018, https://www.blueletterbible.org/lang/lexicon/lexicon. cfm?Strongs=G5321&t=KJV.

25. "manifest (adj.)," *Etymology Online*, last accessed April 23, 2018, https://www.etymonline.com/word/manifest.

26. "Strong's G1538," *Blue Letter Bible*, last accessed April 23, 2018, https://www.blueletterbible.org/lang/lexicon/lexicon. cfm?Strongs=G1538&t=KJV.

27. "Strong's G4851," *Blue Letter Bible*, last accessed April 23, 2018, https://www.blueletterbible.org/lang/lexicon/lexicon. cfm?Strongs=G4851&t=KJV.

28. Under the "Outline of Biblical Usage" heading at: "Strong's G2531," *Blue Letter Bible*, last accessed April 23, 2018, https://www.blueletterbible.org/lang/lexicon/lexicon.cfm?Strongs=G2531&t=KJV.

29. Under the "Outline of Biblical Usage" heading at: "Strong's G5048," *Blue Letter Bible*, last accessed April 23, 2018, https://www.blueletterbible.org/lang/lexicon/lexicon.cfm?Strongs=G5048&t=KJV.

30. "Strong's G4100," *Blue Letter Bible*, last accessed April 23, 2018, https://www.blueletterbible.org/lang/lexicon/lexicon.cfm?Strongs=G4100&t=KJV.

31. Thomas Horn, *The Boy from El Mirage: A Memoir of Odd Beginnings, Unexpected Miracles, and Why I Have No Idea How I Wound Up Where I Am* (Crane, MO: Defender Publishing; 2017), 5–9.

32. "Strong's G1380," *Blue Letter Bible*, last accessed April 12, 2018, https://www.blueletterbible.org/lang/lexicon/lexicon.cfm?Strongs=G1380&t=KJV.

33. "Strong's G4060," *Blue Letter Bible*, last accessed April 12, 2018, https://www.blueletterbible.org/lang/lexicon/lexicon.cfm?Strongs=G4060&t=KJV.

34. *Barnes' Notes on the Bible*, "1 Corinthians 12," *BibleHub*, last accessed April 19, 2018, http://biblehub.com/commentaries/barnes/1_corinthians/12.htm.

35. Thomas Horn, Larry Spargimino, and Donna Howell, *Final Fire: Is the Next Great Awakening Right Around the Corner?* (Crane, MO: Defender Publishing, 2016), 143.

36. Ibid., 145.

37. Ibid., 158.

38. Ibid., 159.

39. Ibid., 158.

40. Ibid., 159.

41. Donna Howell, *The Handmaidens Conspiracy: How Erroneous Bible Translations Hijacked the Women's Empowerment Movement STARTED BY JESUS CHRIST and Disavowed the Rightful Place of Female Pastors, Preachers, and Prophets* (Crane, MO: Defender Publishing; 2018), 300–302.

42. "Strong's G846," *Blue Letter Bible*, last accessed April 12, 2018, https://www.blueletterbible.org/lang/lexicon/lexicon.cfm?Strongs=G846&t=KJV.

43. "Strong's G2406," *Blue Letter Bible*, last accessed April 12, 2018, https://www.blueletterbible.org/lang/lexicon/lexicon.cfm?Strongs=G2406&t=KJV.